Helena
Rubinstein

Helena Rubinstein

The Australian Years

Angus Trumble

LA TROBE
UNIVERSITY PRESS

IN CONJUNCTION WITH BLACK INC.

Published by La Trobe University Press,
an imprint of Schwartz Books Pty Ltd
22–24 Northumberland Street
Collingwood VIC 3066, Australia
enquiries@blackincbooks.com
www.blackincbooks.com

La Trobe University plays an integral role in Australia's public intellectual life, and is recognised globally for its research excellence and commitment to ideas and debate. La Trobe University Press publishes books of high intellectual quality, aimed at general readers. Titles range across the humanities and sciences, and are written by distinguished and innovative scholars. La Trobe University Press books are produced in conjunction with Black Inc., an independent Australian publishing house. The members of the LTUP Editorial Board are Vice-Chancellor's Fellows Emeritus Professor Robert Manne and Dr Elizabeth Finkel, and Morry Schwartz and Chris Feik of Black Inc.

Copyright © The Estate of Angus Trumble, 2023
The Estate of Angus Trumble asserts the moral rights of the author.

ALL RIGHTS RESERVED.

No part of this publication may be reproduced, stored in a retrieval system, or transmitted in any form by any means electronic, mechanical, photocopying, recording or otherwise without the prior consent of the publishers.

9781760644529 (paperback)
9781743823163 (ebook)

 A catalogue record for this book is available from the National Library of Australia

Cover design by Tristan Main
Text design and typesetting by Typography Studio
Index by Belinda Nemec
Cover image: *Helena Rubinstein in a Red Brocade Balenciaga Gown* by Graham Sutherland, 1957. Oil on canvas. © Estate of Graham Sutherland, used by permission.

To three remarkable benefactors, without whom Helena Rubinstein in a Red Brocade Balenciaga Gown *(1956–57) by Graham Sutherland OM (1903–1980) could not have been acquired for the collection of the National Portrait Gallery in Canberra, Marilyn Darling AC, Tim Fairfax AC and Sid Myer AM (The Sid and Fiona Myer Family Foundation), this volume is gratefully and respectfully dedicated.*

Contents

Foreword by Sarah Krasnostein   IX
Author's Note   XIII

*   *   *

Introduction   1

PART I—*VENI, VIDI*
I CAME, I SAW

   1. The Sutherland Portrait   23
   2. Embarkation and Landfall   43
   3. Working with Children   69
   4. Taking the Measure of Melbourne   91

PART II—*VICI*
I CONQUERED

   5. Valaze™   125
   6. To Europe and Back   147
   7. New Zealand   171
   8. Business as Art   191

Epilogue   209

CONTENTS

* * *

Acknowledgements	221
Afterword	225
Endnotes	231
Chronology	253
List of Figures	259
Bibliography	265
Index	275

Foreword

Sarah Krasnostein

'In the professional life of every art museum director or curator,' Angus Trumble writes in the introduction to what unexpectedly became his final book, 'there are acquisitions that one recalls with pride, but only a handful that one suspects may eventually be career-defining or, failing that, those for which one would most like to be remembered. Foremost among the latter, for me so far, is *Helena Rubinstein in a Red Brocade Balenciaga Gown* by Graham Sutherland OM'. Alternately buoyed by his immense curiosity and anchored by his scholarly respect for factual proof, Trumble followed his fascination with the Sutherland portrait all the way back to its subject's origins, which, before his contribution, were shrouded in myth.

Singular in the timing and magnitude of her entrepreneurial success, Helena Rubinstein was the first truly global cosmetics mogul, female or otherwise. At its height, her company employed around 30,000 women. Through her intellect, acumen, bravery, grandiosity, complex personality and sheer force of will, Rubinstein fashioned herself into the staunchly self-possessed *grande dame* forever frozen in Sutherland's sumptuous reds and opalescent greys. Now, in an increasingly waning light, she is remembered as the purveyor *ne plus ultra* of our grandmothers' face creams and lipsticks. Most accurately, however, Rubinstein sold the impossible dream underlying them in a world where women were (as they continue to be) mercilessly judged according to commodifiable criteria that predominantly served the financial interests of men.

'Beauty is power' went the slogan Rubinstein ingeniously invented in 1904 to promote her fledgling business in Marvellous Melbourne. If power is understood as status, autonomy and money, that slogan indeed turned out to be true of Rubinstein, but Trumble invites us to consider whether it was ever true more broadly. 'Beauty might well be power, but power to what end?' he asks. 'What prevailing conditions made it necessary for women to seize upon beauty, or to be urged to do so, and use it as a weapon? What is beauty, anyway?' He welcomes the further questions which arise wherever aesthetics meet gender and commerce. What invisible forces constricted women's lives? Who broke free? And at what cost?

Questioning all received narratives of Rubinstein's life, Trumble traces her unlikely solo journey at the end of the nineteenth century, aged twenty-three, from Kazimierz, Poland, to the minuscule town of Coleraine in rural Victoria. With his characteristic attentiveness, he pieces together her trajectory through the isolated, inchoate – and therefore socio-economically porous – colonies of Australia and New Zealand, a tour which included Queensland's Darling Downs, Melbourne, Sydney, Brisbane, Auckland, Wanganui, Wellington, Christchurch and Dunedin. Long years of granular research allowed Trumble to persuasively make the case for how a young Jewish woman who arrived in Melbourne with no English, little savings and scant social support managed to launch herself from the Empire's most distant outpost to the centres of the universe – London and Paris before the First World War, and later a Park Avenue penthouse where the 'almost entirely self-made businesswoman' burnished the self-mythology that would both survive and obscure her. Through his scholarship, Trumble has not merely filled in the record of Rubinstein's lost Australian years. He has added corrective context and depth of perspective to all biographical accounts which came before, while doing the heavy lifting for any which may come after. He has rescued from obscurity the forgotten facts of female entrepreneurship at the time of Federation. And he has given us a new illumination of daily life, commerce and the Jewish diaspora in Edwardian Australia.

The task of every historian, Trumble writes, is to 'bring under control a mass of fine detail and thread countless polyphonies and antiphonies into a symphonic whole'. He continues: 'part of the excitement of this is that you could easily go all the way back to the beginning and repeat the process in a different key, marshal different melodies, arrange the whole in different movements, but end up with a portrait every bit as faithful (or misleading), a likeness every bit as accurate (or inexact), as the one that I am offering here.' As he was acutely aware, biography – like any history – is inescapably selective and subjective, as dependent on the sensibility of the author as it is on the factual record. Because of Trumble's surgical precision, his empathy and self-awareness, his humour, his grace, his exquisite visual sense, and the sheer scope of his frame of reference, in his hands the facts of Rubinstein's life take on new and startling significance. He draws Rubinstein on the page as Sutherland did on the canvas – in all her human complexity. The woman known for her singular qualities becomes recognisable in her yearnings and her flaws. Her story remains mythic, but the light has shifted. No longer is hers an impossible tale of a warrior Athena springing fully formed into the world. It has become, instead, an object lesson about human generative power – what it is 'to push against an obstacle whilst simultaneously drawing energy from it'. At its heart, this is a book about what it means to be a stranger in a strange land: the potential which such discomfiting displacement can unlock in a psyche, the impact it has on the course of a life, the connections it creates, and the wounds it can inflict.

For the non-fiction writer, one of the consolations of the daunting task of digging through mountains of undifferentiated material – often for years at a time – is the inadvertent excavation of the gold nugget: a whimsical or absurd or shockingly improbable fact from which glitters an energising aspect of human experience. I never had the chance to discuss this particular exhilaration with Trumble, but he described it, perfectly, this way:

History is written by individuals, and I will gladly affirm that my five-year swan-dive into the Edwardian and later worlds of Rubinstein in Australia and New Zealand would not have happened had it not been fuelled by numerous moments of personal delight arising from that form of nostalgia with which we retrieve often surprising, even bizarre flecks of brightly coloured detail out of the jumble of the past: the fact, for example, that in Collins Street, Melbourne, in 1905 you could take from Miss Fredman zither lessons according to Max Albert's normal system. Or those trapeze artists and playful elephants standing on drums with which Elsa Schiaparelli adorned Rubinstein's short Patou pink evening coat for Sydney in 1938. Or Alice Ward and her Egyptological Salon Charmazelle, or Dr Williams' Pink Pills for Pale People …

Each time I happened upon one of these gems, my rapturous first impulse was to text the author, who passed away soon after we discussed his manuscript. And yet, through the magic technology of writing and reading, I feel as though we have remained in conversation, as perhaps he had felt during those hundreds of hours spent peering into the archives for traces of his subject's elusive trail and interior life.

I am thinking of Angus finalising this manuscript at his desk before the sun rose over Canberra on those dark lockdown mornings. Or standing lost in thought on the pretty train platform at Colcraine in his bright socks and handsome shoes, seeing something fundamental about the human experience where everyone else just saw the station. His expansive delight in human experience, art and meaning-making. I am thinking of the years he put into his research – pushing, as Helena had, against an obstacle while simultaneously drawing energy from it. He wrote that he would most like to have been remembered for the Sutherland acquisition. How beautiful it is that this book of fine scholarship will ensure just that.

Author's Note

In the earliest surviving document of Helena Rubinstein's career in business, her application to register her distinctive label as a trademark in Melbourne, in February 1903, she described herself as 'Helena Rubinstein trading as Helena Rubinstein & Co.' Although she did not seek to incorporate Helena Rubinstein Pty Ltd in the state of Victoria until 1909, it is in both senses that I use the term in this volume: the more general sense of 'company' (& Co.) before 1909, and, later, that of a proprietary limited company or corporation.

For reasons that will become clear, mainly arising from the fragmentary, often fugitive character of the surviving documentary evidence here in Australia and New Zealand, from time to time this narrative jumps back and forth by months, years, and even decades. There is no convenient way to deal with Rubinstein's year-long sojourn in Toowoomba in 1900 without straightaway turning for elucidation to Laurie E. Smith in 1904. I have therefore sought to assist the reader by appending a detailed chronology that puts firmly documented events back in their proper order.

For clarity, when quoting from newspapers and other contemporary sources, I have throughout modernised fiddly conventions of late Victorian and Edwardian punctuation, such as 'Mrs. Ward', 'Collins-street', 'to-day', 'to-night', 'St. Kilda', 'M'Guffie', etc. To avoid confusion, I have also corrected the frequent misspellings of 'Rubenstein'. This common tic, still going strong, has proven useful in certain instances because, thanks to the advanced search feature, it has been possible to round up a sheaf of overlooked material simply by seeking 'Rubenstein NOT Rubinstein'.

Kaorite, Koroite, Koroit

In her 1965 memoir *My Life for Beauty*, Rubinstein described her Uncle Bernhard Silberfeld's neighbours riding into Coleraine, Victoria, 'from their stations beyond Kaorite Creek', implying satisfactorily panoramic distances.[1] The correct name is Koroite Creek, formerly Bryan's or Bryant's Creek, which is barely 3.5 kilometres east of Coleraine. The name of Koroite seems to have come from William Young's 15,000-hectare Mount Koroit and Dundas Station nearby (or, at times, Mount Koroite). However, Koroit is also the name of an unrelated small country town about 17 kilometres northwest of Warrnambool, not too far distant. Perhaps unfortunately, all three put in appearances in this narrative.

The illustrations

Probably owing to her notorious vagueness and, at times, obfuscation with respect to the deep past, hitherto the earliest photographs of Rubinstein and other members of her family, when published, have been given wildly varying dates and locations. To take one important example, in the publications accompanying three recent and closely related exhibitions, *Helena Rubinstein: Beauty Is Power* (The Jewish Museum, New York, 31 October 2014–22 March 2015, and the Boca Raton Museum of Art, Boca Raton, Florida, 21 April–12 July 2015); *Helena Rubinstein: Die Schönheitserfinderin* (Jüdisches Museum, Vienna, 18 October 2017–6 May 2018), and *Helena Rubinstein: L'Aventure de la beauté* (Musée d'Art et d'Histoire du Judaïsme, Paris, 20 March–25 August 2019), the family photograph I reproduce as fig. 12,

AUTHOR'S NOTE

carries contradictory captions. New York and Boca: 'Helena, at center, with her mother, Augusta, seated at right, and three of her seven sisters. She is probably about seventeen or eighteen here [which implies 1889/90].' Whereas Vienna and Paris: 'Augusta Rubinstein with her daughters Manka, Regina, Ceska (standing), and Erna (seated). Wilhelm Kleinberg studio, Kraków, 1890.' This agrees with one of Rubinstein's biographers, Maxene Fabe. However, these are further contradicted by Michèle Fitoussi, while Suzanne Slesin is content with 'Rubinstein women' and no date. In my opinion, the standing figure definitely is Helena Rubinstein, and not her sister Ceska. Based on costume and coiffure, the date range could plausibly extend to about 1893, but not much later. However, all of us agree that this photograph was taken in Kraków. I have sought, where possible, to justify and defend each of my other estimates, but in many cases some doubt will remain.

Imperial currency

ONE GUINEA (1 *gn*) = 21 shillings (21*s*) = one pound plus one shilling = £1 1*s* = £1/1/—.
ONE POUND (£1) = one gold sovereign = two half-sovereigns @ 10*s* apiece.
FIVE SHILLINGS AND SIXPENCE = 5*s* 6*d* = 5/6.
FIVE SHILLINGS (5*s*) = one crown = two half crowns @ 2*s* 6*d* or 2/6 apiece.
TWO SHILLINGS (2*s*) = 1 florin (*fl*).
ONE SHILLING (1*s*) = 12 pence = 12*d*.
ONE PENNY (1*d*) = 2 halfpennies @ ½*d* apiece = 4 farthings @ ¼*d* apiece.

Angus Trumble
Canberra, Australian Capital Territory
21 July 2022

Introduction

Beauty is power. This simple formulation, which was such a novel and successful one when Helena Rubinstein began using it to promote her business in Melbourne, Sydney and Brisbane in May 1904, turned out to be literally true of herself, but was it ever true more generally? In a television interview, Golda Meir once remarked with wry good humour but not a little steeliness also that she didn't think going to a beauty parlour would do her much good or be worth the time and money. In other words, for the fourth prime minister of Israel (1969–74), *power* was power. By uplifting the hold-all concept of beauty, were Rubinstein and her company (and their competitors) therefore unwitting agents of repression, imposing upon huge numbers of women all over the world unreasonable and, at times, unfulfillable expectations with respect to feminine beauty that were largely driven by the need to cater to an overpowering male desire? Was Rubinstein even complicit?

'Beauty is power.' Is it? *Was* it? Beauty might well be power, but power to what end? What prevailing conditions made it necessary for women to seize upon beauty, or to be urged to do so, and use it as a weapon? What is beauty, anyway? No doubt many people today would say that most of the answers are contained in the questions themselves. However, 120 years ago, any such Western orthodoxies were yet to evolve rapidly through an accelerating cataract of Edwardian change. Through the course of a long and eventful life,

Rubinstein played a central role in establishing and reinforcing those twentieth-century orthodoxies.

In the professional life of every art museum director or curator there are acquisitions that one recalls with pride, but only a handful that one suspects may eventually be career-defining or, failing that, those for which one would most like to be remembered. Foremost among the latter, for me so far, is *Helena Rubinstein in a Red Brocade Balenciaga Gown* by Graham Sutherland (plate 1). Over the years, I have written about many acquisitions in which I have had a hand, but only Rubinstein has inspired and generated enough to fill a whole book. She has also carried me farthest into previously unknown territories, and into more of those territories than ever before.

I am hardly a historian of cosmetics, or of fashion, or of domestic service in the Darling Downs of southern Queensland, or indeed of labour, hospitality and commerce more generally in Melbourne, Sydney, Brisbane and New Zealand through the decade following Federation. I am also an unmarried gay male white Anglo-Saxon Protestant art historian inquiring, definitely at times also intruding, into hitherto occluded aspects of the closely guarded life of a twice-married Polish–Jewish woman who almost but not quite singlehandedly created from scratch a global cosmetics corporation, at a time when cosmetics were not just frowned upon. They were anathema: almost universally seen as the pathetically meagre arsenal of actresses and tarts. That Rubinstein went to such lengths to create, project and safeguard her own image and, later, her myth, adds further complexity to an already complicated situation. Further, that she did these things in the face of obstacles so numerous and daunting as to be insuperable for an even slightly less determined person is perhaps her greatest achievement. Therefore, to Rubinstein and Sutherland, I owe a debt of gratitude that is impossible to repay other than with what follows. For, upon much reflection, I have concluded that they are *i migliori fabbri* (the better craftsmen).[1]

This book is a portrait in words of a fine portrait and, in strong focus, of the formation of its subject and the origins of her company. It has in

INTRODUCTION

common with portraits in general the fact that there are many blanks and lacunae, especially relating to Rubinstein's eleven formative years in Australia and New Zealand. It has fortunately been possible to uncover and restore quite a few of them but, as with the prudent conservation of a damaged painting, so too it is necessary to stop short of out-and-out reconstruction in the absence of any remnant of the original paint film, although this has hardly inhibited several of Rubinstein's other biographers. However, one of the virtues of blanks and lacunae is that they fire the imagination by giving to areas of light the crepuscular shadows the artist needs to create the illusion of solid forms, tangibles, textures, shapes. In 1956–57, Graham Sutherland brought Rubinstein's Balenciaga gown to vivid life not by slavishly reproducing every stitch and every rhinestone embedded in that rich scarlet fabric, but by a judicious process of highly selective quotation in some places, and sumptuous chromatic generalisation in others. Can we read Sutherland's swagger portrait as a kind of triumphant manifesto? Or is it more of a fortress, with the armature of Cristóbal Balenciaga, set up against her nearest and most threatening competitors?

Selective quotation and sumptuous generalisation: in these respects, Sutherland was doing what every historian has to do – bring under control a mass of fine detail and thread countless polyphonies and antiphonies into a symphonic whole. Part of the excitement of this is that you could easily go all the way back to the beginning and repeat the process in a different key, marshal different melodies, arrange the whole in different movements, but end up with a portrait every bit as faithful (or misleading), a likeness every bit as accurate (or inexact) as the one I am offering here. Like the painting, the book now goes on its way in the hope that with luck, *pace* Horace, it will rise in the esteem of future generations.[2]

Writing about Angela Merkel in *The Washington Post* on 15 July 2021, shortly after the German chancellor's last official visit to Washington DC, senior critic-at-large Robin Givhan carried us into a present that neither Golda Meir nor Helena Rubinstein could possibly have imagined. Recalling an earlier official visit to Washington, Givhan writes of Merkel: 'She delighted in giving Secretary of State Hillary Clinton framed photographic evidence of their shared affection for pantsuits. These two female leaders, in their no-nonsense uniforms, stood side-by-side in 2011 as they admired the picture, which showed the two of them from the torso down, similarly dressed. They laughed at the image – and at the inconvenience of fashion, gender stereotypes and preconceived notions of what power is often presumed to look like.' Meanwhile, Vice-President Kamala 'Harris, too, has laid claim to the sisterhood of the pantsuit, which will someday be as standard, as omnipresent in positions of power, as the brotherhood of the business suit'.[3]

Rubinstein was photographed a number of times entirely at ease wearing trousers, both formally and informally, as in this bold, almost declarative *al fresco* country-drive photograph, her hands thrust into the pockets of her wide-lapelled jacket, the jaunty beret worn just *comme ça* (fig. 1). She seems entirely unafraid of the camera's gaze; even in her stance she seems to 'play to it', evoking something of the mechanic or off-duty chauffeur by the casual way she props her foot on the bumper – yet this also discloses her dainty shoes. And there is a measure of diffidence. We might see her stance as issuing a sort of challenge, but the turn of her head also means that her gaze is pulled back, chin low, suggesting that she is beginning to retreat into a questioning mode, even a degree of private uncertainty.[4] This remarkable image leaves us wondering if the Rubinstein we thought we knew was not far more complex – and paradoxical.

We shall see that even prior to the establishment of her company in Melbourne at the beginning of 1903, Rubinstein exhibited an appetite and stamina for risk that, in turn, stimulated a Janus-like degree of confidence in herself and, in due course, her enterprise, that surely makes her story relevant today. From the beginning of her career in business until the very end, Rubinstein thrived on twin impulses: a dynamic of unapologetic emulation when it suited her, being unafraid of her many competitors; and a clarity and conviction with which she successfully differentiated herself and even drew strength from them.

INTRODUCTION

Figure 1. Helena Rubinstein on holiday in France,
with Chrysler Plymouth and Peugeot automobiles, c. 1932.

Rubinstein is not an anachronism. She conceived and developed her business entirely for women, modern women. She employed mostly women, approximately 30,000 of them, in her salons, laboratories and factories at the height of the business in the era of President Dwight D. Eisenhower. She aimed solely to meet feminine needs and desires. Not four years after starting her business, she had reached into all six states of the new Commonwealth of Australia, and no fewer than five New Zealand cities. In both jurisdictions, women's political and social rights were more advanced than in almost any other part of the world, and certainly far more advanced than in the imperial capital. Through the five decades in which she built her empire, Rubinstein never turned her back on the two countries that in 1907 gave her a springboard into London, Paris and eventually New York. She kept control of the company until she died in 1965, never contemplating retirement. However, the importance of Australia and New Zealand in the saga of

Rubinstein has largely been overlooked by her European and American biographers. At best, most of the pertinent details have been lost in an unremitting parade of error and unintended misinterpretation.

The trans-Tasman importance of Rubinstein, meanwhile, has all but been forgotten in Australia and New Zealand. During the long period in which I have been researching and writing this book, I have met many people, mostly young people, who have never heard of Rubinstein. On the other hand, a distinguished former colleague of mine, Ruth Wilson, treasures the memory of working for, promoting and eventually managing the well-stocked Helena Rubinstein counter of an Australian department store, with its distinctively incentivised and progressive workplace culture. This was in South Australia in the early to mid-1980s, immediately prior to the acquisition by L'Oréal of the Helena Rubinstein brand. At a time when many questions relating to ethics and sustainability in fashion, gender identity, women and power, glass ceilings, misogyny and above all #MeToo – to say nothing of the stubborn persistence of anti-Semitism – animate much contemporary public debate and private discussion, Rubinstein assumes quite startling relevance.

If today we join a long queue to purchase (from $90) a small bottle of Clinique Smart Clinical Repair™ Wrinkle Correcting Serum (CL1870 Laser Focus Complex™), which repairs, resurfaces, 'replumps' and promises 'a 32 per cent reduction in stubborn lines', we are quite literally buying into a highly profitable commercial narrative, almost every part of which Rubinstein created in Australia and New Zealand 120 years ago. It would have given her much satisfaction to know that, nearly sixty years after her death, not only does she remain topical, many who followed in her footsteps have paid her the ample tribute of unabashed imitation while wearing, largely thanks to Rubinstein's hearty appetite for it, only a small fraction of the risk, or none at all. It is timely, then, to consider the company she kept.

* * *

Helena Rubinstein was one of those people whose long life brims with transcontinental encounters that capture the imagination. The caveat, here, is that often one feels one couldn't make it up, and she frequently did. So did many other people.[5] Nevertheless, we can independently place Rubinstein in known locations on particular dates, sometimes with distinguished statesmen and those close to them; great European and American writers and artists; composers and performers; scientists such as her compatriot Marie Curie; stars of the stage and screen; pioneering couturiers and leaders of society. Rubinstein's friendship with Pablo Picasso, though wary, lasted for forty years. Her mostly enjoyable, decades-long feud with Elizabeth Arden lately reached Broadway in the musical *War Paint*. In 1959, Israeli foreign minister Golda Meir personally accepted the gift of the Helena Rubinstein Pavilion for Contemporary Art in Tel Aviv, provided Rubinstein agreed to build, equip and staff a factory in Israel. Lunch followed with Prime Minister David Ben-Gurion. Later still, Rubinstein consulted Sir Edmund Hillary in relation to developments in apiary, his day job, and the exciting skin-nourishing properties of royal jelly. The Georges Pompidous sublet the granny flat in Rubinstein's famous house in the quai de Béthune on the Île Saint-Louis, and remained there after Pompidou became prime minister of France in April 1962. He and Madam Pompidou preferred not to move into the prime minister's official residence, the Hôtel de Matignon. Rubinstein was an early and prescient investor in the Xerox corporation.

Rubinstein's first marriage, in London in 1908 to another Polish Jew, Edward Titus, whom she met in Sydney, carried her into the Paris of Gertrude Stein, F. Scott Fitzgerald, Ernest Hemingway *et cetera* and, later, the cultural, artistic and literary worlds of Greenwich Village. In 1929, Titus became the first publisher in France of D.H. Lawrence's *Lady Chatterley's Lover*. Three years later, in September 1932, the last issue of his journal, *This Quarter*, was devoted to surrealism. It is something of a roll call. The contributors included Tristan Tzara, Paul Éluard, Luis Buñuel, Benjamin Péret, André Breton, Max Ernst, Yves Tanguy, Man Ray, Giorgio de Chirico and Salvador Dalí.

It is said that in Paris in the 1920s, James Joyce offered to write copy for Rubinstein's products in the style of *Ulysses*, claiming that 'women will be so puzzled they will rush out and buy'.⁶ Whether or not this anecdote is true – which I rather doubt – its persistence may nevertheless stand as emblematic of a longstanding and continuing male habit of declining to give Rubinstein credit for her enormous success in business and more generally refusing to acknowledge the independence, agency and purchasing power of modern women.

Rubinstein's first son, Roy, was born at home, 24 Grafton Street, London, in December 1909; a second son, Horace, followed in May 1912, when Rubinstein was not quite forty years old. The marriage, which was always turbulent, broke down towards the end of World War I and after years of sporadic transatlantic separation finally ended in divorce in 1932, the year of surrealism. Anaïs Nin narrowly avoided being named co-respondent. Rubinstein's second marriage in 1938 to the much younger Georgian émigré Artchil Gourielli-Tchkonia completed her social ascent. Thereafter, she rejoiced in the style and title of 'Princess Gourielli'.⁷

Perhaps the most impressive aspect of her life is that Rubinstein followed a long trajectory that led from a Polish ghetto to a Park Avenue penthouse triplex, via imperial Vienna, colonial Australia and New Zealand, Britain and France, that successfully avoided, indeed soared over and past, a handful of the greatest cataclysms of the late nineteenth and twentieth centuries. Kazimierz, the old Jewish quarter in Kraków, sheltered her family from the terrible Russian pogroms following the assassination of Tsar Alexander II in Saint Petersburg in 1881. Rubinstein defied the economic malaise of Melbourne and Victoria during the 1890s and 1900s. She found sanctuary and prospered in the United States of America throughout World War I, while her London and Paris businesses would appear to be among the few upon which that unprecedented industrialised slaughter made little impact. She sidestepped the Wall Street crash and the ensuing Great Depression. She avoided the Nazi occupation of Paris, rode out World War II and survived the Holocaust.

Not that these did not touch or affect her, sometimes directly. Her sister Regina Kolin perished in Płaszów or Birkenau or Auschwitz or on the streets of Kazimierz. This may well explain (if any explanation were needed) why, in later years, she so fiercely protected and advanced the interests of Regina's three children, Oscar, Henry and Mala Kolin, who became known as Mala Rubinstein. However, it is important to grasp that by the time Graham Sutherland painted her portrait in 1956–57, although her business was under considerable pressure, Rubinstein was entitled to feel that her very survival, her many achievements and her great wealth were far more than a matter of luck.

Wisely, for example, in December 1928, with a share price nudging $70, she sold a substantial interest in her American company to Lehman Brothers. Following the Wall Street crash and its terrible aftermath, in 1931 she bought it back, all of it, for approximately $3 a share – in cash. This was a painstaking exercise in persuasion. Rubinstein wrote to as many small shareholders as she could locate, most of whom were women, and explained that Lehman Brothers had failed to understand her company – which was true – and that its prospects depended upon being under her direct control, which also turned out to be true. On its own, this would not have been enough to wrest that control from Lehman Brothers. What she was asking from those small shareholders was almost preposterous and certainly illegal. If you believe in my products, she said, nothing less than selling your shares to me will ensure their survival and protect the future of the company. The speed with which by this unconventional technique she reacquired a sufficiently large interest in the company persuaded Lehman Brothers that, measured against far more pressing Wall Street priorities in that dark hour, Helena Rubinstein Incorporated was not worth fighting for. They conceded defeat and sold the rest of the company back to her.

Equally wisely, and prompted by her failure to close the Vienna operation before the Anschluss in March 1938, within a year Rubinstein had removed herself and her collection of modern and African art from Paris to New York, well before the arrival of the Nazis. She also made sure that most of her extended family were safely brought to America – this at a time when members of long-established wealthy Jewish families in France could not be made to believe that they might, could or would be in any danger.

Given these exceptional circumstances, and having once again found sanctuary in America, one can only imagine the anger and dismay that Rubinstein must have felt when in 1941, having set her heart upon leasing the 36-room triplex penthouse in 625 Park Avenue on the northeast corner of East 65th Street in the Lenox Hill neighbourhood of Manhattan, she was told that the building's cooperative board did not accept applications from Jews. In 1915, she had been prevented from opening the New York premises she wanted because of an even more blanket restriction against Jews that was somehow made to apply to much of the length of Fifth Avenue. She had no choice but to settle instead for 15 East 49th Street. Even in 1941, however, on the Upper East Side of Manhattan this type of blatant anti-Semitism was not uncommon, but Rubinstein's reaction to it was. Without hesitation, she bought the whole building. Thenceforth, those who had declined to accept her money had no choice but to pay it to her in rent or move house. 625 Park Avenue remained her principal residence for the rest of her life.[8] Throughout Rubinstein's career, there are many other examples of equally bold decisions and shrewd personal and business judgements.

The eight-part estate sale that ran over many days at Parke-Bernet Galleries in New York after her death in 1965 makes for fascinating reading.[9] Rubinstein was an ambitious, pioneering collector of Oceanic and African art, in which project she was much assisted by advice from the British sculptor Jacob Epstein, and of modern and contemporary art, furniture, decorative arts and rare gems and other jewels – scattergun but at times inspired. She owned numerous sculptures by her compatriot Elie Nadelman; that his monumental plaster *Horse* (c. 1911–15) should have found its way into the collection of the National Gallery of Australia in Canberra is a particularly satisfactory twist(fig. 2).[10] Apart from Graham Sutherland, many other not always famous artists painted, drew and photographed her, almost without exception less well than Sutherland did. These include Paul César Helleu, Christian Bérard, Marie Laurencin, René Bouché, Raoul Dufy, Emmanuele Castelbarco, Louis Marcoussis, Roberto Montenegro, Pavel Tschelitchew Man Ray, Cecil Beaton, William Dobell, Salvador Dalí, Andy Warhol and Pablo

INTRODUCTION

Figure 2. Helena Rubinstein in the 'treasure room' of her Park Avenue apartment with *Horse* by Elie Nadelman and carpet designed by Jean Lurçat, 1936, photographed by George Maillard Kesslère.

Picasso.[11] In a way all this feels very *Travesties* by Tom Stoppard, but it is real.

Before any of this, Rubinstein lived in Australia from 1896 to 1907, and her company began its life in February 1903 as two upstairs rooms in O'Connor's Chambers, 138 Elizabeth Street, between Little Collins and Bourke streets, in Melbourne.

* * *

The National Library of Australia has transformed the way we write social history (and every other sort) through Trove, its immense searchable collection of digitised newspapers.[12] With practice, it is now possible to find stray but vital snippets such as this slight paragraph in 'Gossip from Women's Clubland' in the *Queensland Figaro and Punch*:

Miss Helena Rubinstein, the pretty Polish girl who has lately been staying in Brisbane, is a cousin of the celebrated composer.[13]

Days, weeks, months of careful scrolling through microfilms in the dark might never have yielded this. Now the software takes you straight to it. We can run, but nowadays we simply cannot hide – and this was as true in 1904 as it is in 2023. In this case, Rubinstein's brief sojourn in Brisbane in 1904, a return visit, has hitherto escaped notice, but according to *The Brisbane Courier* she arrived there by train from Sydney on the Wednesday.[14] Suffice to say, there is not a scrap of evidence to support the flamboyant claim that Rubinstein was related to the celebrated Russian pianist, composer and conductor Anton Grigorevich Rubinstein, whose works were ubiquitous in Australian concert programmes through the 1890s and 1900s. However, it is noteworthy that she appears not to have persisted with the story – which would have been almost impossible to verify or disprove in Brisbane at the time, but far too easily exposable in the longer term. Wisely, she dropped it.

The value of Australian colonial newspapers cannot be overstated, particularly the plethora of dailies and illustrated weeklies that were being published in huge numbers at the turn of the century. Compared with today, Melbourne's press was enormously diverse and fully inter-colonial, indeed international. Consistently accurate and measured in its lengthy, syndicated news coverage, it reflected many shades of opinion across a wide spectrum that extended from the ultra-conservative landed interests to the most radical trade unions. This is not to say that the press did not regularly blur the boundary between detached reporting and friendly advertorial. On the contrary, we shall encounter numerous instances in which Rubinstein shrewdly exploited the latter. Perhaps most importantly, the dense advertising columns of Melbourne's papers retained many of their original vital uses, as a way of tracing missing persons or seeking to redirect unclaimed letters (that most forlorn phenomenon of colonial life), or as a means of more or less covert communication.

INTRODUCTION

The Melbourne press doubled as a Federation post box, message bank, billboard, calendar, megaphone, whispering gallery and echo chamber. It was not yet even partly supplanted by the telephone, of which in Australia in 1901 there were still only 33,000 in use.[15] The Marconi Company's first Australian two-way radio station did not open at Queenscliff, Victoria, until 1905.[16] For the time being, the newspapers continued to serve almost every purpose and most forms of public and even private communication. From the hundreds of affecting, evanescent messages that fill the daily personal columns therefore dangle numberless severed threads of microhistory.

Rubinstein's many similarly slight and fragmentary appearances in the Australasian press from 1900 to 1907 furnish valuable pieces of intelligence that exist nowhere else.[17] For the rest of her life, Rubinstein had every reason to feel confident that these would be as elusive as needles in haystacks, indeed far more so. She could never have imagined them being so easily and so liberally harvested. Now that we may do so, the problem is not one of location and retrieval so much as facing up to the daunting challenge of sifting, sorting, weighing, interpreting and contextualising – of giving form to what has so often seemed an ethereal, even fugitive presence in Australia at the time of Federation.[18] Among those sheaves of information, however, the most colossal and easily the most important was the annual fruit of a piece of private enterprise, compiled by hand.

In 1861, John Sands in Sydney and Dugald McDougall in Melbourne established an intercolonial business partnership that passed through their respective descendants and endured for more than a century. Sands & McDougall were by far the largest stationers operating in the Australian colonies, supplying every form of paper, account book, ledger, form, ticket, bill, envelope, bottled ink, printing and bookselling service upon which all commercial and government ventures depended, from the smallest shopkeeper to the largest banks and colonial or state and Commonwealth agencies.[19] Of their various almanacs, gazetteers, maps and other publications, however, their annual *Melbourne and Suburban Directory* lifted them into the realm of an intercolonial search engine on a par with Google.

Sands & McDougall's *Directory* was an immense list of every business, landlord and tenant in every premise, running the full length of every Melbourne street. Beginning at number 1 on the north or eastern side of each street, the list continued all the way up to the highest odd number at the other end of the street, and thence back to the beginning at number 2 (or the equivalent) on the opposite south or western side, working all the way up as before. This formidable undertaking was accomplished by a small army of Sands & McDougall 'walkers'. Combing Melbourne's crowded grid of streets and densely populated buildings, in which the majority of tenants were sole practitioners occupying single rooms, Sands & McDougall's walkers noted down full names and professions of every occupant, up to and including each building's caretaker.

The *Directory* was an awesome logistical, editorial, indexing, typesetting and printing undertaking on an industrial scale. It was published every January, and was therefore almost immediately obsolete, so the task of compiling, checking and revising the next year's edition began as soon as the previous one was bound and distributed. It carried a healthy retail price of £1 – happily subsidised by the sale of thousands of advertisements at the head and foot of almost every page, and a brace of full-page ads at the front, at the back and in the middle, the solicitation and coordination of which was on its own a vast enterprise.

Prior to the arrival of the telephone book, which was far less comprehensive, Sands & McDougall became an indispensable resource for post offices, municipal authorities, the metropolitan police, and commissioners of taxation (among many others). The additional value of the uninterrupted run of directories between 1896 and 1907, however, is that they provide a bird's eye view of Rubinstein's movements between premises, and a glimpse – fleeting, certainly, but reliable – of the scores of people with whom she rubbed shoulders and kept company.

Thus, in the *Directory for 1904*, reflecting data collected during 1903, we find Helena Rubinstein & Co. occupying second-floor rooms in the Fourth Victoria Building at 243 Collins Street. Her neighbours on that floor included a Miss O.A. Snowball, 'artist'; Madame Berrill, *costumière*; Miss G.F. Gaunt and Miss I. Lindsay Kirkland's 'School of Physical Culture'; Michael Cohen, general merchant; Thomas Kellaway, tailor, as well as the workroom of Thorne & Littlewood, bootmakers.[20] So light are these various footprints that in many instances the *Directory* constitutes their only enduring residue. Miss Snowball, incidentally, was a painter on china. In that same year, the art critic of *The Australasian* admired her fish service with tureen.[21]

It would be naïve in these cases to infer anything more than the mere fact of proximity. No doubt, the majority were ships passing: in corridors, on staircases and in the lift – Sands & McDougall confirm that indeed there *was* a lift – and keeping themselves to themselves, as in any office building today. However, Sands & McDougall permit us to observe Rubinstein taking three rapid 'steps up', in quick succession, over a little less than three years between February 1903 and the end of 1905. Indeed, the *Directory* provides almost the only surviving hard evidence of another personal and professional link that may well shine a thin but penetrating ray of light into the very origins of Rubinstein's business. Later prisms refract a lot more light than that, but from a much greater distance and across a far wider spectrum, such that the quality of the light tends to be cloudy, even deceptive. An excellent example of this is supplied by Patrick O'Higgins.

*   *   *

Patrick O'Higgins worked for Helena Rubinstein almost continuously from 1951 until her death in New York on 1 April 1965. According to her sometime amanuensis, an ambitious young Irishman, the flurry of welcome publicity surrounding the exhibition at the Tate Gallery in London of both surviving versions of Graham Sutherland's 'controversial' portrait of Rubinstein in the third quarter of 1957 prompted Madame to set O'Higgins to work on her ghosted memoir, *My Life for Beauty* (1965).[22]

In the years following her death, O'Higgins wrote his own, impressionistic *Madame: An Intimate Biography of Helena Rubinstein* (1971), which in many ways amounts to a camp torrent of not exactly hostile but unremitting insinuation.[23] Despite having been one of Rubinstein's legatees (receiving also an annuity for life), O'Higgins did not hesitate to refer uncharitably to Rubinstein's dentures; her greed; and her shabby treatment of both husbands, her two sons, her many other employees, and of himself.[24] Indeed, O'Higgins blamed her for causing him to suffer a nervous breakdown. He emphasised her unpredictable oscillations between flamboyant extravagance and habitual meanness. He also carefully noted what amounted to expenses fraud, plagiarism, customs irregularities, and various other examples of, at best, sharp business practice. There are many not particularly subtle flecks of anti-Semitic detail, as when O'Higgins coldly attributes to Rubinstein's second husband, Artchil Gourielli-Tchkonia – who, he says, 'had the appetites, the manners, the rough humour of a peasant smiled upon by good fortune' – the following remark: 'My wife very rich, very clever Jewish *Hausfrau!*'[25] Note the deftness with which Patrick O'Higgins managed thus to sideswipe both husband and wife simultaneously. At the same time, his book is laden with inaccuracies, errors, and distortion.

Although the memoir is unfriendly, nevertheless various photographs document the undoubted closeness of the working relationship that existed between Rubinstein and O'Higgins. One, in particular, which was taken in Paris in the autumn or winter of 1960, brings out some of the complexity of that relationship (fig. 3). Forced into close proximity by being seated in the back seat of a limousine, suggesting that O'Higgins was seated in the middle and a third passenger was on his other side, on one level he and Rubinstein seem perfectly comfortable at close quarters. She is swathed in a fur coat with an eccentric matching hat, this ensemble worn over a smart suit and many jewels. However, O'Higgins, likewise in hat, coat and woollen scarf over a neat suit and tie, is captured listening to her with serious intentness – his head turned sharply, his eyes fixed directly upon her, his jaw set. These hint at deference and concentration, even tension. Rubinstein is speaking, but her eyes do not engage with his. They stray beyond. A power relationship is at play. Given that by this date O'Higgins had worked for Rubinstein for nearly ten years, we should give him credit for those years of service.

INTRODUCTION

Figure 3. Helena Rubinstein and Patrick O'Higgins in Paris, 1960.

By his own account, O'Higgins's responsibilities spread haphazardly across a wide spectrum. He was not an executive of the corporation, but he was far more than a personal or executive assistant. In old age, Rubinstein came to trust and depend upon him as a travelling companion, confidential secretary, mouthpiece, barometer, runner of important business errands and punching bag. Therefore, we should neither dismiss out of hand some of the criticisms he published after her death, nor too easily impugn his point of view, even though in later years he was perfectly prepared to impugn hers.

The situation with O'Higgins is complicated, and is perhaps best summed up by the dustjacket blurbs he managed to extract from Cecil Beaton ('A witty and heartfelt valentine to an old monster'), from Anita Loos ('Her story would seem like a hilarious joke except she rolled up a hundred million dollars') and above all from Diana Vreeland, editor-in-chief of

American *Vogue*: 'Patrick O'Higgins's deep respect and love for the old girl really comes through. He has done a wonderful book on her.' Done is right.

These two unindexed books, *My Life for Beauty* (1965) and O'Higgins's *Madame* (1971), did much to establish and reinforce the myth of Rubinstein near the end of her life and shortly after her death, and also effectively covered her tracks, above all through the vital years of 1896–1907, when she conceived and created the first iteration of her business. However, in apparently seeking also to debunk the myth, fortunately O'Higgins gives us sufficient glimpses of independently verifiable detail to lend some credence to those parts of her story that in later years Rubinstein strove to suppress. Subsequent efforts to reconstruct those years either side of Federation have resulted in much confusion.[26] It is the aim of this volume to correct some of the more egregious errors, and to fill in some – but unfortunately by no means all – of the gaps.

What is so baffling, given what she went on to achieve, is the degree to which the many people whose paths we know Rubinstein crossed in Australia and New Zealand between 1896 and 1907 seldom, if ever, made any explicit or enduring reference to those encounters in later years, by which time hers was a household name. Whether or not this was a consequence of the fact that most men never seem to have taken her seriously, and many men still don't, our understanding of Rubinstein's formative years in Australasia will long remain a work in progress.[27]

This book began its life in 2015, the day Graham Sutherland's portrait of Rubinstein was delivered to the National Portrait Gallery in Canberra, where I was then director, and the moment I hurried down to the basement and watched, delighted, as it emerged from its crate. The book has evolved through a number of stages, each separated by several years. An admiring remark in the New Zealand press, quoting Julius Caesar, commended itself as the helpful division into two parts entitled, respectively, '*Veni, Vidi* (I came, I saw)' and '*Vici* (I conquered)'. Chapter 1 begins with the portrait that has prompted and inspired this book. Chapters 2 and 3 deal with Rubinstein's origins and her years in Australia before she started her business (1896–1903).

INTRODUCTION

Chapter 4 forms a hinge, a fulcrum, in which we consider the improbable commercial company she was proposing to keep in Melbourne from February 1903 onwards, while Chapters 5 to 7 look closely at her earliest successes in business and her rapid expansion into all six states of Australia and five New Zealand cities on both islands. Chapter 8 doubles back to the Sutherland portrait and a few of its distinguished predecessors and contemporaries. In each case, I suspect even readers who know a great deal about Rubinstein in her transatlantic commercial heyday and later years – Rubinstein the art collector and fashion plate, swathed in Elsa Schiaparelli or Cristóbal Balenciaga – will be surprised by the unlikely character and speed of her initial ascent in Australia and New Zealand. A work in progress, perhaps, but it is worth remembering that Rubinstein herself was, until the last decade of her life, the quintessential work in progress, and an active participant in the formation of her own legend. That we may know as much as we now do about her Australasian years is therefore a stroke of good fortune.

While labouring away in the early 1980s on his official biography of Lord Mountbatten, Philip Ziegler found it necessary to prop a card on his desk that read: 'Remember, despite everything, he was a great man.'[28] At times, I have found it necessary to do something similar for Helena Rubinstein. She was often maddening, and remains so. Occasionally, one wishes she had not amassed quite such an enormous collection of truly ghastly 'opaline glass', shelf upon groaning shelf of it, and concentrated instead on her rich holdings of African art – the Kota and Fang reliquaries, for example, or objects on a par with her superb Cameroonian 'Bangwa Queen', which so captivated Man Ray. In 1966, her estate yielded the first dedicated auction sale of African art ever to take place in the Western market. It is now taken far more seriously than it was at the time. For each of her missteps as an art collector there are far more flashes of inspiration. Her impressive group of early Picassos and Braques place Rubinstein at the epicentre of cubism. The large group of Mexican paintings she hungrily acquired soon after 1940, when she met Frida Kahlo and Diego Rivera in the San Ángel studio in Mexico City, likewise shows Rubinstein breaking new art-collecting ground, while remaining committed to the Paris moderns: Amedeo Modigliani, Max Ernst, Joan Miró, Henri Matisse, Kees van Dongen ...

Against her many and most outrageous fibs, there remains a larger narrative the thrust of which is consistent and undoubted. She constantly surprises. I know of no individual or corporation who embraced the idea of all lower-case typography and signage before she did. Thus 'helena rubinstein' became a sort of e. e. cummings *avant la lettre*. By the 1950s, her executives were holding up to ridicule the wealthy mogul who ran around her offices switching off the lights to save electricity, and rummaging in wastepaper baskets for things that could be reused or recycled. Nobody is laughing today. From the very beginning, in 1903, Rubinstein showed herself to be a master of publicity, the deft wrangler of a pliant press. At length, by the 1920s, the handsome return on her substantial investments in newspaper advertising did much to transform the transatlantic advertising industry itself. She was a phenomenon, a force not of nature but of artifice. So let us now swan dive into one of the great lives of the twentieth century, mindful that whenever we think we have alighted upon the formative or indeed the canonical Rubinstein, several others are likely to sprout up in her place. How very pleased she would have been, while being careful to conceal the pleasure.

PART I—*VENI, VIDI*
I CAME, I SAW

A Beauty Boom. – Into the big busy islands of New Zealand comes a Viennese beauty culturist with many laurels, with sheafs of flattering introductions, with all the triumph and glory of a fair Alexander. For like the great ancient warrior, Mlle Rubinstein came, saw, and conquered. Her victories cover the six States of the Federal Commonwealth.

The New Zealand Times, Wellington, February 1907.[1]

1

The Sutherland Portrait

'The last portrait of me done by Graham Sutherland,' Helena Rubinstein wrote shortly before her death in 1965, 'portrays me as an eagle-eyed matriarch! At first I hated it, but with time the picture has grown on me. And I remind myself that some art critics have likened it to a Renaissance masterpiece ... I had never seen myself in such a harsh light. Yet later, when they were exhibited at the Tate Gallery, although I scarcely recognised myself through Sutherland's eyes, I had to admit that as paintings they were indeed masterpieces.'[1]

A portrait in the Western tradition is a kind of paradox: the product of a fruitful collaboration between artist and subject, a likeness observed, given freely or, at times, guardedly, and fixed in time and space. Yet the portrait travels thereafter into the constantly evolving realms of memory, history and taste. From the day it is carried out of the artist's studio, the portrait passes through cycles of reinterpretation, the original encounter seen in ever new light, often shifting to different countries and continents, none of which the artist or his subject could ever have envisaged. For the rest of their lives, both may also gradually diverge from that original encounter, opening up ever-greater temporal and physical distances between each of them and their portrait. Having begun its life as a likeness *now*, the portrait shifts that likeness back through an inexorably receding *then*. Sometimes, if for a while there is no physical distance – when, for example, the portrait hangs in the subject's own house, or remains in the hands of the artist – the temporal distance only becomes the more apparent. At length, the portrait is bequeathed to an ever-widening posterity, sometimes in light of growing fame, or else the gathering dusk of obscurity, or sometimes both at once.

Graham Sutherland was one of the most distinguished British artists of the twentieth century. In his second volume of autobiography, Kenneth Clark described how Sutherland told him during World War II that in future he wanted to paint portraits, an ambition which, at the time, Clark greeted with scepticism, even bewilderment.[2] Halfway through the calamitous twentieth century, portraiture did not seem to be anywhere near the vanguard of contemporary British art. The most lionised mid-century portrait painter was Augustus John OM RA. As president of the *retardataire* Royal Society of Portrait Painters in Carlton House Terrace, Augustus John seemed to belong to another, increasingly superannuated age. By mid-century the tide seemed to have turned against portrait painting in Britain.

Sutherland at first made his reputation as a surrealist, and as a master of Pembrokeshire landscape, focusing on wild escarpments and the gnarled roots of ancient trees. Through Clark's influence Sutherland was brought into the War Artists' Scheme within the Ministry of Information, focusing mainly on bomb damage in London, tin-mining in Cornwall, coal-mines, limestone quarries, and on documenting the damage inflicted by the Royal Air Force on German bomb depots in occupied France. None of these anticipated, any more than his pre-war surrealism did, Sutherland's determination to paint portraits.[3]

Sutherland's reputation, output and confidence grew steadily during the late 1940s and 1950s. His portraits of Somerset Maugham (1949, Tate) and Sir Winston Churchill (1954, destroyed) were among the most celebrated works of British contemporary art in the post-war years. He went on to paint Lord Beaverbrook, Lord Sackville, Clark himself, Lord Goodman, Maximilian Egon zu Fürstenberg, Konrad Adenauer, Pierre Schlumberger, Baron Élie de Rothschild, and Daisy, the Hon. Mrs Reginald Fellowes.[4] This is the company Rubinstein and her portrait by Sutherland were keeping in 1957. Sutherland was in 1960 appointed to the Order of Merit.⁵

Recalling his earliest encounters with Rubinstein in England in 1956, when she was eighty-three, just before she made her final journey to Australia and New Zealand, Graham Sutherland wrote to Patrick O'Higgins:

> I have an acute 'sense' of her presence – even now – of the contained energy burning away behind the stillness. I sensed that she was suspicious of people and, in a curious way, even distrustful of herself – of her taste perhaps. My impression was strong in thinking that neither pictures, furniture nor objects meant more to her than a foil for electric, contained and strong vitality. She had fallen you will remember and the blue-black of the bruises on her face might well have been maquillage! It was on the second visit that I discovered what to do, because at the time I was able to observe her buying – and bargaining – over a table-full of costume jewellery by the gross and I drew her, unaware of my presence, in her Balenciaga dress, looking like an empress ... showing that rare, almost deprecating, but *enchanting* smile; it gave me the material in which I was able to work. She was, in a word – magnificent – minute and monosyllabic, with the force of an Egyptian ruler. She had a good many self-doubts and half-yearnings for some other life, half-glimpsed, which enabled her to say, 'I could do without all my money. If I were suddenly poor again, I could live perfectly happily.'⁶

Suspicious; distrustful of her own taste; bargaining over 'costume jewellery by the gross'; empress; Egyptian ruler; 'all my money'; 'If I were suddenly poor again ...' Leaving aside the question as to how Sutherland might have formed the impression that Rubinstein ever *had* been poor, one that she herself had long been at pains to dispel – apparently with some justification – we shall return to the difficult and complex question of cliché and not even always encoded anti-Semitism.

As Anthony Julius has written, the subtlest forms of anti-Semitism in England and elsewhere have given rise to a sort of paranoia, to which he himself readily owns:

> Jews succeed against the grain; there is a certain resistance to them that is rarely expressed, and never legislated. Anti-Semitism in England breeds Jewish paranoia. You don't see it coming; and when it's gone you're still not quite sure what it was. To understand what is going on in England, you need a very nuanced sense of the anti-Semitic, one which overlaps with an Anglo-Jewish self-definition.[7]

However, those subtle forms of anti-Semitism also have a sinister tendency to seep, at times undetected, into the ostensibly positive estimation of Jewish subjects. 'Part of the ambivalence of anti-Semitism', Julius goes on, 'is that it slides into a certain kind of regard for Jews.' It is a vital question, therefore, to ask: Is this what was going on, and is maybe still going on, in the encounter between Graham Sutherland and Helena Rubinstein? Indeed, does reading carefully for signs, for residues, of anti-Semitism implicate us in the identification, the delineation, of ethnic and racial difference, which is in turn so obviously fraught with danger?[8] There is no easy answer. Perhaps the best that can be said is that it is important to keep asking the question, to be aware that it exists, and to allow oneself to be troubled by it. Any careful examination of a Jewish life in history involves a degree of outside scrutiny of which Rubinstein, in this instance, had every reason to be wary, indeed suspicious; every reason to presume that it brought with it measures of not always latent hostility, ranging from the faint, the mild, even the unconscious, all the way to the positively lethal.

* * *

In the section of his book that deals with the creation of Sutherland's portraits, Patrick O'Higgins made perhaps one of his most careless errors. Rubinstein's journey to England, he said, followed the death in April 1958 of her younger son, Horace Titus, from a heart attack in Greenwich, Connecticut.[9] However, the encounter between Rubinstein and Sutherland took place two years earlier, in 1956, *before* Horace Titus died. Instead, it was for her second husband, who died suddenly on 21 November 1955, that Rubinstein was in mourning. O'Higgins went on to suggest that it was in a letter of condolence, received 'ten days after Horace's death', that his friend the photographer Cecil Beaton passed on the fateful suggestion that Sutherland wished to paint Rubinstein.[10] Her ensuing journey to England O'Higgins characterises as a consolatory diversion which Rubinstein, 'comatose in satin sheets', resisted at first until, he suggests, the idea that Sutherland had never yet painted 'an important woman' led personal vanity, even hunger for publicity, to supplant an all-encompassing but, it turned out, only temporary grief.[11]

Even before Rubinstein met Sutherland, O'Higgins continued, the task of negotiating a fee was in London allotted to Boris Forter, 'Ceska Cooper's principal business associate and manager ... a wily White Russian whose acute financial brain, patience, and tact balanced Mrs Cooper's many eccentricities' – Ceska Cooper being Rubinstein's sister, by then in charge of the London and South African branches of the business.[12] It was to be a *commissioned* portrait. Presumably encouraged to do so, the Sutherlands extended to Rubinstein an invitation to lunch at their home in West Malling, roughly halfway between Sevenoaks and Maidstone in Kent. The meeting was a success. Sutherland drew Rubinstein more or less constantly during the week that followed. She then facilitated a further week of sittings at her house in the quai de Béthune in Paris. Rubinstein proceeded there ahead of the Sutherlands, and it was there that she had the fall to which Sutherland referred in his letter to O'Higgins, a fall that resulted in such bad bruises as to require heavy applications of additional rouge and kohl. 'The effect was extraordinary. She appeared for lunch', recounted O'Higgins in his characteristically unpleasant way, '[again] in the elaborately embroidered Balenciaga dress looking like Theda Bara cast as Count Dracula. "Her make-up is sensational!" Graham Sutherland could hardly contain his enthusiasm.'[13]

There can be no question that Sutherland derived considerable excitement from seeing Rubinstein as a sort of Byzantine empress. He was not alone. The trope crops up in many other places. O'Higgins recalled a chance post-war re-encounter in a hotel dining room at Villefranche when, incredibly, Jean Cocteau 'raised his arm like a Roman Centurion and greeted Rubinstein thus: "*Je salue l'Impératrice de Byzance!*"'[14] Later, Roderick Cameron made it clear that at times the analogy dripped with sarcasm. She was, he thought, 'a great middle-European peasant lady standing firmly in profile armoured by her own astuteness and hard work in the carapace of glitter, enamelled in beads and jewels, [and] looked like some formidable twentieth-century Byzantine empress'. For 'middle-European peasant lady', read Jew.[15]

In January 1938, Cecil Beaton, whose especially chilling anti-Semitic credentials are well documented, had described Rubinstein in his diary even more crudely as 'an old Polish frog ... with a huge casket of jewels. I have never seen such a collection, and she clicks her teeth and shrugs "Only rubbish. Much more in Paris" – but they are jewels that would belong to a kingdom, not a private individual.'[16] Not even a month later, Beaton lost his job at American *Vogue* when it was discovered that he had inscribed what David Mellor describes as 'microscopic anti-Semitic doodlings' in the margin of a drawing in the February 1938 issue that made it necessary for Condé Nast to recall 150,000 copies of the magazine and print a corrected run. It is to their credit that they did so. Writing in 1977, Keith Roberts wrote: 'Sutherland had the wit to see the old lady of eighty-six [*sic*] as a proud survivor, the shrewd Empress of a Kingdom of Illusions.'[17] As recently as 1982, Sutherland's biographer Roger Berthoud could state that Rubinstein's portrait conveyed 'the imperious air of a potentate and the ferocity of a bird of prey'.[18] Such assessments tell us more about the men who made them than about the character of Rubinstein. There can be no question that to anti-Semitism, at times explicit but more often than not subtle, we may also add plain misogyny.

Though deeply unattractive, Beaton was an especially interesting observer because, again in the 1930s, he created a surrealistic photomontage in which he cleverly and seamlessly superimposed Rubinstein's face onto the head of what appears to be an eighteenth-century life-sized marble bust on plinth with epaulettes, the bust of a military gentleman (fig. 4). Beaton contrives to replace Rubinstein's coiffure with the bust's marble one, a bag wig, the ribbon of which takes the place of her signature chignon. He festoons the lapel and lace kerchief with many jewels – the earrings are her own – while the bust itself is placed over and adjacent to at least five substantial prints after paintings by Jean-Antoine Watteau. The bust pins them down, and partly obscures all of them, while in turn they deprive the bust of any architectural or interior setting. The shadow of her profile is made to fall obliquely across the sky of the nearest print, and with crude, unflattering emphasis upon her anamorphically lengthened nose. The crisp white border of that print also forms an approximately lozenge-like cartouche within which the bust is, at the same time, accommodated.

Figure 4. Surrealistic photomontage, 1930s, by Cecil Beaton. Reproduced from the lost original by Charmante Studio, 210 Fifth Avenue, New York.

The fact that this photomontage survives in the Helena Rubinstein collection in the Fashion Institute of Technology in New York proves that she herself once owned and kept it, but it is unique in being, to my knowledge, the only surviving image in which Rubinstein was made to take possession of and inhabit any aspect of the eighteenth century. True, she had dallied with Louis XIV furnishings in her first New York salon at 15 East 49th Street, and her estate sale contained numerous pieces of French furniture and *objets de vertu*. However, she had long since made a point of embracing instead the smooth whiteness, chrome and clean straight lines of high Modernism.[19] The montage, slightly fey but not entirely unflattering, hardly gives the impression of an 'old monster' or 'an old Polish frog', and although Beaton grumbled about the amount and degree of doctoring he was required to do to his own portrait photographs of Rubinstein – the inches she insisted he take off her waistline, for example – in every case he was more than willing to go ahead and follow instructions.

In the smaller version of her finished portrait by Sutherland, Rubinstein is seated with what strikes me as incomparable dignity and splendour. She is erect, strong, silent, and, as Cameron noted, heavily bejewelled – suffice to say that there are, in this instance, no 'beads'. Her head is held high, while the strength of her arm and the tension in her wrist continue all the way down to her glossily lacquered fingers' ends, the nail of her left index finger carefully sharpened into something like a talon – and I use that word advisedly but with caution.

The artist was obviously fascinated by his subject, the cast of her head, the strength of her octogenarian neck, the line of her nostril, the sense of shrewd determination with which he endows her eyes and mouth and chin, the blackness and the thinness of her hair, dragged with such force into her chignon. There is, at the same time, a palpable sense of tautness and containment in the pose, which Sutherland himself remarked upon, as well as a degree of tension that is reinforced by the disciplined geometry to which the artist held himself. His preparatory grid of steep ruled diagonal and intersecting horizontal lines is clearly visible in places beneath the relatively thin paint film. One wrist does not rest over the other. It is, rather, as if the left strains downwards over the right, and the right pushes upwards in equal measure, both serving to fix her shoulders and set her elbows. She may be calm and still, but Rubinstein is far from relaxed.

In Melbourne in 1957, the late Rowena ('Binny') Lum recorded a long, deferential interview for radio with Rubinstein that survives among many others in the collection of the National Film and Sound Archive of Australia in Canberra.[20] Although Rubinstein gradually builds a head of steam, the interview begins with the same containment and caution that Sutherland himself noted elsewhere in his letter to O'Higgins. Rubinstein was, he said, 'a real mystery woman … for the most part, monosyllabic'.[21] Indeed, Sutherland resorted to that last word twice. It is relatively unusual to be able to compare voice and sustained speech, intonation and inflection, with a contemporaneous finished portrait of the speaker, but in this case Lum's interview and Sutherland's portrait have in common a discernible measure of tension. Confronted by a public platform on which to perform, and a corresponding mass audience (as distinct from a mass market), Rubinstein tended to be abashed, cautious, wary. She was equally shy, even insecure, in private. It seems she reserved for her husbands, sons and executives private moments of candour but also, as the years went by, explosions of increasingly tyrannical rage.[22] Her favourite social diversion was playing bridge, and with much concentration and minimal small talk. Indeed, proficiency at bridge became for her executives almost a condition of their employment. Her game was aggressive. She liked to win.[23]

* * *

By the time he painted her in his studio at Trottiscliffe, about four kilometres northwest of his house at West Malling, Sutherland had drawn and sketched Rubinstein many times (fig. 5). Some of these drawings were deposited by the artist's widow, Kathleen Sutherland, in the prints and drawings department at the British Museum, and they reveal not only the degree of care with which Sutherland observed his subject, but also the swiftness and consistency with which from the outset he settled upon the attitude and orientation of her head. Later, in 1960, Sutherland returned to his subject and, working with the Curwen Studio in London, created three lithographs, two of which are therefore reversed(fig. 7).[24] The first 1956 sittings took place at first in the comfortable sitting-room of Rubinstein's suite at Claridge's in London. According to O'Higgins, she was 'enshrined in cushions', with her feet propped on all four London telephone directories. 'There were masses of flowers and a real log fire burned in a splendid fireplace.'[25]

Figure 5. Three portrait studies of Helena Rubinstein by Graham Sutherland, 1956.

Figure 6. *Portrait of Helena Rubinstein*, 1956, by Graham Sutherland.

Figure 7. *Portrait of Helena Rubinstein III*, 1960, by Graham Sutherland.

Rubinstein sat for Sutherland for another week about a week after that, in May 1956, this time in her house in Paris.[26] Post-war travel from England to France still being relatively restricted, the Sutherlands jumped at the chance when Rubinstein proposed to help make it possible, and to pay their expenses. Sutherland returned to Paris in the autumn. There is some disagreement as to when he finally decided upon the Balenciaga gown, but all agree that the gown provided him with the defining framework for his finished pictures. At the end of that second week Sutherland sought and was granted permission to snip a piece of exquisitely embroidered fabric overlaid with sequins, glass beads and rhinestones from inside the hem of her gown, so as to be able to reproduce it as faithfully as possible. That swatch measured several square inches. He also cut a wisp of her hair and took samples of her lipstick, rouge and eye shadow.

Apart from the superb drawings and studies he executed quickly, Sutherland produced three versions of his portrait of Rubinstein. The first, not yet finished, was destroyed in a fire in the artist's studio on 15 December 1956; the Sutherlands were both heavy smokers. "'Don't I smell burning?" she [Kathleen] called up. "I'm just burning the bloody studio down," Graham called back, and the canvas went out of the window.' Some ash from a lighted cigarette had ignited vapour arising from his methylated spirits.[27] Afterwards he worked on two fresh versions concurrently. Both were finished by April 1957.[28] On 14 April, 'the *Sunday Times* scooped the Beaverbrook press with a Felix Man photograph of Graham at work on the seated version'.[29] Apparently responding to this, Cecil Beaton wrote enthusiastically to Sutherland: 'It looks superb, a staggering likeness of the old bird. She's pretty marvellous, and you've given her the proper treatment, and not cheated on her baldness or her glamour.'[30] Sutherland wanted to know which version Beaton preferred, and urged him to visit Alfred Hecht's, his framer in the King's Road, to see both portraits in the flesh. Beaton responded with equal enthusiasm: 'Upon close study I came very definitely to the conclusion that I *much* preferred the sitting picture. It has more depth and vitality, more solidity, and the face is more vibrant ... the whole exercise has been a *tour de force*, and

I'm sure the old bird will reap great rewards from her cleverness in inveigling you into the project.'[31] This closing remark was sarcastic: Cecil Beaton did not hesitate to take credit for successfully choreographing the encounter.

The second, significantly larger version, which shows Rubinstein standing imperiously, her hands firmly planted on her hips, is arguably the less powerful – as Beaton rightly suggested. However it is also, as John Hayes puts it, the more truculent and obviously proprietorial, straying in the direction of coarseness.[32] (plate 2) It also differs from the smaller version in that Sutherland chose to place Rubinstein against a shallow enclosing space that consists of wainscot panelling, the upper half of which is blocked in with broad, desiccated verticals that recall mid-career Francis Bacon, whom Sutherland knew well.[33] However, in Sutherland's hands this technique and the effect of it are, I think, at odds with his far more exacting treatment of the standing figure of Rubinstein and her magnificent head. The contrast between them is slightly jarring. In any event, this larger version was soon afterwards purchased by Lord Beaverbrook, together with a number of drawings, and in 1959 formed part of the core collection of the newly established Beaverbrook Art Gallery in Fredericton, New Brunswick.[34]

The smaller version in Canberra is markedly more regal, and benefits from a plain, mostly smooth, thinly painted blue-grey background – a high-keyed void into which the figure looms with not a little drama. It also benefits from the comparatively elongated proportions of the canvas, something it shares with the earlier portrait of Somerset Maugham, but with a consequent loftiness of space into which Sutherland lifts his subject. In both versions, which are slightly larger than life-size, Rubinstein holds that curious small fan, an accessory with which Sutherland allowed himself more than a hint of personal stylisation – as if something small and dry and spiky has been plucked from one of his contorted surrealist landscapes from many years earlier, or from one of his thorny bushes, and carefully slotted between Rubinstein's thumb and forefinger. It is a clever compositional device in both versions, not only providing Rubinstein with something to handle, but also serving to soften the otherwise over-emphatic horizontal line that passes through her waist. In the Canberra version, the spry verticality of the fan works better than in the Beaverbrook picture, and also maybe serves as a gentle rebuke, post hoc, of the artist's own severity with regard to his unflattering portrayal of Rubinstein's nearest knuckles and of that startling sharpened fingernail. It is also the nearest we get to any suggestion, any evidence, of tremulous motion in a portrait that is in every other respect imbued with stillness. A careful preparatory drawing and the Felix Man photograph, in both of which it is nowhere to be seen, prove that Sutherland's fan was a last-minute addition, but that from the outset the fingernail was an important compositional device.

From the beginning of the second phase of her career in England immediately before the outbreak of World War I, it was part of Rubinstein's genius that she fully grasped the importance to her business and to her brand of boldly projecting her own glamour – in costume, maquillage and coiffure, the better to attract sustained publicity and, in turn, gain commercial traction. True, there were hints of this already in her approach to the business in Melbourne, but it was not until she established herself in London and Paris that the strategy took shape and then took off. In later years, her astonishing wardrobe was wholly strategic, beginning with the House of Worth in Paris and continuing through Paul Poiret, Jacques Doucet, Captain Edward Molyneux, Madame Suzy, Lanvin, Agnès, Chanel, Schiaparelli, Dior, Givenchy and Cristóbal Balenciaga, as in this instance. Approaching the age of ninety, in 1962 she purchased a purple ensemble from Yves Saint-Laurent's first solo collection after his departure from the House of Dior.

We have seen that it was Sutherland's idea that his subject should be portrayed wearing her full-length crimson brocade gown designed by Cristóbal Balenciaga, a choice with which Rubinstein was obviously comfortable. This he did with superb fluency, brilliantly conveying both richness of texture and hue; the stiffness and weight of the fabric and the complexity of the design. The ensemble, consisting of the gown and a matching coat which Sutherland did not paint, survives in an altered, shortened state in the collection of the Costume Institute at the Metropolitan Museum of Art in New

York, having been presented in 1969 by Rubinstein's niece Mala Rubinstein.[35] (plate 3) Details illustrate the degree to which Sutherland rejoiced in its design and captured the essentials (plates 4, 5).

Balenciaga may have sourced this magnificently embroidered fabric from Gustav Zumsteg at the House of Abraham in Zurich, and although Rubinstein owned gowns by Balenciaga that were created with fabric from René Bégué of the Maison Rébé, this piece was not one of them. Rubinstein had been an important client of Balenciaga since 1939, when for that year's winter collection in Paris 'he created a series of evening gowns directly inspired by Velázquez's portraits of the Infanta Margarita and her ladies-in-waiting. For *Harper's Bazaar*, George Hoyningen-Huene photographed two of these gowns against canvases by Pablo Picasso and sculptures by Constantin Brancusi' in Rubinstein's house in the quai de Béthune.[36] The emphatic horizontality of the waistline whence the full long skirt radiates out and spirals downwards in stiff crimson folds over her crossed legs – right over left in elegant counterpoint to the orientation of her wrists – serves to fix the viewer's eye. We are by this device made to see Rubinstein upwards from below, and also to be persuaded that hers is, surely, the complementary view *de haut en bas*. Which is not to suggest that she does not simultaneously give the impression of thoughtful introspection. Both things are happening, and that duality endows the portrait with its undoubted psychological complexity. It is something of a paradox.

As with her wardrobe and her eclectic approach to interior decoration, so too it was with her jewels. Rubinstein had long been famous for them, and for the flamboyant way she used large quantities of jewels to enhance and dramatise her appearance. At times she seems to have revelled in giving the impression that she wore all her jewels at once. Eyewitnesses were consistent in recalling the clatter of many bangles on both wrists preceding her into any room. In his portraits, Sutherland obviously took great care faithfully to execute her diamond and pearl cluster-drop earrings, the famous seven-strand necklace consisting of 369 graduated baroque pearls, and the huge plump cabochon gemstones set in her rings.[37]

Figure 8. Helena Rubinstein posing at the Tate Gallery with both versions of her portrait by Graham Sutherland, 1957.

According to the jewellery designer Kenneth J. Lane, 'If you look at the Sotheby Parke-Bernet catalogue of the [posthumous 1965 jewellery] sale, you'll see there were lots of remarks about flawed stones and old settings – they weren't really serious pieces.' To which Lindy Woodhead correctly adds, first, that Rubinstein's most distinguished pieces of jewellery were bequeathed to her surviving sisters and other members of her extended family and were therefore not included in the New York sale, and that she 'didn't buy jewellery to keep it in bank vaults, she wore it, and she wore it well. She was passionately fond of large showy settings and knew perfectly what she was doing when she bought stones that were less than perfect.'[38] Rubinstein was also fond of mixing precious and costume jewellery, as if to display casual disregard for the monetary value of the former and to uplift the purely aesthetic, often surprising effects of the latter. As with her Balenciaga gown, Sutherland obviously derived much enjoyment from the task of capturing her jewels, lending to the underside of one or two of the biggest pearls, for example, a warm blush of light reflected up off the red brocade. He had had few opportunities to tackle sumptuous effects such as these; most of his subjects had been men.

Rubinstein's immediate reaction to both of Graham Sutherland's paintings when she first saw them at Hecht's in London, well before the end of the summer of 1957, was not ambivalent so much as hostile. O'Higgins dates this to 'a dank, dark November day', however correspondence in the collections of Tate and the Beaverbrook Art Gallery shows not only that the paintings were on loan to the Tate Gallery from 1 October (at the latest) but that the larger version was already by then the property of Lord Beaverbrook.[39] Approaching her eighty-fifth birthday, and perhaps being amply reminded of it, cannot have helped. '"Oh, my God! ... Look at me." She turned her back on both portraits, "... so old! So savage ... a witch!"' (fig. 8)[40]

Earlier, before the end of May, Sutherland had sent photographs to O'Higgins, who responded with the suggestion that the artist might consider 'softening' or lifting the sagging chin line, adding that for business reasons Rubinstein needed to look 'ageless'. For decades, her publicity and portrait photographs had been routinely doctored to this end. Sutherland baulked at this *démarche*, responding from Venice on 3 June, 'My portraits are objective – neither idealised nor caricatured, as everyone knows. If I start softening etc. etc. it is the beginning of the end. To say nothing of the fact that I cannot invent new necks without spoiling the paintings. On the other hand I grew very fond of Madame while working, and I would like her – from her business point of view (because I know she is *far* too intelligent to mind otherwise, for reasons of personal vanity) – to be happy.'[41] Further, he undertook to see what could 'honourably be done'. Close and careful looking at the paint film, however, suggests that, thank goodness, Sutherland stood his ground and made no subsequent alteration.

Figure 9. Helena Rubinstein posing *en fête* with (left to right) Viscount and Viscountess Hambleden, Douglas Cooper, Nela Rubinstein, Kathleen Sutherland, Artur Rubinstein and Graham Sutherland, Grafton Street, Mayfair, 25 November 1957.

Evidently recovering from the initial shock, in which she also noted that her left profile was her '*bad* side', Rubinstein soon arrived at a reasonably tolerable accommodation. On 25 November, wearing her Balenciaga gown but a different suite of jewels,[42] she hosted a reception for Sutherland in Grafton Street, and was photographed there *en fête* with the Sutherlands, Viscount and Viscountess Hambleden (of the W.H. Smith fortune), the celebrated concert pianist Artur Rubinstein, his wife Nela, and the Australian-born critic and art collector Douglas Cooper (fig. 9). It was Cooper who, years earlier, referring to Sutherland's studies of the head of Somerset Maugham, described these as exhibiting 'the same sort of expression of the process of growth and struggle as he found in the rugged surfaces and irregular contours of a boulder or a range of hills'.⁴³ He might easily have applied the same observation to Sutherland's portraits of Rubinstein. Another photograph taken on the same occasion shows the artist and his subject seated at close quarters on a small reproduction Louis XV settee discussing the fabric of her gown (fig. 10). If body language can be any indication, in these surroundings Sutherland appears far less comfortable than Rubinstein – almost abashed, deferential. Madame, after all, was on this occasion on her home turf.

Figure 10. Helena Rubinstein and Graham Sutherland,
Grafton Street, Mayfair, 25 November 1957.

Compared with the many portraits by other artists that preceded it, Graham Sutherland's is by far the stateliest, and comes closest to representing for Rubinstein a sort of apotheosis in dignified old age. However, in order to attain that happy state, you do have to start somewhere.

2

Embarkation and Landfall

In May 1907, Helena Rubinstein lodged with the Commonwealth Department of External Affairs in Melbourne her application for naturalisation as a British subject (fig. 11). Those documents survive in the collection of the National Archives of Australia in Canberra and form an invaluable framework for her Australian sojourn, but the contents are far from reliable.[1]

According to her neatly signed statutory declaration, Rubinstein was born in Kraków (true) in the northernmost Austro-Hungarian province of Galicia (i.e. modern Poland: true) on Christmas Day (true) in 1879 (*not* true). Notwithstanding, 'I make this solemn declaration conscientiously believing the same to be true, and by virtue of the provisions of an Act of the Parliament of Victoria rendering persons making false declarations punishable for wilful and corrupt perjury.' By then, Rubinstein was residing in not just respectable but fashionable lodgings at 'Arcadia', 17 Spring Street, Melbourne, facing the Treasury Gardens. She conducted her business, the Valaze Institute, in Messrs W.H. Glen & Co.'s Music and Piano Warehouse at 272–274 Collins Street. She had invented the fetching middle name of 'Juliet' and gave as her profession 'importer' – which was not strictly speaking true either, not just yet. Although it purported to come from Russia, Dr Lykuski's skin food Valaze™ was concocted with the aid of the firm of Felton Grimwade in Flinders Lane, which is how Frederick Sheppard Grimwade JP 'of Harleston, Caulfield' came to stand sponsor.

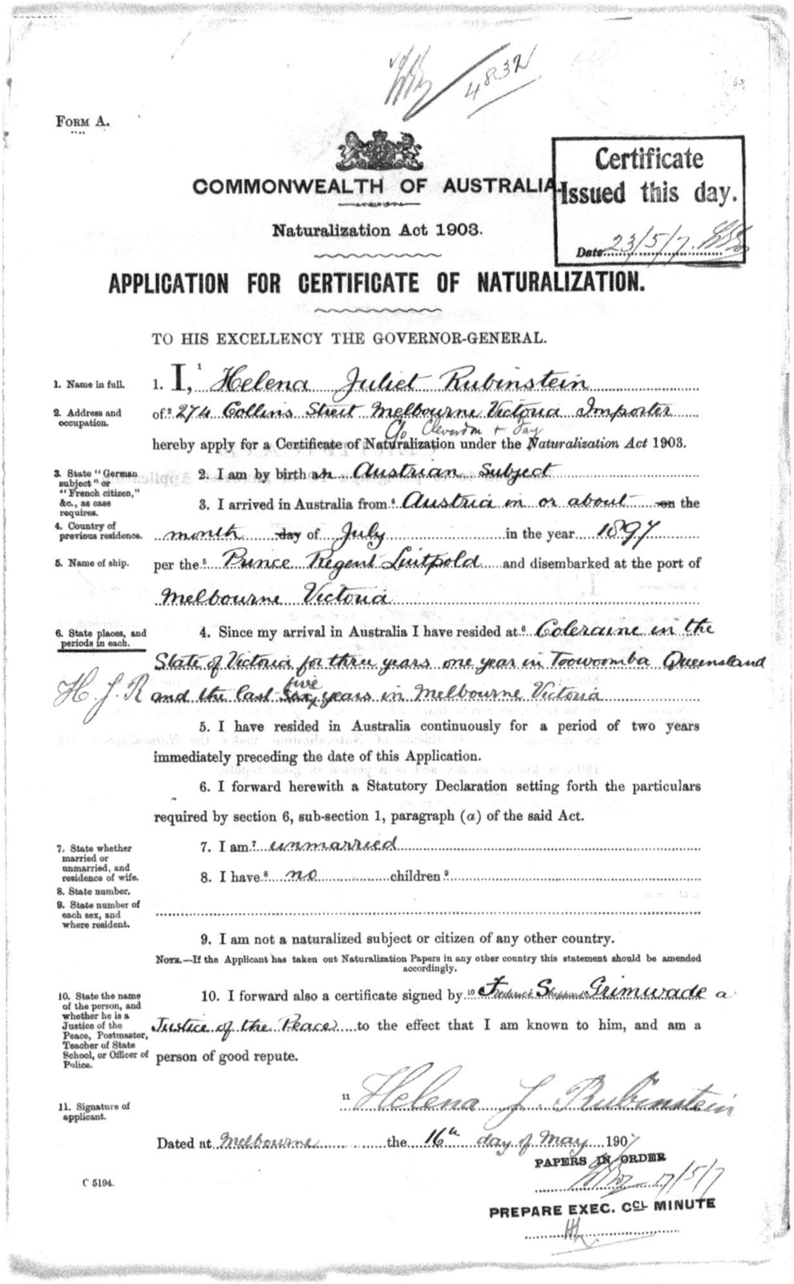

Form A.

COMMONWEALTH OF AUSTRALIA

Naturalization Act 1903.

Certificate Issued this day.
Date 23/5/7

APPLICATION FOR CERTIFICATE OF NATURALIZATION.

TO HIS EXCELLENCY THE GOVERNOR-GENERAL.

1. Name in full. 1. I, *Helena Juliet Rubinstein*
2. Address and occupation. of *274 Collins Street Melbourne Victoria Importer* C/o Cleverdon + Day hereby apply for a Certificate of Naturalization under the *Naturalization Act* 1903.
3. State "German subject" or "French citizen," &c., as case requires. 2. I am by birth *an Austrian Subject*
4. Country of previous residence. 3. I arrived in Australia from *Austria on or about* on the *ninth* day of *July* in the year *1897*
5. Name of ship. per the *Prince Regent Luitpold* and disembarked at the port of *Melbourne Victoria*
6. State places, and periods in each. 4. Since my arrival in Australia I have resided at *Coleraine in the State of Victoria for three years, one year in Toowoomba Queensland and the last five years in Melbourne Victoria*

5. I have resided in Australia continuously for a period of two years immediately preceding the date of this Application.

6. I forward herewith a Statutory Declaration setting forth the particulars required by section 6, sub-section 1, paragraph (a) of the said Act.

7. State whether married or unmarried, and residence of wife. 7. I am *unmarried*
8. State number. 8. I have *no* children
9. State number of each sex, and where resident.

9. I am not a naturalized subject or citizen of any other country.

NOTE.—If the Applicant has taken out Naturalization Papers in any other country this statement should be amended accordingly.

10. State the name of the person, and whether he is a Justice of the Peace, Postmaster, Teacher of State School, or Officer of Police. 10. I forward also a certificate signed by *Frederick Sherman Grimwade* a *Justice of the Peace* to the effect that I am known to him, and am a person of good repute.

11. Signature of applicant. *Helena J. Rubinstein*

Dated at *Melbourne* the *16th* day of *May* 190*7*

PAPERS IN ORDER

PREPARE EXEC. CO. MINUTE

C 5194.

Figure 11. Helena Rubinstein's application for naturalisation as a British subject, May 1907

The firm of Felton Grimwade came into being in 1867, when in partnership Alfred Felton and Frederick Sheppard Grimwade purchased the wholesale drug house of Youngman & Co. Through the next twenty-five years, the new firm prospered. Despite the financial collapse of 1891 and the ensuing depression, Felton Grimwade remained the largest and most profitable pharmaceutical company in the colony, with thriving subsidiary interests in New Zealand and Western Australia. Felton Grimwade also established companies that fed into and/or supported their chain of supply, most importantly the Melbourne Glass Bottle Works (1872), one of the important forerunners of Australian Consolidated Industries (ACI). From a large and bustling three- and four-storied factory and warehouse that stretched between 349 and 351 Flinders Lane and Flinders Street, Felton Grimwade had long been able to concoct, formulate and manufacture many different pharmaceutical products, wet and dry, and to distribute them to retail chemists and others wholesale, in their own fit-for-purpose jars and bottles.

In the last quarter of the nineteenth century, the term 'pharmaceutical' embraced many kinds of product, such that their operation offered Rubinstein *either* a convenient one-stop wholesale manufacturer and supplier upon whom to rely in giving her affordable substance to the genie of Valaze, *or* a reliable source in bulk of refined lanolin, of which Felton Grimwade were also wholesalers. Quite possibly both.[2] Lanolin, from the Latin words for wool and oil, is in fact a wax that is secreted by the sebaceous glands of sheep. It is a form of natural waterproofing that prevents fleeces from getting cripplingly saturated, but it has long been recognised as beneficial to human skin. In 1885, Felton Grimwade had gone into partnership with the Melbourne pharmacist Joseph Bosisto, whose eucalyptus oil distillery on the bank of Dandenong Creek supplied them with the primary ingredient with which they manufactured the first 'indigenous' Australian product to be exported in bulk to Britain – Bosisto's Eucalyptus Oil for various medicinal and antiseptic purposes.

As early as 1877, Felton Grimwade were manufacturing and distributing a product known as Mrs Allen's World's Hair Restorer, which 'never fails to restore Grey Hair to its youthful colour, imparting to it new life, growth, and lustrous beauty. Its action is certain and thorough, quickly banishing greyness. It is not a Dye. It ever proves itself the natural strengthener of the Hair. Its Superiority and Excellence are established. The genuine only in pink wrappers.'[3] At the turn of the century, Felton Grimwade were relying less and less on sole-trading customers such as Mrs Allen and Helena Rubinstein, but those customers had long been the bread and butter of Flinders Lane.[4]

From the beginning, Rubinstein's principal claim about Valaze was that it had been formulated by an acquaintance or friend of her mother's, a great Russian or Polish or occasionally Hungarian chemist or doctor or skin specialist named Dr Josef Lykuski or, at times, 'Lykusky' – on each and every point Rubinstein could never quite make up her mind. Yet Dr Lykuski is a lively presence in all of Rubinstein's publicity. By 1930, she had added a brother, and in 1965 she was even claiming that the eminent doctor had accepted her invitation to sail to Melbourne for a while. We can only speculate whether this not-necessarily-implausible adjustment was intended to cover against any possible future discovery that Valaze was formulated locally and not expensively imported from Russia. In fact, the recipe, which O'Higgins claimed to have seen on a sheet of paper Rubinstein showed him towards the end of her life, consisted of lanolin, vegetable oil, mineral oil and ceresin wax, with cheap scent, possibly rosewater, to cut or neutralise the woolly smell of the lanolin. Woodhead suggests that ceresin wax was an unlikely ingredient of cold cream, and that it probably did not go into Valaze.[5] However, Bennett has shown that this was not the case.

Ceresin wax is an odourless mineral substitute for beeswax. It has a relatively high melting point and reduces the sweating or bleeding of oils in emulsions, both qualities that help to stabilise any cold cream, especially one that is used in a hot climate. Cosmetic grades of refined lanolin, meanwhile, had been used in Germany from about 1880; its medicinal benefits had been advocated by the Berlin pharmacologist Professor Oscar Liebreich. Indeed, the use of lanolin was so commonplace by 1900 that the Melbourne *Leader* included it in their recipe for a home-made 'Cold Cream for the Face':

Take 20 grains of powdered gum-arabic, 1 oz. of pure white vaseline, ½ oz. of pure lanoline and ½ oz. of rosewater. Beat up the gum-arabic with a little of the rosewater. Then add, by degrees, first a little of the vaseline, then a little of the lanoline, then more rosewater, and so on, till the whole is beaten to a smooth cream. This cream is invaluable to those whose faces are inclined to be rough and crack when east winds visit us. It should be well rubbed into the skin after the night's wash.[6]

As we shall see, in 1903 Rubinstein described herself unequivocally in her trademark application as 'manufacturer', but the most important point to grasp at the outset is that her product was neither unique nor especially unusual. The great Dr Lykuski therefore furnished an important backstory with which to create and maintain an exciting commercial point of difference.

In her application for naturalisation as a British subject, Rubinstein revised the date of her arrival in Victoria from 1896 to 1897, although she named the right ship, the *Prinz-Regent Luitpold*. She stated that she had spent three years in Coleraine, one year in Toowoomba in southeastern Queensland (which would bring her up to 1900–01, and was true), and then 'six five' years in Melbourne, all up 'ten nine' years resident in Australia. These corrections were all neatly initialled. On the face of it, this leaves at least two years in Australia unaccounted for – or only eighteen months (more or less) if Rubinstein were taking into account her fact-finding mission to Europe in 1905. In September of that year, she dragged her sister 'Cäcilie' (Ceska Rubinstein) and her cousin Lola Beckmann back to Melbourne aboard the steamer *Karlsruhe*.[7] The remaining missing eighteen months are those Rubinstein spent in domestic service in Toowoomba and, upon her return to Melbourne, waitressing at the Maison Dorée oyster saloon in Swanston Street and the Chicago and Winter Garden Tea and Luncheon Rooms in the Block Arcade, Collins Street.

Rubinstein's naturalisation papers were lodged on her behalf by the respectable firm of solicitors Cleverdon and Fay of 95 Queen Street,

Melbourne. According to the various wax-pencil annotations and rubber stamps, the governor-general, Lord Northcote, duly signed her certificate of naturalisation on 22 May 1907, thus turning Helena Rubinstein into a British subject. These documents effectively formed her ticket of leave, for they opened the way to Edwardian Mayfair, whither, with five years' worth of accrued capital amounting to a little more than £12,000, she proceeded immediately, and shortly afterwards to 255 rue Saint-Honoré in Paris. However, these documents succeed in occluding the most remarkable aspects of her Australian sojourn and therefore, I think, of her achievement as an almost entirely self-made businesswoman. The supreme irony is that the stories Rubinstein managed to air-brush out of her own myth are the very ones that most effectively burnish it today.

* * *

Chaja (Helena) Rubinstein was born at home on 25 December 1872 in a small second-floor flat, 14 Szeroka Street, Kazimierz, the Jewish quarter of Kraków in occupied southern Poland. To Lindy Woodhead we owe a considerable debt of gratitude for establishing Rubinstein's date of birth with absolute certainty.[8] The building at 14 Szeroka Street is a neat, compact little block with a café on the ground floor, three tall windows on the first, and two small dormer windows on the second, projecting from a steeply pitched roof. Today the building is painted an attractive shade of pale green, and it keeps company with neighbouring buildings of similar size, compactness and simplicity of design. It is neither conspicuous and imposing nor markedly humble or impoverished. It sits squarely in the middle.

Throughout her life, Rubinstein fibbed outrageously about her age, except, it seems, in her later American passports.[9] When she sailed to Melbourne in August–September 1896 aboard the *Prinz-Regent Luitpold*, the ship's manifest notes her age as twenty. She was in fact twenty-three.[10] When she returned to Melbourne aboard the *Karlsruhe* in September 1905, she owned to twenty-four. She was actually approaching thirty-three.[11] In her 1907 application for naturalisation as a British subject, she gave as her year of birth 1879. She therefore professed to be twenty-seven years old, but was in fact thirty-four.[12] When she married Edward Titus at the General Register Office, Strand, on 28 July 1908, with characteristic chutzpah, Rubinstein owned to being twenty-eight years old when she was thirty-five.[13] By this time, she was at least being consistent. Later, the gaps widen; in Artchil Gourielli's 1938 petition for naturalisation as an American citizen, Rubinstein gave 25 December 1886 as her date of birth (a fourteen-year differential). As late as October 1957, when she was nearly eighty-five, the *Daily Telegraph* was given to understand that she was seventy-four.[14]

The opening sentences of her 1965 memoir adhere to this pattern, but this time in reverse: 'I have always felt that a woman has the right to treat the subject of her age with ambiguity until, perhaps, she passes into the realm of over ninety. Then it is better that she be candid with herself and with the world. I am well over the mark, actually, ninety-four, but that does not mean that my spirit and my stubbornness have left me.' Rubinstein was not yet ninety-two.[15]

Personal vanity always swayed Rubinstein, more often than not for strategic business reasons, so it would be easy thus to account for this cavalier degree of vagueness. However, it is important to keep in mind that when she arrived in Australia, indeed long before, and in many jurisdictions, it may well have been *necessary* to lie about her age. When, in the late 1950s, James Pope-Hennessy was writing his official biography of Queen Mary,[16] one of the innumerable interviews he conducted was with an octogenarian retired butler, a Mr Hough, who in 1893 went to work as steward's-room boy and under-footman to Queen Mary's parents, the Duke and Duchess of Teck, at White Lodge, Richmond Park. 'Asked how old he was at the time, Mr Hough did not rightly know, about 17 he should fancy. The trouble in those days was that in private service you always had to alter your age – you were too young for some places, too old for others; hence you ended by really forgetting how old in fact you were.'[17] If this fascinating observation applied to young men trying to make their way in the late-Victorian domestic labour market in Britain, it was equally applicable in the Australasian colonies and *doubly* applicable to women and girls.

There was little regulation of employment in colonial Victoria. State education, at least, since the landmark *Education Act* of 1872 had been compulsory for all children up to the age of fourteen, and compared with other jurisdictions this was a remarkably ambitious piece of legislation. However, there is evidence that laws against the exploitation of child labour were being routinely flouted: 'Missing, since 8th June 1900, from 6 Bridport Street, South Melbourne, Boy, 13½, fair', ran one bleak ad in the missing friends and messages column. 'Anyone harbouring *or employing* will be prosecuted.'[18] Many advertisements for legitimate 'situations vacant' in Melbourne at around the time Rubinstein arrived there made explicit requirements with respect to age:

GIRL, 18, assist house work. Fernshawe, Westbury Street, East St Kilda ...
GIRL, young, tidy, assist light house work, just left school preferred [i.e. at least 14 years]. 438 Queen Street ...
GIRL, smart, about 14, useful, sleep home; wages 4s. Luncheon Room, 397 Lonsdale Street West.[19]

There are thousands of similar examples in the Melbourne press at the time of Federation. We find them also applying to governesses and waitresses, in both of which capacities Rubinstein served for several years.

Even more galling was the fact that there were regular *bons mots* in the press that mocked women for making claims about their age that were considered implausible: 'London newspapers say Amy Castles is nineteen years of age', sneered *Table Talk* in January 1902. 'This is evidently Greenwich time.'[20] Being a rising Australian dramatic soprano, and not quite twenty-two, Castles' adjustment (if she made it herself rather than having it made for her) seems relatively modest compared with Rubinstein's, but the wider economic and social contexts are important to grasp. Edwardian working women were often forced to lie about their age.

Kazimierz was an ancient ghetto. Owing to the complex military and political history of nineteenth-century Poland, and Eastern Europe more generally, Kraków was to some degree insulated from, but not unaffected by, the Russian pogroms following the assassination of the Tsar in St Petersburg in 1881. Modern Poland was then divided between Prussia, Austria and Russia. Kraków was a magnet for displaced Eastern European Jews seeking a stable, comparatively tolerant urban centre with, crucially, a well-respected old university – the Uniwersytet Jagielloński, the alma mater of Copernicus. Kraków also afforded plentiful opportunities for trade throughout the Austro-Hungarian Empire, of which it was for the time being, with Prague, an important northern outpost. Until the Nazi occupation and the Holocaust systematically destroyed it, the large Jewish community in Kraków looked to Kazimierz as its hub. The neighbourhood sustained about 120 synagogues, prayer houses, ritual bathing and other facilities, but the Jewish community had spread far beyond its boundaries. By the 1870s, the Jews of Kraków, about a quarter of the whole population, were rapidly becoming fully Polish, while Kazimierz was becoming overcrowded and was increasingly seen as either poor or ultra-conservative or both.

Helena Rubinstein was the eldest of the eight surviving daughters of Naftaly Hertzel ('Horace') Rubinstein, originally from Dukla, a small town about 200 kilometres southwest of Kraków, in the foothills of the Carpathian Mountains, close to the border between modern Poland and Slovakia. Rubinstein *père* may have been prompted to depart by the onset of a cholera epidemic that mowed through the town between 1865 and 1867. His wife, Helena's mother, was Gitel ('Augusta', i.e. Gusta) Rubinstein, and their other seven daughters were Pauline, Rosa, Regina, Stella, Ceska, Manka and Erna. Four brothers and two other sisters died in infancy. As John Poynter has remarked, Rubinstein was positively Napoleonic in exploiting this ample stock of younger siblings. One by one, they were summoned from Kraków and roped in as her business rapidly grew.[21]

Hertzel Rubinstein was a middle-class egg and kerosene merchant of mixed abilities, and Gusta Rubinstein was one of the *nineteen* children of Rabbi Sale (Solomon) Silberfeld and his wife Rebecca, of whom thirteen survived infancy, childhood and adolescence. Rabbi Silberfeld's other occupation is given variously as 'moneylender', 'banker' or 'speculator'. It could have been some modest combination of all three, of which the designation 'banker' is the most dubious.

By the 1930s, Rubinstein was inclined to characterise her childhood home as at least middle-class, even prosperous. By that time, she gave credit to the famous Polish actress Modjeska (Helena Modrzejewska) for either introducing Dr Lykuski to Gusta Rubinstein when Rubinstein was a little girl, or for spontaneously pressing Valaze upon her mother.[22] Neither picturesque scenario was true. Modjeska had sailed to the United States several years before Rubinstein was born, and the Rubinstein family never lived 'in a large old house near Rynek Główny (Rynek Square), close to the University'.[23] Instead, their second-floor flat in Szeroka Street was cramped, even if, according to the 1890 Kraków census, they did by then accommodate one servant. Hertzel Rubinstein kept a shop not far away, at 13 Józefa Street.[24] Nevertheless, there is no reason to disbelieve Rubinstein when she recalled:

> It was a house filled to overflowing with the overstuffed furniture of the nineteenth century, and the varied collections of a father who had a passion for papers and books. Oil lamps were used to light the rooms, and in winter we kept warm by the towering porcelain stoves which burned night and day.[25]

What Rubinstein cleverly implies here is an appreciable difference in scale and affluence. In fact, the household would appear to have been economically precarious. The Rubinsteins moved house at least four times, presumably driven to do so by the needs of a rapidly growing family. From 14 Szeroka Street they moved to a flat in 25 Bozega Ciala in about 1878, then back to a different flat in Szeroka Street, number 18, then to 2 Wazka Street, and finally to their biggest flat at number 2 Bartosza Street, where the servant was noted in the census.[26] Degrees of poverty being relative and often difficult to discern, we may conclude that, if not poor by Kazimierz standards or indeed by standards more generally, the Rubinstein family was not by any means as prosperous as Helena Rubinstein later implied (fig. 12). The fact that in the 1880s and 1890s they never lived outside Kazimierz is significant. However, we may infer that they were 'aspirational'. Three of Gusta Rubinstein's brothers, Bernhard, Louis and John Silberfeld, migrated to Australia between 1870 and 1886.

Figure 12. Helena Rubinstein, standing, with three of her seven sisters and their mother, in Kazimierz, Kraków, c. 1890–92.

Rubinstein must have gained from her father some basic experience in wholesale and retail. In 1965, she recalled having successfully negotiated for her father the release of a wagonload of eggs that were stranded in hot weather at the city gates due to a religious holiday, possibly *Szawuot*, or Shavuot.[27] Subsequently, Rubinstein learned much from her more prosperous Viennese relatives and her three uncles in the Western District of Victoria, but her claim to have studied medicine in Kraków for a brief period was bogus. Women were not yet admitted to the medical or any other school in the Jagielloński. She may have undertaken some rudimentary training as a nurse or assistant in the old Kazimierz infirmary, but nothing more formal than that. The distaste she expressed for 'the first whiff of antiseptic' and 'the sights and odours of the sickroom' have the ring of authenticity, as does her exceedingly rare admission of failure: that is, in the attempt to pursue her 'medical studies'.[28] Even so, in her 1957 radio interview with Binny Lum, perhaps emboldened by the long distance between Melbourne and London in one direction and approximately the same distance to New York in the other, Rubinstein felt able to refer not only to the fact that she had studied medicine and that her father had wanted her to be a doctor, but also that she had studied chemistry.

Following an unsuccessful attempt by her parents to arrange a marriage, and some sort of conflict arising from the loss of her first love, the shadowy Stanisław, a medical student who for some reason was deemed unsuitable, at a certain point Rubinstein left her parents' home.[29] At first, she remained in Kraków, living in the household of her aunt Rosalie Silberfeld Beckmann.[30] It was more likely through Mrs Beckmann than her mother that presently Rubinstein moved to Vienna, where she spent a while living with another of her Silberfeld aunts, Helena Splitter, from whom she may have been inspired to Germanise the given name they shared, substituting Helena for the Polish–Jewish Chaja (חיה). Frau Splitter's husband Liebisch and his three brothers were successful furriers.[31]

In 1893, Vienna was the capital city of a wealthy empire that controlled much of Eastern Europe, from the Balkans to modern Poland and from the Swiss border to the western Ukraine. At its not entirely stable core was the union of the two ancient monarchies of Austria and Hungary. The Austro-Hungarian Empire also embraced what are now the Czech Republic, Slovakia, Slovenia, Croatia, Bosnia and large chunks of southern Poland, Ukraine, Rumania (Transylvania), northeastern Italy and many other substantial pockets of territory around the periphery. For the time being, its many languages, ethnicities and faiths produced in predominantly Catholic Vienna a magnificent intellectual and cultural flowering that continued up to the outbreak of World War I.

The pomp and grandeur of Vienna's built environment was an unapologetic celebration of imperium. The newly completed Ringstraße, the mother of all encircling grand boulevards, was Vienna's haughty rebuttal of Haussmann's Paris. The River Danube, only exceeded in length by the Volga in Russia, was a famous ribbon of myth that fastened the whole of Europe to Vienna and her empire, from southern Germany near the Swiss border to the Black Sea. 'An der schönen, blauen Donau' by Johann Strauss II (Opus 314) had since 1866 placed the proprietorial stamp of Vienna upon the 'beautiful blue Danube', and in the form of an exhilarating, enormously popular Viennese waltz, which was danced all over the world.

There had been a substantial Jewish community in Vienna since the twelfth century. By the end of the nineteenth century, in a population of 1.3 million, 118,000 souls, nearly 9 per cent, owned to being Jewish, but their contribution to the Viennese economy was out of all proportion. Based on the 1934 census, Georg Glockemeier calculated that 51.6 per cent of Viennese doctors were Jewish; 60 per cent of bakers; 75 per cent of bankers; 40 per cent of jewellers; 34 per cent of photographers; 40 per cent of café proprietors; 85 per cent of lawyers; 31 per cent of dentists; 73 per cent of wine merchants; 67 per cent of furriers, and so on.[32] As well, Vienna was a centre of radical Jewish thought. Theodor Herzl, the father of Zionism, studied law at the University of Vienna. When Helena Rubinstein arrived there, Sigmund Freud was well established in private practice at Berggasse 19.

As in France and many other places, the prominence, visibility and success of the Jews of Vienna gave rise to anti-Semitism. It had always been there but had long been mostly latent. It was all too easy to ignore. However, Viennese anti-Semitism was a ticking timebomb. Provincial and municipal elections in 1889, 1890 and 1891 showed it to be sharply on the rise, and prominent liberals were so alarmed by its viciousness that a well-organised *Verein zur Abwehr des Antisemitism* (Association for the Defence Against Anti-Semitism) was established in 1891 to fight against it. Nevertheless, few Viennese Jews could possibly have imagined then, the terror following the *Anschluss*, or that on *Kristallnacht*, 9–10 November 1938, no fewer than ninety-two Viennese synagogues and countless Jewish businesses would be destroyed by the Nazis. At least three of Helena Rubinstein's Splitter cousins, whom she had helped look after in Vienna when they were small children, were deported and murdered in Auschwitz or Flossenbürg.

The household of Liebisch and Helena Splitter gave Rubinstein much more than a fleeting glimpse of cosmopolitan Vienna at the height of its sophistication in the 1890s. Just as many aspects of life in colonial and Federation Australia and New Zealand drew energy and supreme confidence from being a part of the British Empire, it is vital to bear in mind that when she arrived in Melbourne, Rubinstein had already experienced essentially the same dynamic in Vienna. That dynamic shapes and works upon the individual in subtle ways. She does not necessarily think, if attending a recital in the Sofiensaal or a performance at the Wiener Hofoper, and afterwards strolling down the Kärntnerring, that she is the glad beneficiary of the Habsburg imperial project, or the proud subject of a great polyglot empire extending from Sarajevo to Prague and from Salzburg to Lviv. Nevertheless, the confidence that Rubinstein exhibited throughout her later career cannot have been dampened by her formative experience of Vienna, any more than it was in any way stifled in Australia and New Zealand.

In August 1896, at around the time when for unknown reasons the Splitter fur business packed up and moved from Vienna to Antwerp, Rubinstein travelled alone by steam train from Vienna to Genoa, an uncomfortable if picturesque 24-hour journey that skirted the Alps by way of Styria, Carinthia and Friuli-Venezia Giulia, and right across Northern Italy from the Veneto

Figure 13. The Bremen-based Norddeutscher–Lloyd fast twin-screw steamer *Prinz-Regent Luitpold* in Sydney Cove, c. 1900.

across Lombardy and down into Liguria.[33] From there she sailed to Australia aboard the almost brand-new, relatively small Bremen-based Norddeutscher–Lloyd fast twin-screw steamer *Prinz-Regent Luitpold* (fig. 13).

Embarking at Genoa on Tuesday 11 August, the 36-day voyage brought her to Melbourne in the colony of Victoria, arriving there early on Wednesday 16 September 1896.[34] Why did Rubinstein go to Australia? It was certainly not to create a company. She was instead setting out on an urgent mission of mercy. This conformed to a well-established pattern of going to the aid of close relatives, but the geographical displacement was infinitely greater. Her cousin Eva desperately needed help.

Cousin Eva Silberfeld had gone to live with the Rubinstein family in Kazimierz in the early 1870s. Her mother died when she was a little girl, and Eva was an only child. Her father, Gusta Rubinstein's brother Bernhard

Silberfeld, migrated to Australia to seek a better life, and entrusted his only daughter to his sister's care until such time as Eva could rejoin him. It would be naïve to suppose that Gusta Rubinstein did not take full advantage of Eva's extra pair of hands, once she was old enough, to help with the youngest children, who continued to materialise regularly through the 1870s and into the late 1880s. In her 1965 memoir, Rubinstein said that she had grown close to Cousin Eva. Helena looked up to Eva, who was five years older. They kept up a regular correspondence after Eva sailed to Australia not later than 1888.

In about 1891, aged about eighteen, Rubinstein left her parents' home and went to live with her mother's sister in another part of Kraków. Rosalie and Moritz Beckmann had nine children aged thirteen years and under. It would be equally naïve to suppose that Rosalie Beckmann did not, however affectionately, set Rubinstein to the same hard domestic work. It is possible that that was why she was sent or summoned in the first place. The decision to leave her parents' home may therefore have been taken for her. When Rubinstein arrived in Vienna in about 1893, Helena and Liebisch Splitter had five little boys between eight and two years old, as well as a newborn infant. No doubt Helena Splitter likewise availed herself of the help that Rubinstein was by then so well accustomed to providing.

In the meantime, events in the life of cousin Eva Silberfeld had unfolded badly in Australia. On 19 May 1889, Eva married Louis Leopold Levy, 'commission agent' or 'commercial traveller', according to Jewish rites in Drummond Street, Carlton. The marriage was a disaster, although it produced three sons. In 1892, Levy was insolvent, having accumulated insupportable debts as a jewellery salesman.[35] For a while he worked for Bernhard Silberfeld's much younger brother John, which is presumably how Levy met and paid court to Eva. In 1896, Eva Levy petitioned the Supreme Court of Victoria for a *decree nisi* divorce on the grounds of habitual drunkenness, violence and desertion, which apparently took place in 1893, when she and the children sought refuge under her father's roof in Whyte Street, Coleraine, in the Western District of Victoria.[36] It seems Louis threatened to kill her on two occasions, one of them during her third pregnancy. The divorce was granted only a few days before Rubinstein set sail from Genoa.

Towards the end of her life, Rubinstein was inclined to characterise her move to Australia as an escape from Poland, where, following the disappointment and heartache of losing the shadowy Stanisław, she said there was nothing left for her. However, in 1896 Rubinstein had every right to feel short-changed, even oppressed, by the family pattern of dispatching her, or letting her be summoned, to lend unpaid assistance to successive batches of her mother's many Silberfeld nieces and nephews. In the circumstances, one might speculate whether, not quite ten years later, the recruitment of her cousin Lola Beckmann in Kraków was for Rubinstein a sort of quid pro quo. However, the situation with Eva Levy was different. Rubinstein was responding to an urgent call for help from a cousin in distress to whom for years she had been devoted.

Lindy Woodhead is puzzled by Rubinstein's decision to embark at Genoa rather than Bremen or Hamburg via Kraków.[37] The 414-kilometre local train service from Vienna to Kraków took nearly eight interminable hours because it stopped everywhere. The fastest, though not the most direct, onward route from Kraków to Bremen was by way of Warsaw and Berlin, but that meant having to enter the easternmost territory of the Russian Empire. Although she would leave it almost as soon as she entered, nevertheless going by that route meant that Rubinstein would have had to carry an Austro-Hungarian passport with a visa issued within the previous six months by the consular section of the Russian Embassy in Vienna. However, to 'persons of the Jewish faith the visa is only granted in special circumstances', which in practice meant never.[38]

Although by 1896 many European governments recommended carrying a passport, passengers by land or sea did not yet need one to cross most European frontiers except those of Russia and the Ottoman Empire. Therefore, from Kraków Rubinstein would have had to go the long way round via Breslau (now Wrocław), Dresden, Leipzig, Magdeburg and Hanover. Setting out from Vienna, Genoa was therefore the far more convenient point of embarkation. It also had the virtue of bypassing the ports of Antwerp or Rotterdam, Southampton and possibly Marseilles, therefore saving on the cost of the berth, the equivalent of £32, a little more than the *annual* wage of a waitress in colonial Melbourne. The voyage would be shorter and cheaper, certainly, but not by much. One senses, here, the kindly intervention of Helena Splitter in providing a welcome subsidy prior to Rubinstein's departure. This was the first time in her life that Rubinstein had seen an ocean, the sapphire blue Ligurian Sea and the spectacular Riviera di Ponente extending westwards from Genoa. It was also the first time that she had sailed anywhere on a ship, much less halfway around the world.

Rubinstein was one of fifty-three saloon-class passengers aboard the *Prinz-Regent Luitpold*. There were 152 passengers in steerage and only a handful in first class. Conditions for saloon-class passengers were comfortable and as entertaining as they wanted them to be, even if the voyage were not in any case a source of wonder to a young Polish–Jewish woman who had only ever known landlocked Kraków and Vienna. The Norddeutscher–Lloyd line was the second-largest in the world after P & O, and its ships were famous for being on average the fastest. Even so, ports of call involved off-loading passengers and boarding new ones; taking on fuel, fresh food, water and other supplies. This took time, so transit passengers had the opportunity to join day-long excursions on dry land or to escape from the other passengers and explore each port at their relatively unhurried leisure.

The first stop was the Bay of Naples, in the glorious shadow of Vesuvius. The heat of Naples in August can be overwhelming, but for Rubinstein it was merely a first instalment. All subsequent ports of call, ever hotter, were either under British control or served a British colony. Most were Conradian. Much of the rest of the voyage was therefore a hybrid experience of, on the one hand, global Britain at the height of her maritime power and, on the other, increasingly oppressive tropical heat.

The ancient port of Alexandria on the western verge of the Nile delta was nominally under the flag of the Ottoman Khedive, but Britain exerted tight control over Egypt. Likewise, Port Said was under Anglo-French administration because of the strategic importance of the Suez Canal, but its busy traffic made it the crossroads and pivot of Europe, Africa and Asia. Vessels passed through the canal in single file, so passengers could expect to wait for several days before the *Prinz-Regent Luitpold* took her turn. A day trip from Port Said by train, trap and camel to inspect the Great Pyramid of Giza was therefore not only feasible; it was almost obligatory.

No doubt there were passengers for whom the eastern Mediterranean and the Levantine seaboard, or even the marvels of ancient Egypt, held little or no fascination, or indeed the canal itself, a wonder of modern engineering with its fifty-kilometre sections of ramrod straightness, an incongruous channel of water cut right across the northwestern Sinai. However, I suspect those passengers were rather few. The psychological impact of this long eastward and southward voyage also lay in its weird combination of tedium and shipboard routine, an incessant cycle of enormous meals with the same people at close quarters, day after day, week after week, and, in between, deck games, endless rounds of bridge and almost nightly dances, which Rubinstein remembered enjoying.[39]

Rubinstein was travelling alone, and she was shy. A social hazard on board ship was therefore that she might soon become a magnet for the well-meaning, the garrulous, the inquisitive or even the predatory. Acquaintanceships formed quickly in the excitement of departure, or the novelty of quoits or deck croquet, might soon be regretted. Few techniques of tactful avoidance were available to single women in saloon class, sandwiched as they were between first class on the uppermost deck and the no man's land of steerage. Language skills (or lack of them) could certainly be helpful, but escape was impossible. Any sense of confinement, even entrapment, however, was offset by the slow-motion rollercoaster of changing conditions and the unfamiliar scent and scenery of ever more exotic ports.

The prevailing daytime temperature on the sluggish soupy waters of the Gulf of Suez and the Red Sea in August was an overpowering 39°C (102°F). It was not much cooler at night. This was a source of accumulating torment to everyone, but especially passengers occupying northeast-facing cabins. The *entrepôt* and waystation of Aden conjured up the hot dry mythic world of Arabia – the scent of coffee and black pepper in the old spice market; the upward lurch and roaring of camels; the angular profile of Yemeni fishermen's transom-sterned dhows – but it also held the promise of the Indian Empire. The crossing of the Gulf of Aden and the Arabian Sea, a busy shipping route for pilgrims undertaking the Hajj from all corners of South and Southeast Asia, could also be stifling so that, when finally reached, the huge melting pot of Bombay (Mumbai) provided a welcome point of disembarkation, diversion and relief. With luck, catching your first offshore glimpse of the sun rising over Bombay, an orange disc in the sultry haze of dawn, the shore silhouetted with date palms, was a famous rite of passage for new arrivals, while Bombay Harbour, teeming with activity, was the commonest point of entry to India.

The onward leg down through the Laccadive Sea to Colombo in Ceylon (Sri Lanka) took Rubinstein to the equatorial tropics and into the September monsoon, which brought afternoon rainfall so heavy that experiencing it for the first time was like making the unexpected discovery of rain itself. Weather permitting, one might take tea on the broad terrace of the Grand Oriental Hotel or the famous Galle Face. A few days after leaving Colombo, passengers were enjoined to submit to Neptune's messy ritual of 'crossing the line' of the Equator, whence a long, seemingly endless southeasterly run across the vastness of the Indian Ocean ensued, by far the longest stretch of the voyage. Depending on passengers' sea legs, rough conditions could confine them to their cabins for miserable days on end. Rubinstein was lucky. She remembered the Indian Ocean as having been 'languid'.[40] With disembarkation at the port of Fremantle in Western Australia, one extreme of hot steamy wet emerald green was supplanted by another of mild dusty dry blue-grey green and brown beneath a huge dazzling cobalt blue Australian sky.

The ship continued down past Cape Leeuwin to the busy pastoral port and whaling station of Albany, and onwards across the Great Australian Bight.

Finally passing up the Gulf of St Vincent to Largs Bay and Port Adelaide, yet again the union flag flew from the Customs House flagstaff. The final stage of Rubinstein's voyage was only a few more days, down into Bass Strait, past Cape Otway, through the heads at Point Nepean, and up the shipping channel of Port Phillip to Hobson's Bay and Railway Pier at Port Melbourne.

One cannot but conclude that this voyage must have been a transformative experience for the young Rubinstein. Upon reaching Sydney on her second-last return visit in 1938, she was proud to inform the press that since 1896 she had gone on to sail the same route *six more times*, and at least once or twice across the Pacific, which is almost as far. She added that her transatlantic crossings alone amounted to a staggering 167 to date – interrupted only by the Great War.[41] After World War II, Rubinstein happily shifted to travel by air, to South America, to Russia, and finally in 1957 to Hong Kong and Japan and for the last time to Australia and New Zealand. It is difficult to think of any other woman born in the second half of the nineteenth century who had in the course of a long lifetime travelled greater distances, or more often. Not even Dame Nellie Melba or Anna Matveyevna Pavlova, both peripatetic, attained anything like the enormous tally of nautical miles that Rubinstein relentlessly accumulated. Yet it was her first voyage from Genoa to Melbourne that ignited her passion for travel; in later years, long ocean voyages provided the only extended periods in which Rubinstein could be persuaded to rest.

In her memoir, Rubinstein stated that her purpose in sailing to Australia in August 1896 was to join her Uncle Louis Silberfeld and his only child, her cousin Eva Levy.[42] Rubinstein went on to say that before too long relations in Coleraine soured between uncle and niece.[43] This may have been true, but it is far from being the whole story. There were three Silberfeld uncles in Victoria (three of her mother's eighteen siblings), but Rubinstein hardly mentions the second and never the third. She *did* mention an unnamed 'distant cousin' who proposed marriage in Australia, but this cannot have been any of her uncles' progeny so that cousin remains a mystery.[44] The strangest part is that Cousin Eva was Bernhard's daughter, not Louis's, and, even stranger, it was in Bernhard's house in Whyte Street that she settled in Coleraine, not Louis's, because by that date Louis – unmarried and childless – had permanently removed himself to the nearby hamlet of Merino. Why did Rubinstein make this curious substitution? The answer may be simple. Throughout her life, she was notoriously vague with respect to *all* names, something that she freely admitted and Patrick O'Higgins repeatedly emphasised.[45]

* * *

Although they were born in Kraków, the three Silberfeld brothers all sailed to Victoria from London or Gravesend, but separately and at long intervals.[46] As Polish Jews, the Silberfelds were still relatively unusual in colonial Victoria, as indeed was Rubinstein herself. Jews had formed part of the Australian settler community ever since the arrival of the First Fleet in January 1788. However, the main influx in Victoria took place during and after the Gold Rush beginning in the second half of 1851, when the local population of Jews started to rise from only 200 in 1848 to about 3000 in 1861 – Hebrew congregations kept extremely good records. These were mainly Anglo-Jewish migrants, whose mercantile activities reflected sometimes long periods of at least partial assimilation in Britain. Some of the most prominent entered public life.

It was not until after successive Russian pogroms following the assassination of the Tsar in 1881 that the first substantial wave of Eastern European Jews began to arrive in Victoria, including Elcon Baevski and his brother Simcha, the future Sidney Myer. Like Rubinstein, Baevski reached Melbourne in 1896. Simcha followed in early April 1899, having sailed from Antwerp aboard the *Karlsruhe*.[47] However, of the increase in the Australian Jewish population from 9125 in 1881 to 21,615 in 1921, only about 3000 were Jewish refugees from Eastern Europe, a relatively small number compared with the huge wave of migrants who made the much shorter voyage across the Atlantic to the United States, Canada, Mexico, and Central and South America. Moreover, a direct effect of the depression of the 1890s was a temporary decline in the Jewish population of Victoria from 6459 in 1891 to 5907 in 1901.⁴⁸ Britain's Jewish population, by contrast, increased seven-fold through the twenty years following 1881, from 35,000 to roughly 250,000, prompting Westminster to pass the *Aliens Act 1905*, which substantially restricted further immigration. That the Silberfeld brothers should all have sailed by way of Britain is consistent with the experience of many later Eastern European Jewish migrants to Australia.⁴⁹ Nevertheless, for the time being, Polish, Russian and other Eastern European Jews were relatively scarce in Victoria.

What was not quite so unusual was their choice of destination. As Suzanne Rutland has pointed out, in the 1860s 60 per cent of the whole Australian Jewish population was concentrated in Sydney and Melbourne. However, the remaining 40 per cent were a vital and visible presence in the nineteenth-century towns of rural New South Wales, Victoria and pockets of southern Queensland.⁵⁰ It is no accident that Sidney Myer began his mercantile career with the small drapery business that Elcon and he set up in 1900 in Bendigo in central Victoria.⁵¹ However, not all country towns sustained congregations or built synagogues, and eventually the challenge of maintaining Jewish life, education and traditions led in most cases either to their abandonment through complete assimilation or else to relocation to the two biggest cities.⁵² Bernhard Silberfeld eventually chose the latter path.

From the moment she alighted at Port Melbourne on Wednesday morning, 16 September 1896, Helena Rubinstein was most unusual in several respects. She was a young unmarried Polish Jew. She had no discernible profession or vocation. She must have had enough resources to secure her saloon-class berth aboard the *Prinz-Regent Luitpold*, to make contact with the Silberfelds upon or ahead of her arrival, and to receive instructions after a day or two lodging in Melbourne about how to get herself from Melbourne to Coleraine by train. However, she had little else to fall back on.

In the southern spring of 1896, the journey by train from Spencer Street Station in Melbourne to Coleraine was still pretty arduous. Passengers bound for Ararat and beyond did not always go directly through Ballarat, but depending on the freight might go the longer way to Ballarat via Geelong. From Ballarat, the train continued to Ararat via Beaufort. Passengers then changed to the Ararat–Portland line and, skirting the spectacular eastern side of the Grampians (Gariwerd), alighted at Hamilton via Dunkeld. The last leg to Coleraine was on a *third* train, but that relatively short journey – one daily service in each direction – could nevertheless take hours and hours because of successive ninety-minute siding stops for loading and unloading goods.

Figure 14. Helena Rubinstein in Vienna, c. 1895.

One of only a few studio photographs of Rubinstein that predate or date from her time in Australia survives in the Helena Rubinstein Collection in the Library of the Fashion Institute of Technology in New York, which proves that she held onto it until the end her life (fig. 14). It was taken in

Vienna some time before 1896 and shows her wearing an unpretentious dress with a beaded bodice, a high neck, leg-o'-mutton sleeves and a simple straw hat with a few feathers decorating the crown. She wears it at a jaunty angle, the brim upturned. The impression this photograph conveys is partly demure and contained. Although it is impossible to see it now without knowing what lay ahead for Rubinstein, one cannot help discerning in it a sense of strong determination. Her eyes, especially, have an intentness and a focus that cannot but have arrested any official of H.M. Customs and Excise at Railway Pier or a member of the staff of the Victorian Railways in the bustling ticket office at Spencer Street Station. Demure, even restive, but determined also: already, and to the extent that she reveals anything at all, the youthful Rubinstein projects here a complex mixture of apparently contradictory qualities.

3

Working with Children

In 1965, Helena Rubinstein recalled her first impression of Coleraine: 'The sun was strong, the wind was violent. The never-ending sweep of pasture, broken here and there by a blue gum tree, presented a very different picture from the one I had imagined.'[1] This begs the obvious question, what did she imagine? However, with characteristic guardedness Rubinstein never provided an answer. Owing to this, and to many other references to the heat and dust of Australia, Coleraine has suffered from a widespread general misconception in the mostly American, English and French Rubinstein literature, according to which the scorching desert wind and desolation of this 'outback' town either propelled Rubinstein towards face cream or stimulated a demand among weather-beaten local women for the Polish or Russian cream that she already used herself.

In 1972, Maxene Fabe, describing Rubinstein's journey from Melbourne to Coleraine in September 1896, managed to distil more errors into a single sentence than anyone before or since: 'For now she must take a long ride via teeth-rattling stagecoach [sic] through the mountains [sic] along the dusty inland road past endless herds [sic] of bleating sheep and bony cattle to reach the frontier [sic] outpost [sic] of Coleraine.' Lindy Woodhead speaks of 'a typical, small, pioneering outback town'. Even as recently as 2013, Nicky Haslam could refer to Coleraine as 'an outback township above Melbourne.'[2]

Coleraine is no more outback than Wiltshire resembles Oklahoma. The country between Hamilton and Casterton, Victoria, is every bit as emerald green and cuddly as the other part of the valley of the River Wannon that is closer to Murndal, sixteen kilometres away. Even at the height of the severe recent drought, when residents of Coleraine were deeply concerned about the scarcity of water, by comparison with southern New South Wales the surroundings gave the strong impression of greenness and relative prosperity. Water was still flowing over the Wannon Falls, although there was certainly less of it. This is glorious, rolling sheep and cattle country – the envy of most Australian graziers elsewhere, and firmly embedded in that famous stretch of the continent that in late June 1836 had inspired Major Thomas Mitchell to name this area *Australia Felix*.

This is not to suggest that Rubinstein's recollection of Coleraine was not genuine and heartfelt. We can safely say that, arriving there in September 1896, a 23-year-old Polish–Jewish woman who had known only Kazimierz and the melting pot of imperial Vienna at the height of its sophistication must have looked upon Coleraine and the surrounding district as, at best, a frightening *tabula rasa*. When suffering from homesickness or fatigue or encountering, as she must have done in those first few months, a language barrier, Rubinstein would have been forgiven for thinking that she had landed on the moon.

Rubinstein's Uncle Bernhard Silberfeld apparently started his mercantile career in Melbourne in partnership with an L. Richards. Richards and Silberfeld, waterproof clothing manufacturers, occupied upstairs premises in a two-storied wooden building on the southwest corner of La Trobe and Elizabeth streets.[3] The partnership appears to have dissolved after July 1884, when a fire broke out in their workroom and gutted the whole building.[4] Bernhard Silberfeld had decided by then, or even earlier in 1884, to make a fresh start in the Western District of Victoria. At first, he kept a general store at Tahara, about nineteen kilometres south of Coleraine, where, no later than 1886, Louis Silberfeld joined the mixed business. That hamlet has today all but vanished. Bernhard and Louis then shifted to Coleraine. This may have triggered Eva Silberfeld's long delayed immigration and reunion with her father. Bernhard took the lease on McLean's General Store at 107 Whyte Street. However, for reasons unknown the Silberfeld brothers' partnership was formally dissolved in April 1887, whereupon Louis moved to nearby Merino and set up on his own.[5]

Bernhard continued trading in Coleraine and prospered. On New Year's Day in that year, he was listed in the *Hamilton Spectator* among the stewards due to officiate at the New Year's Day Races in Coleraine.[6] His 1892 letterhead read: 'B. SILBERFELD, STOREKEEPER. Gents' Clothes made to measure at the shortest notice.' He and/or Louis appear to have doubled as part-time oculists for a while, and we know that they engaged in fairly ambitious moneylending.[7]

All three brothers applied for letters of naturalisation as British subjects in colonial Victoria. Their papers survive in the National Archives of Australia.[8] As with Rubinstein's own application, these documents are full of vagueness and inconsistency, particularly with regard to dates of birth. But what of Cousin Eva? We have seen that it was to rush to her aid at the time of Eva's divorce in 1896 that Rubinstein sailed to Australia. A pathetic coda appeared in *The Argus* on Monday 2 January 1928:

> The police are anxious to communicate with relatives of Louis Leopold Levy, whose body was found on the railway line at Kensington on Friday night. It is believed that Levy lived in Victoria Street, North Melbourne, and had recently been discharged from a mental home. According to statements made to the police, Levy was a passenger on a train. Near Kensington he attempted to touch a passing train and fell onto the line.[9]

Eva Levy died in the Mercy Hospital in East Melbourne on 6 May 1947.[10] She was eighty, a good five years older than her famous cousin, although in 1965 Rubinstein described Eva as having been a few years younger than her.[11] We do not know if they kept in touch in later years; to be fair, given the unusual circumstances, Rubinstein's silence may well have been tactful and/or intended to be discreet. The stigma surrounding divorce in the grim era of the *Matrimonial Causes Act 1857*, to say nothing of the sullen cloud of silence that then hung over cases of aggravated domestic violence, cannot be overstated.[12] Eva Levy and Rubinstein shared the unusual experience of successive episodes of more or less voluntary displacement, and as young unmarried Jewish women assisting their nearest relations. For both, Coleraine represented a dramatic resumption of that same strategy, in which dire necessity played the dominant part.

It is difficult to draw many conclusions about Rubinstein's relatively fugitive uncles and her cousin Eva. There are signs of tension – according to Patrick O'Higgins, Rubinstein claimed that Uncle Louis (more probably Uncle Bernhard) 'took liberties', and according to John Poynter, she shocked her English teacher by asking, 'What does "bugger" mean? My uncle calls me that.'[13] It has also been suggested that bitter conflict arose from the fact that Rubinstein was never paid any wages for working for her uncle, other than in board and lodging. She had long experienced the expectation that family obligation and duty outweighed most other considerations. Perhaps the patience that was first imposed upon her in Kazimierz was running out. However, there are, I think, hints of clannishness also – of blood being thicker than water, despite everything. Did Bernhard and Louis part company or expand into two branches of the same business (possibly three with John)? Most importantly, the Silberfelds allow us to see Rubinstein's immigration, work, business acumen and eventual naturalisation as conforming in many ways to a well-established family pattern. Even her fact-finding mission from Melbourne to Hamburg, Vienna, Paris and London and back in 1905 followed the example of John Silberfeld's activities ten years earlier, when he shuttled several times between Adelaide and Bremen before vanishing from Australian records.

Upon her arrival in Coleraine, Rubinstein spoke the southern Polish dialect of Eastern Yiddish, Polish, German and a little French, but very little English – possibly none at all. She is said to have attended a local school, a solitary adult in a large class of children. She worked for her Uncle Bernhard in Whyte Street and lent Eva a much-needed hand with the three little Levy children – work that was no less arduous, probably more so. While Rubinstein was later vague about what she did in Coleraine, she was careful to lay some emphasis upon her appearance:

> To the hard-working, kindly Australians, the little girl from Poland must have looked like someone from another world. Anxious to make a good impression on my relatives, I had taken great care over my appearance, and I arrived wearing one of my most elegant white pleated dresses, with a large straw hat and, of course, wearing high-heeled button shoes. I also carried my parasol, but I found it quite impossible to keep the dust out of my eyes and, at the same time, hold it over my head in the correct European manner... My uncle's neighbours, who had ridden in from their stations beyond Kaorite [*sic*] Creek[14] to welcome me, politely admired my inappropriate clothes... Stubbornly I dressed up for every possible occasion, and I even defied Eva's sound advice by continuing to wear my impractically high-heeled shoes on a terrain that had never been intended for anything so frivolous.[15]

The Coleraine Racecourse, where Uncle Bernhard was a steward, is a charming spot just beyond the eastern edge of town. This was where the famous Great Western Steeplechase was run every May.[16] Rubinstein cleverly created a wrong impression by referring here to her uncle's friends riding into town from their 'stations' beyond Koroite Creek, implying that this was a sort of epic cross-country slog over vast distances. However, Koroite Creek is hardly more than a stone's throw from the Coleraine Racecourse. The 'stations', meanwhile, were almost certainly small holdings, which proliferated on the outskirts of Western District towns in the 1890s.

By her own account, Rubinstein brought with her from Poland twelve pots of her mother's face cream, and much interest arose among the women and girls of Coleraine.[17] If, as seems distinctly possible, she became convinced that lanolin from local merino fleeces might be used to improve her mother's formulation, there is no evidence that she acted upon the idea before she opened her first rooms in Elizabeth Street, Melbourne, at the beginning of 1903.

It has been estimated that up to half the weight of a newly shorn merino fleece consists of the raw grease from which lanolin is afterwards refined. A frequent observation since well before Federation has been that although their work is in almost every other respect back-breaking, shearers, wool classers and tar boys tend to have soft, smooth hands. According to a 1909 feature article entitled 'The Wool Land' in *The Sydney Morning Herald*, 'The skin of a shearer's hands is always soft, almost like a woman's, because the grease actually manicures him.'[18] It would not have been difficult for Rubinstein to absorb this piece of common knowledge in the grazing community of Coleraine, but alas we have no hard evidence that she did so with any immediate or practical object in mind. What we can be sure of, however, is that every spring a small army of shearers descended upon the district and were a conspicuous presence in Coleraine's three hotels, four bootmakers, two saddlers and Bernhard Silberfeld's mixed business.[19] The Silberfelds' Whyte Street shop, no less than every other business in Coleraine, was bound to the core agricultural industry of the region, and Rubinstein was well aware of it.

In about 1899, aged twenty-six, Rubinstein left the Silberfeld–Levy household. Local tradition has it that prior to leaving the district, she fled Coleraine and worked for a while for a Jewish merchant in nearby Sandford, near the confluence of the Wannon and Glenelg rivers, not far from Casterton. Soon afterwards, however, Rubinstein boarded the train to Hamilton, and never went back.

* * *

According to a throwaway, undocumented line in a lecture published in the *Victorian Historical Magazine* in 1961, Rubinstein worked for a while

(c. 1899–1900) as governess to the children of the squatter, grazier and oarsman Steve Fairbairn at Meltham, his estate near Gheringhap outside Geelong, south-west of Melbourne: 'It is said that his sons were brought up there, and that their governess was the now celebrated Miss Helena Rubinstein.'[20] This claim has proven impossible to verify, although it is worth noting that the lecture was originally delivered at Meltham itself, and the claim was made not long after Rubinstein's final visit to Australia and while she was still very much alive, as indeed were Steve Fairbairn's younger son Ian, and his elder son's widow Angela. None of them chose to contest it.

What we can be sure about, however, is that for about two years after she left the district of Coleraine, Rubinstein worked as a governess in at least two other households, both prosperous, one in Toowoomba on the Darling Downs of southeastern Queensland and one in the bayside suburb of St Kilda in Melbourne. This was an occupation for which Rubinstein had every reason to feel amply qualified. Approaching her twenty-sixth birthday, for as long as she could remember much of her energy had been marshalled in such work, first, in aid of her father and mother and seven younger sisters in Kazimierz, then nine Beckmann cousins elsewhere in Kraków, six even smaller Splitter cousins in Vienna, and, lately, three little Levy cousins in Coleraine – Reg, Fred and Theo, who, when she arrived there in September 1896, were six, five and three years old – a grand total of twenty-five small children in four separate high-maintenance batches. She had known no other way of life, which may well explain how the ambition to create her business and tread her own path was first ignited and in due course took such tenacious hold.

Governesses were mostly young, well-educated, middle-class women who were employed to supervise the early education of children at home. In many cases, governesses were a cheaper and more convenient alternative to sending children to boarding school. From 1862, when the Female Middle Class Emigration Society was founded in London, many British governesses obtained cheap, flexible loans with which to finance unassisted passage to the Australasian and other colonies, where they pinned their hopes on starting a new, respectable life. In repaying their loans to the

Society, many of these governesses wrote accounts of their experiences. Their letters contain often bleak accounts of the scarcity of 'situations', and of hardship more generally.

For some, this bold exercise in relocation went according to plan. It was especially bold because the path they chose was so singular. These impecunious young women set sail with the expectation of being able to find adequately remunerated employment in a good, hopefully enlightened household, and that their charges would prove to be manageable, healthy, receptive to instruction (often in many disciplines), and well behaved. If the children were not well behaved, the governess depended upon their parents to give her the support to impose discipline at her discretion.[21] Upon almost every single point, governesses risked disappointment. For some, the venture went badly wrong. In every case, these governesses had little to fall back on but their own resourcefulness. Many of them disappeared into the melting pot of colonial life. Governesses and nannies (for younger children and infants) were not technically servants. However, they were worked just as hard as servants, were paid as little as servants and were often treated like servants.[22]

Colonial governesses oscillated with varying degrees of discomfort between the drawing-room and the servants' hall, but they were mostly bound to the schoolroom or the nursery, administering lessons, when they were not accompanying their charges on outings. Governesses were expected to be genteel and well educated.[23] Indeed they often provided instruction in languages, music, mathematics and other disciplines. Their social position was a lot higher than that of nursery maids and other domestics. However, it was nevertheless often economically precarious, and being marooned between the drawing-room and the servants' hall meant that governesses were effectively excluded from both, and importantly lacked the pecking order and systems of support that existed in the latter – the pecking order being below stairs every bit as rigid as it was upstairs. Increasing competition for positions among impecunious and/or distressed gentlewomen held governesses' salaries down. In most cases, a higher standard of dress and deportment was expected than could be achieved with an annual salary of only £20 or £30.[24] Governesses were also at times subjected to 'deprivations, hardships, enforced subjugations to distasteful principles and regulations' such that, depending upon the location of the household, employers might be obliged simply to take what they could get.[25] It is far from certain that Helena Rubinstein did not belong in this category.

Conversely, governesses were at times obliged to settle for circumstances that struggled to meet the unwritten requirements of 'a good home'. According to one distressed governess, writing at length in March 1899 about several resident positions in rural New South Wales,

> My duties were to teach English, music, French, elementary Latin, plain and fancy needlework, and, if possible, dancing and singing to four pupils; and in my spare time (if I had any) to assist in making and mending – salary £26 per annum. I was told that though the salary was small it was a good home. My next and last interview was for a governess to a family who lived 400 miles [664 kilometres] away, and the duties were to teach all English subjects, music, French, drawing, calisthenics and club exercise, assist in making and mending, superintend the washing and dressing of the children, make the nursery beds and prepare the nursery meals – salary £25 per annum. Must sign for six months or forfeit fare. Can any one tell me why governesses, who are mostly refined girls, are expected to do so much, when servants, cooks, &c., have their special duties and no more, and are allowed a great deal of freedom? The salaries offered to us are fit for nurse-girls, whose only duty is to look after baby.[26]

It should not surprise us that, even if in about 1899 Rubinstein had already decided to take up the occupation of governess, she set about doing so from a direction entirely different from the path taken by the many beneficiaries of the Female Middle Class Emigration Society. Her own education was at best rudimentary. She was not a native English-speaker, but she did speak German and French, which were far more useful to her in Australia than Polish. Rubinstein had the advantage of already being in the colony, and could lay claim to much relevant experience with small children. However, when in about 1899 she took the train from Coleraine or Casterton to Hamilton (and onwards), she had no guarantee of being able to find work as a governess. She faced stiff competition from better-educated, more genteel applicants. If she anticipated or encountered any anti-Semitic prejudice, we have no evidence of it. That she succeeded at all is a mark of considerable enterprise. More importantly, the boldness of her decision to leave Coleraine demonstrates Rubinstein's serene tolerance of superabundant risk.

With regard to Meltham, Steve Fairbairn himself made no mention of the remarkable fact that Rubinstein had been governess to his young sons in his hearty sportsman's memoir *Fairbairn of Jesus* [College, Cambridge]: *An Autobiography* (1931).[27] It is possible that he simply did not know; if he did, it seems inconceivable that he would not have at least mentioned her. By 1931 her fame was widespread. Either way, Rubinstein cannot have stayed in the Fairbairn household for long. Perhaps this first stint with the little Fairbairn boys was not a success.

Two purely circumstantial factors lend *some* credence to the Meltham episode, and the possibility that Rubinstein worked there. Then as now, Geelong and Ballarat were the centres to which the towns and rural communities of the Western District of Victoria looked more directly than to Melbourne (and vice versa). They were logical destinations for any refugee from Coleraine. The Fairbairns' extensive Queensland interests, meanwhile, open up a route to Toowoomba that is far more plausible than the elaborate old chestnut Rubinstein implanted in her earliest Valaze publicity and again in her 1965 memoir, namely that she had worked as governess to the children of a lady she met in 1896 on board the *Prinz-Regent Luitpold*. That lady, she claimed, was the wife of an aide-de-camp to the governor of Queensland, Lord Lamington.[28] In the middle of 1903, to 'Iris', Melbourne correspondent of the Adelaide *Critic*, Rubinstein let it be known that:

Miss Rubinstein arrived in Australia a few years ago as governess in a vice-regal family. Like most Austrians, Miss Rubinstein was a linguist. While filling the post the remarkable qualities of her pure complexion led to comment. She was asked what she used for her skin. She was amused, but mentioned only a soap and skin-food her mother sent her from Russia – a skin-food prepared by Dr Lykuski, a European specialist. Miss Rubinstein was asked to procure some for the Governor's wife ... When, two years later, the Governor left his State, Miss Rubinstein came to Victoria and became governess in a leading squatter's family out Western way.[29]

In the absence of Lord and Lady Lamington, who had left Queensland at the end of 1901, Rubinstein could be fairly confident that these claims would pass unchallenged, although, as we shall see, there were plenty of people in Toowoomba who could have refuted them, and with vigour. However, as with various other strands of her narrative, there is a minuscule grain of truth to this one. It certainly brings Rubinstein to within range of Harlaxton House, the Lamingtons' hilltop retreat on the outskirts of Toowoomba in the southern summer of 1899–1900. However, we now know that Rubinstein was instead causing something of an uproar at Astonette, Drayton Road, the residence of Mr and Mrs Evelyn James Metcalfe.

When Rubinstein described herself as having been 'governess in a vice-regal family', what she avoided saying was that she had been governess to the children of the sister of the wife of a military gentleman attached to a vice-regal household, some 125 kilometres away. In January 1898, Mrs Metcalfe's youngest sister Beatrice (*née* Brodribb) married Captain Charles Pyne of the Royal Warwickshire Regiment. Captain Pyne had been aide-de-camp to Sir Henry Wylie Norman, governor of Queensland (1889–95), but was promoted by Norman's successor, Lord Lamington, to be his incoming Excellency's private secretary (1896–1901). Presently we shall conclude from invaluable testimony recorded in a most unexpected quarter that Rubinstein had plentiful opportunities to come into direct contact with Mrs Pyne and the Metcalfe children's Pyne cousins. All were frequent visitors to Wyalla, the splendid Toowoomba home of their Brodribb grandparents, but there is no trace of a Miss Brodribb aboard the *Prinz-Regent Luitpold* in 1896.

Mr and Mrs Metcalfe and Mr and Mrs Fairbairn moved in the same, relatively closed Queensland social circle, the Fairbairns shuttling between Brisbane, Melbourne, Geelong and their remote cattle station and those of Mr Fairbairn's many siblings. Both couples crop up regularly in the social and golfing pages through the 1890s and 1900s, with tantalising proximity to each other, and to several vice-regal households.[30]

At the time of Federation, most state governors and governors-general of the Commonwealth arrived in Australia with no prior knowledge of their respective seats of government. They and their household staff, a high proportion of whom were young unmarried British army officers, looked upon the colonial upper class as the natural pool from which to populate the blank social calendar of their respective Government Houses. How else was one supposed to know Who was Who? The colonial upper class, meanwhile, came to regard the vice-regal circle as one to which they enjoyed automatic if not exclusive access. The relationship was symbiotic.[31]

As well, vice-regal households in neighbouring colonies enjoyed a special sort of bond. They tended to know each other and had plentiful opportunities to meet and to exchange juicy social and political gossip. In the circumstances, it is hardly surprising that impecunious but promising and well-connected British officers discovered in that same pool a ready supply of wealthy brides. Mrs Metcalfe's youngest sister made one such marriage, as did two of Steve Fairbairn's many nieces.[32] Ships passing, perhaps, and thin though this gruel undoubtedly is, nevertheless we can place the Fairbairns and the Metcalfes, if not in the same pew, certainly in the same Queensland church – which was not a church so much as a cathedral.

Any such colonial upper-class social network, such as it was, benefited their servants and other employees as much as it supported Mrs Fairbairn and Mrs Metcalfe. But there were complications. If, as I have suggested, Rubinstein's brief tour of duty at Meltham might not have been a success,

Mrs Fairbairn faced a dilemma. The easiest way to rid herself of such a problem was a glowing reference, to smooth for Rubinstein the fastest possible path into another household. *Plus ça change*. However, by doing so, Mrs Fairbairn ran a social risk, if Rubinstein proved to be as unsatisfactory to Mrs Metcalfe as she had been to Mrs Fairbairn.

There were other shades of possibility. If Rubinstein had instead been a boon to the Fairbairns, another household in desperate need of a governess might not hesitate to poach a particularly good one. As a rule, one simply did not go about poaching other ladies' governesses. In an emergency, however, one did what one had to do. The greater the emergency, the more one was prepared to bend or even break the rules. Mrs Metcalfe was heavily pregnant when her husband engaged Rubinstein. Time was running out.

This raises another possibility. As David Hansen has so memorably put it, at the outermost fringes of the Empire, from time to time pianos washed up on the beach.[33] The Australian colonial upper class was far more accustomed to social anomaly, muddled conventions, mixed usage and strange or surprising new arrivals than was its aristocratic prototype in Britain. It follows that, even if she materialised in Geelong or Toowoomba without any references, the young Rubinstein stood a far greater chance of securing employment as governess to the Fairbairn children at Meltham or the Metcalfe children at Astonette than she would have done in almost any other English-speaking jurisdiction. Being most unusual was not necessarily a disadvantage. Indeed, the Metcalfes may have derived some satisfaction from having obtained the services of a governess whom their children could be enjoined to address as '*Fräulein*', as we shall see they certainly did.

* * *

Toowoomba occupies a magnificent position atop the Great Dividing Range, effectively the easternmost edge of a great undulating plateau known as the Darling Downs, about 125 kilometres west of Brisbane. It lies in a bowl-shaped eerie at the head of the dramatic Lockyer Valley. Toowoomba was the principal hub of the Darling Downs, mainly looking west to the pastoral runs, many of which were huge. Toowoomba is to those great properties, that huge swathe of country, as Geelong and Ballarat were to the Western District of Victoria.

Queensland squatters built their elegant townhouses in Toowoomba; sent their children to boarding schools there; sought specialist medical attention, and (when practicable) the lying-in hospital. They raced their thoroughbred racehorses at Toowoomba. They established their families permanently in town. They created institutions of learning and charity. The railway from Brisbane to Sydney went via Toowoomba so as to intercept passengers connecting from distant termini right the way across rural Queensland. Its public buildings and lively commerce bespeak a particular pride, and Toowoomba was for more than a century the principal centre of agricultural industry, supporting foundries, tanneries, every sort of manufacturing upon which Queensland graziers depended, and without which a far more inconvenient journey to Brisbane down on the coastal plain would have been necessary. Toowoomba was the Simla of colonial south-eastern Queensland.

Sadly, the greatest Toowoomba villas and townhouses are mostly gone, and the few that remain are in a sorry state of decline. Their once magnificent gardens and grand acreages of park and grounds have long since been carved up. In my hunt for any sign or remnant of Astonette, the best I could do was to locate one or two gigantic trees in an otherwise crowded neighbourhood and conclude, correctly, that these once formed part of their magnificent garden in Drayton Road (which was renamed Anzac Road soon after World War I). Mr and Mrs William Beit's 1895 Ascot, meanwhile, which is in Newtown, a short walk away, *has* survived. The quite indescribable ballroom wing at the rear is also known as 'the folly', for fairly obvious reasons. The style is Darling Downs Baroque with Moorish cum Tyroleo-Novgorod grace notes.

According to a long article in *The Darling Downs Gazette* in June 1900, the case of E.J. Metcalfe v. Olive Keys in the Toowoomba Police Court solves the mystery of what Rubinstein was doing there in 1900–01.[34] The plaintiff,

Mr Evelyn Metcalfe, a gentleman of independent means, summoned the defendant for absconding from his hired service. She, Olive Keys, had lasted only one month as the Metcalfes' cook. Late on the evening of 23 May 1900, Miss Keys and two other domestics departed without prior warning. They left behind a note that read:

> To Mrs Metcalfe. No doubt you will be surprised to find us gone, but we made a promise that if one went we would all go. You will find in here a pound for a week's wages for two. You will have the other. Remember this, if you want to keep girls you need never expect Britons *while you keep a (Boer) bore*, for Britons never shall be slaves. God Save the Queen. [my italics]³⁵

Rubinstein was at this time governess to Mr and Mrs Metcalfe's daughter José, while Mrs Metcalfe (Wynnie Prudence, *née* Brodribb) was expecting another child, Debonnaire Prudence, who arrived in 1901 – both of whom, incidentally, are a keyword-searcher's dream.[36]

According to the defendant, Rubinstein made a habit of entering the kitchen at Astonette and issuing orders in a most imperious, peremptory and interfering manner. Who were Olive and the others to obey, Mrs Metcalfe or Miss Rubinstein? Miss Rubinstein had also been severely critical of Olive's cakes, which Mrs Metcalfe had earlier professed to like. The cakes appear to have been the straw that broke the camel's back. According to Olive's testimony, Miss Rubinstein hotly protested that Mr Metcalfe *disliked* her cakes, and instructed Olive to desist from baking them. The topical reference to Mrs Metcalfe's 'Boer bore' evidently arose from only the sketchiest idea of where exactly Rubinstein came from. As she spoke German and was addressed as '*Fräulein*', Olive and the others may have concluded that Rubinstein was German and therefore loosely aligned with the Afrikaners. If so, they were wrong. At any rate, this settles the question – Rubinstein was by May 1900 already honing her administrative skills as governess to the Metcalfe children at Astonette, Drayton Road, Toowoomba.

The *Toowoomba Chronicle and Darling Downs General Advertiser* took up the story on Saturday 28 July 1900.[37] The police magistrate had earlier fined Olive Keys £1 for leaving her position as cook in the Metcalfe household without giving reasonable notice under Section 3 of the *Master and Servant Act 1889*. Miss Keys boldly appealed against this penalty to the civil jurisdiction of the district court, which sat at Toowoomba on 19 and 20 July 1900. His Honour Acting Judge L.E. Groom dismissed the appellant's case on the grounds that, first, Miss Keys had departed Astonette in secrecy and at night without giving any prior warning to Mrs Metcalfe; second, that it could not be found, on the evidence, that the interference of the governess, Miss Rubinstein, was of such an intolerable nature as to justify their abrupt departure; and third, that the mere fact that Miss Keys was told to take orders from Miss Rubinstein was not in itself enough to justify the defendant in her action – implying that Olive's cake defence was insufficient. Mrs Metcalfe was perfectly entitled to give orders through others she might place in charge of her household. If a servant could on any caprice absent herself and simply forfeit a week's wages the object of the Act would be frustrated. His Honour then referred to the case of *Neighbour v. Moore*.[38] So that was that.

Acting Judge Groom soon rose far above this in almost every respect obscure matter, and became Sir Littleton Groom, the long-serving federal member of parliament for Darling Downs from 1901 to 1929, and a senior cabinet minister in successive Commonwealth governments from 1905 to 1914 and, finally, sixth speaker of the House of Representatives (1926–29), the first to preside over John Smith Murdoch's newly completed Provisional Parliament House in Canberra.[39] I wonder if, in his recollection, he ever made the connection between that interfering governess in *Metcalfe v. Keys* and the *châtelaine* of 24 Grafton Street, 255 rue Saint-Honoré and 15 East 49th Street? The fascinating part, though, is that through later decades the Metcalfes themselves never seem to have grasped what Rubinstein, their sometime governess, went on to achieve. Given the uproar surrounding *Metcalfe v. Keys*, one might conclude that they simply preferred to forget – were it not for the valuable testimony of Laurie E. Smith.

* * *

At some point between Rubinstein's departure from Toowoomba in autumn 1900 and July 1904, a young woman succeeded her as governess or nanny at Astonette (in fact a combination of both roles), in this case to the younger Metcalfe daughter, Debonnaire, who was by then three and a half years old. Her name was Laurie E. Smith, and by an incredible stroke of good fortune she kept a diary. That valuable document of a prosperous early childhood in Federation Queensland survives in the collection of the John Oxley Library in Brisbane.[40] Writing with child-like simplicity, Nanny Smith intended this charming chronicle, with its pressed flowers and a few watercolour and other illustrations, eventually to be a keepsake for Debonnaire ('baby').

Laurie's diary mainly deals with the various doings of baby – her health, sleep, play, diet and interactions with Daddy, Mammie, aunts and uncles, other children, family friends and relations – to say nothing of Simpkin, 'such a great cat', whose death and slightly alarming obsequies and interment occurred on 7 and 8 October 1904.[41] The immense value of Laurie's diary, though, is that it produces a granular picture of the comfortable domestic arrangements at Astonette in the aftermath of the *Metcalfe v. Keys* debacle; indeed, Laurie brings home its full ramifications. When, under cover of darkness, Olive and the others walked out of Astonette in 1900, the immediate burden must have fallen heavily on Rubinstein's shoulders. There is no reason to suppose that Wynnie Metcalfe, being heavily pregnant with Debonnaire, or else lately delivered of her, had ever so much as boiled a kettle, or knew what to do with an egg.

The staffing arrangements at Astonette included the housekeeper Mrs Cory; 'Cook'; Annie the housemaid or lady's maid; Minnie the laundry maid; Valentine and George the gardeners; as well as Debonnaire's older sister José's non-resident tutor or governess, Miss Jackson, and her dancing teacher, Miss Marley. An unnamed dressmaker regularly visited Mrs Metcalfe. Her work was presumably beyond Laurie's capacity, although Laurie ran up blouses for Mrs Metcalfe and devoted one day per week to pattern-cutting, sewing and mending – mainly clothes for the children. She worked with a sewing machine, at times struggling to keep up with the workload.[42]

Baby Debonnaire is regularly enjoined to greet the postman, as well as the fruit man and the butter boy. She also pays regular visits to the stables to say hello to the ponies, David and Molly, and Papa's chestnut mare, Polly, who was something of a local celebrity: 'one of the best buggy horses in the district'.[43] A good deal of attention is paid to Debonnaire's dolls Mary, Louie and Tommy (among others). Life was mainly confined to Debonnaire's nursery, where Laurie also slept, except when she was ill; when Debonnaire was ill, Laurie attended throughout. Games took place on the wide verandahs, or in the garden, or sliding about with other children on the highly polished floor of the ballroom at the Beits' Ascot.

What we would call Laurie's job description is daunting. Laurie oversaw every aspect of the care of baby, a 24-hour responsibility. She supervised all nursery meals and oversaw dressing, undressing, bath-time, bed-time, hymns and prayers. She read aloud; gave rudimentary lessons; provided instruction and practice in French conversation; imposed discipline when needed; and kept a watchful eye over sometimes high-maintenance play – including running races in the garden. She administered medicines: senna tea with sugar; castor oil (with a chocolate chaser) and mustard foot baths for colds.[44] From time to time Laurie delivered baby to her parents in the drawing room for an hour or two at tea time, or before bed, but apart from those formalities everything Laurie did must strike the modern reader as indistinguishable from what most mothers or carers now do.

On top of all this, Laurie organised elaborate beach picnics at Southport. She supervised outings, which also doubled as responsible errands to the bank, to pay household bills and so on. Laurie arranged flowers throughout the house. She chaperoned the children to church on Sundays. She took José to the dentist to have her wires painfully removed. There were visits to the post office; to nice Mr Norris and Mr Ridgeley the chemists; to Laidlaw & Peak the grocers; to J.H. Jones the drapers; to Bain's photographic studio in Queen Street; to the Toowoomba Steam Laundry; and to

T.K. Lamb & Co., the confectioners and cake shop in Ruthven Street, for a nourishing sponge.

On these occasions, Valentine the gardener doubled as groom, harnessing David to the governess's tub cart, while naturally Laurie took the reins. The drive from Astonette into town is a long steady descent. It required some skill handling the reins with one hand and using considerable elbow grease with the handbrake in the other. Returning from town required a confident whip hand. As well, Laurie took the children surprisingly often to the churchyard, where they freshened up or replaced the flowers on Grandfather Frank Brodribb's newly dug grave, as well as that of half-brother Theo's mother Isabel, the first Mrs Metcalfe.[45] Laurie was reading aloud Beatrix Potter's *The Tale of Peter Rabbit* not eighteen months after its first trade publication by Warne & Co. in London in October 1902. Astonette had a telephone.

This was the charmed little world, fearfully circumscribed but wealthy and clannish, into which Rubinstein was lifted during her year in Toowoomba in 1900, and there is no reason to suppose that her duties were materially different from Laurie E. Smith's. True, in 1900 José Metcalfe was six years old; she turned seven in November, so attendance upon the nursery cannot have been as arduous. Still, the broader framework of responsibility must have been more or less identical, and Rubinstein must have known many if not most of Laurie's *dramatis personae*.[46]

In this important context, Laurie's diary contains perhaps the most fascinating residue, and within the space of a single sentence. Exactly coinciding with the end of Rubinstein's brief consulting stint above Messrs William A. McGuffie & Co., the pharmaceutical chemists in Queen Street, Brisbane, to which we shall return in greater detail, on Thursday 20 October, Laurie noted:

> Debonnaire ... went to bed to rest & then she was made clean & pretty & went with Mammie & José to the station to see José's old governess 'Fräulein' pass on her way to Sydney.[47]

If this is not an explicit reference to Rubinstein, we would need to consider the odds against two former German-speaking governesses in the Metcalfe household travelling overland by train from Brisbane to Sydney via Toowoomba on the same day. This is not proof, but I find it overwhelmingly persuasive, and suggests that the Metcalfes retained memories of Olive Keys's 'Boer bore' that were sufficiently affectionate as to bring them to greet Rubinstein, however briefly, on the platform and in the bustling refreshment rooms of the Toowoomba Railway Station, more than four years afterwards. If so, the reunion must have been particularly affecting, because it was either the first time Rubinstein had ever met Debonnaire, or the first since she was a newborn infant. It is also remarkable that the only known reference to Rubinstein in any contemporary non-official Australian manuscript source was noted down for the benefit of a little girl, and by Laurie E. Smith, a hardworking nanny whose cheerfulness and devotion shine from every page.

* * *

Towards the end of 1900 or in 1901, Rubinstein made her way from Toowoomba to Melbourne. Her departure seems not to have been collateral damage caused by the case of *Metcalfe v. Keys*, or by the unwelcome publicity in the press that arose from it. According to oral tradition, once again, it was as a governess that Rubinstein straightaway entered the service of a prominent Jewish businessman, Moritz Michaelis, at his spacious home, Linden, in Acland Street, St Kilda.[48] At this time the Jewish community of Melbourne was mostly concentrated in town, close to the Melbourne Hebrew Congregation in Bourke Street, but there were other pockets. We have already seen that in 1889 Louis and Eva Levy married according to Jewish rites in Drummond Street, Carlton. That locality would grow in importance as a Jewish neighbourhood, but not until the 1920s. The more prosperous, however, were moving out to the bayside suburb of St Kilda, where Rubinstein followed, at least for a while.

The connection with Mr Michaelis was apparently sought and successfully made through a relative of Michaelis's, Maurice Max Shaumer, who had for a while been in partnership with Uncle John Silberfeld. Woodhead argues that it was through Michaelis that Rubinstein made contact, in turn, with Frederick Sheppard Grimwade.[49] As with all forms of oral tradition, the detail is maddeningly unclear. True, the firm of Michaelis, Hallenstein & Co. were successful manufacturers of glue and processors of gelatine, and to that extent their operations overlapped with those of Felton Grimwade in Flinders Lane. We know that the firm of Michaelis Hallenstein sourced possum skins from Coleraine for their glue lines, but it would be absurd to suppose that this can have been the avenue by which Rubinstein came to be governess in the household of Moritz Michaelis. There was also in 1900 a considerable cultural and social gulf separating the Grimwades' Harleston in Caulfield from Linden in St Kilda, despite their relative physical proximity.

There is, as well, a problem of chronology. In 1900, Moritz Michaelis was eighty years old; he died on 26 November 1902. If Rubinstein had served in his household as a governess it must have been for his grandchildren, the three sons of his second son (and sixth child), Edward Michaelis.[50] Soon afterwards, Rubinstein is to be found in Elizabeth Stern's boarding house at 29 and 30 Grey Street, St Kilda. This is the only evidence we have that Rubinstein sought any particular adherence to, or association with, the local Jewish community. As far as I am aware, after her departure from Kraków she was never in any way religious or observant. However, the processes of assimilation could be gradual. At the time of Federation, those processes, those stages, were themselves evolving through any number of personal responses to local circumstances that depended upon where you happened to live. Edwardian Australia provided a substantial measure of freedom to maintain the old ways, to abandon them or to tread a middle path. It has so far proven impossible to locate Rubinstein with any precision on this satisfactorily broad and tolerant spectrum.

Between August 1896 and the southern winter of 1901, Rubinstein had travelled alone by train from Vienna to Genoa. She had experienced the long voyage to Australia. She had caught her first glimpse of Melbourne. She had been embedded in four separate households with small children, having previously been embedded in three others, two in Kraków and one in Vienna. In three of the Australian households she had been employed as governess. She had returned to Melbourne from Toowoomba. As she approached her twenty-ninth birthday, Rubinstein exchanged the, at best, socially ambiguous position of governess in the Michaelis household in St Kilda for the much harder and less well-remunerated position of 'waitress' in town. She had come to Australia, and she had already seen much. However, this was not even the end of the beginning.

4

Taking the Measure of Melbourne

Perhaps the most impressive aspect of Helena Rubinstein's first three years in business (1903–06) is that from the outset she prospered in Melbourne despite the pre-existence of a great deal of direct local competition. Even before she entered it, she knew that her milieu would be crowded. Many of her future competitors were long-established. Some of them had for years enjoyed close and friendly relations with the press. Rubinstein was a new arrival for whom the cultivation of press publicity meant starting from scratch. What was to be her point of difference? What commercial leverage would she have at her disposal? How might she separate herself from the Greek chorus of face-cream and, Thespis-like, step forward and take her rightful place downstage centre? It is hard to decide which is the more remarkable, the fact that she did it or the fact that she managed to do it so quickly. Crucially, Rubinstein had a good eighteen months to take the measure of the commercial and professional company she was proposing to keep. The range and character of that mixed company reward close scrutiny, as indeed her own close scrutiny in 1901 and 1902 clearly rewarded Rubinstein.

Melbourne at the time of Federation

The Melbourne to which Rubinstein made her way from Toowoomba in the moment of Federation was still the second most populous city in the British Empire. Despite the ill effects of the crash of 1891–92, the speed of Melbourne's growth in the fifty years following the discovery of massive quantities of gold in 1851 was unprecedented. The European population of Melbourne grew from only 23,000 to half a million.[1] Paul Huège de Serville has shown how, with the rise of Victoria's bubble of wealth, the pre-existing social elites of Melbourne and Port Phillip, such as they were, also rose.[2] The strange mixture of late Regency fugitives and dandies and more or less bona fide 'gentlemen' who clustered around the Melbourne Club in October 1836 did not rise by degrees; after 1851, they soared, and to dizzying heights, in wealth and influence and jealously guarded exclusiveness.[3] In 1891–92, the prudent avoided disaster, but the improvident and meretricious were ruined. We have already seen the impact of the ensuing depression of the 1890s, and of the coincidental Federation drought. Recovery was long and slow and flat. Indeed, the population of Victoria fell sharply, many people seeking work elsewhere and many others crossing the Bight to join the new gold rush to Coolgardie in Western Australia. In the fifteen years following 1891, Victoria lost as many people as she had gained between 1860 and 1890.[4] At the same time, in Melbourne in 1900 unemployment remained high, around 10 per cent (down from 28 per cent of trade union members in 1893). There were also aftershocks in the form of brief periods of recession, in 1901, 1903 and 1908. Having decades earlier exceeded Sydney's in size and wealth, Melbourne's population was finally overtaken in 1905. Through the first decade of the twentieth century, Victoria's economy hardly grew.

However, despite all that, in 1900 the underlying, accumulated wealth of Victoria remained more or less intact; the problem was simply one of inertia, sluggish return on investments, and vast resources tied up in feeble trusts, government bonds and under-performing agriculture. By then, perhaps shocked into this mode by the economic crisis, the highest stratum of

Melbourne society formed a tightly closed ceiling whose impenetrability rivalled even that of the Athenæum, Balliol or the House of Lords. In this respect, the uppermost social fabric of colonial Melbourne exhibited a weave that was, despite everything, in her own estimation, proudly different from Sydney's. In the midst of economic malaise, for years upper-class Melbourne derived much comfort from seeing herself, inaccurately, as a rich and costly brocade compared with Sydney's stolen chintz.

But what about the lower, much broader ranks? Beneath such an airtight lid, and despite the flat economy, there existed in Edwardian Melbourne a virtual pressure cooker of metropolitan life. In many ways this held up a mirror to the imperial capital but with far greater social elasticity. Female students were first admitted to the University of Melbourne in 1880 – to Oxford not until 1921, and to Cambridge more than twenty-five years later, in 1947. Likewise, the push for women's suffrage was far more advanced and successful in the Australasian colonies than at home in Britain.

Trans-Tasman societies at the time of Federation afforded opportunities for Edwardian settler women that existed almost nowhere else – political, social, academic, professional, commercial. In 1903, Vida Goldstein became (with three other women: Selina Anderson, Nellie Martel and Mary Moore-Bentley) the first in the British Empire to be nominated and stand for election to parliament. Vida Goldstein's heritage was, like Rubinstein's, Polish–Jewish. Before 1877, her father Jacob Goldstein had run a general store in Warrnambool, a little more than 130 kilometres southeast of Coleraine. Goldstein stood for election to the Senate as an independent candidate for the state of Victoria (unsuccessfully as it turned out), but she went on to stand for parliament another four times: in 1910, 1913, 1914 and 1917, twice for the Senate, as before, and twice for the House of Representatives. However, her first campaign took place in Melbourne a good two years *before* Christabel Pankhurst was arrested in London and sent to Royal Holloway for interrupting a Liberal Party meeting by shouting her demand for votes for women. By 1911, all Australian states had enacted legislation that gave women the right to vote. All women over the age of twenty-one in England,

Scotland and Wales would have to wait until 1928 before they were able to vote on an equal footing with men.[5]

Alas, we have no evidence that Rubinstein engaged with or responded to any of these developments in any particular way, but roughly coinciding with the full duration of her Australasian sojourn, they must at least have touched her, as indeed they affected all European women in Australia and New Zealand. Roughly twenty years after her departure for London, however, in 1928 Rubinstein wrote: 'The cosmetic business is interesting among modern industries in its opportunities for women. Here they have found a field that is their own province – working for women with women, and giving that which only women can give – an intimate understanding of feminine needs and feminine desires.' Her experience of life in Edwardian Australia and New Zealand cannot but have pushed Rubinstein in this direction.[6]

Theatre and entertainment in Melbourne had for decades been vigorous. In 1863–64, the famous but ageing Charles and Ellen Kean undertook a lucrative tour of the Australian colonies and the United States, beginning in Melbourne. As Marguerite Hancock has rightly observed, the aim of the tour was to make enough money to provide for the Keans' comfort in retirement, certainly not the last time a Melbourne season would be undertaken specifically for that purpose – and relying upon large audiences positively thirsting for stars from London, even comparatively superannuated ones.[7] Lyster's Opera Company soon followed, as did J.C. Williamson's Theatre Royal and Her Majesty's, Sarah Bernhardt's and Nellie Melba's sensational tours, and so on. We shall see that Rubinstein was quick to exploit a testimonial sought from, or more likely proffered by, Williamson's star Nellie Stewart, despite or perhaps precisely because she had seen palmier days.

Melbourne had long established, fostered and sustained numerous institutions of culture and learning, art and music. There were also charitable clubs and societies of every description. The sheer size and number of suburban town halls reflected the strength of demand for large spaces for many such public uses. As well, the Edwardian population could see her pre-existing wealth amply reflected in the rest of Melbourne's ostentatious public buildings;

the metropolitan cable tram and railway systems; the advent of the telephone and other advanced infrastructure. If the machinery of commerce no longer roared, it was managing to tick over in a more or less *laissez-faire* manner.

In this, it was much assisted by the coming of Federation. From May 1901, pending the location and construction of a new seat of national government in New South Wales (not closer to Sydney than 160 kilometres), the new Federal Parliament met in Spring Street.[8] For the time being, Melbourne was the Commonwealth of Australia's new capital city. The economic impact of this was significant, but the symbolism and the atmosphere and the change of mood were transformative.

The creation of the Commonwealth of Australia was almost universally regarded by its settler population as, for good or ill, the strengthening of a proud and useful link in the global chain of the British Empire, the largest the world had ever known and upon which the sun never set. Most Australians and New Zealanders saw themselves as British and looked to Britain as home, even if a steadily growing proportion of them had never been there, and even if a worsening sectarian division existed between the Protestant majority and the large Irish Catholic minority, a division further exacerbated by class and labour conflict. On the whole, however, Australians went on subscribing to British illustrated weeklies. They read pressing news from London in every daily newspaper. State education made sure that their children's mental arithmetic was aligned with imperial weights, measures, pounds, shillings and pence. Their social habits, courts, justice system and institutions of local, state and federal government replicated those of Westminster. This general outlook formed the background to everything. More, it conferred upon every part and portion of Australian life a degree of confidence and ambition that found constant expression, perhaps most obviously in the built environment. It is impossible to imagine, for example, the enormously ornate 500-room Federal Coffee Palace going up in Collins Street, Melbourne, in 1888, without the energies pouring inwards from British imperium, energies that were so passionately funnelled into the creation of something quite so ambitious and absurd (fig. 15).

Figure 15. Federal Coffee Palace, Collins Street, Melbourne, c. 1890–92.

True, Australian nationalism made room for significant points of difference, but these were largely contained within a persistently defining framework of Britishness, colourful antipodean scions, as it were, grafted onto the mature rootstock of English oak, Scottish ash or Irish alder. In 1906, in the case of *Attorney-General of the Commonwealth v. Ah Sheung*, the newly established High Court of Australia went so far as to say: 'We are not disposed to give any countenance to the novel doctrine that there is an Australian nationality as distinguished from a British nationality.'[9]

Rubinstein's decision to move from Toowoomba to Melbourne, and ultimately to exchange the position of governess for that of waitress, was extremely bold because it bucked much wider demographic trends. At first, she worked at the Maison Dorée restaurant and oyster saloon at 158 Swanston Street.

Subsequently, she worked in the Chicago and Winter Garden Tea and Luncheon Rooms, an artists' haunt in the Block Arcade in Collins Street. It is possible, as Woodhead suggests, that she worked in both at the same time, although I think this is unlikely.[10]

The harsh working conditions and low pay of waitresses generated a lot of discussion in the Melbourne newspapers in 1901. In January, the proprietor of the Standard Dining Rooms in Chapel Street, Prahran, was fined 2/6 (with the much higher sum of £4/4/6 in costs) on a charge of having caused Euphemia Murdoch, a waitress, to work seventy-four hours during the first week of December 1900, the legal limit being sixty hours.[11] Cases of unfair or peremptory dismissal, non-payment of wages, and other instances of over-work were reported regularly.[12] This reflects the advent of better employment laws and conditions under pressure from the Eight-Hour and Labour movements in Victoria, but it also suggests that, while hospitality and amenities for dining were on the rise in Edwardian Melbourne, those who waited tables, particularly women, languished almost at the bottom of the food chain. Only barmaids occupied a lower position. For Rubinstein, there is no question that this represented a sharp descent of several rungs on the social, if not the economic, ladder. According to labour market figures published in December 1900 in *The Queenslander*, governesses earned £35 to £50 per annum, while waitresses earned 12s to 16s per week.[13]

It is tempting to speculate whether in 1901 Rubinstein made the transition from governess in Toowoomba and St Kilda to waitress in the heart of Melbourne as a temporary concession through the necessary months it would take to establish the business she already had in mind. The issue of timing supports this idea. If, as seems likely, her waitressing work began no later than the southern winter of 1901, Rubinstein had just eighteen months in which to raise capital, to find and lease the best premises she could afford, and in the most promising location.

At the same time, she needed to secure a reliable supply of her product from Felton Grimwade, and to agree upon its formulation, character, size, name and presentation. She needed to do some pretty extensive publicity groundwork and to turn her mind to the design and content of her label. That she should have gone to the trouble of registering this as a trademark suggests that Rubinstein approached the establishment of her company with a relatively long and well-organised run-up, and at least some resources with which to start off. Above all, she must have approached all these tasks with the clearest possible idea of what her company would look like, and how it would turn a profit.

The pecuniary impact of the shift from governess to waitress may not have been as sharp as it at first appears. If Rubinstein had earned £35 per annum in Toowoomba, *The Queenslander*'s lower estimate, and 12s a week in Melbourne, the latter sum amounted to a little more than £30 per annum. However, waitressing work was far heavier, noisier, and much less respectable and more insecure even than the occupation of governess. The waitress had to tolerate smoke, damp, heat and noise. She was perforce obliged to run the gauntlet of the chronically drunk, who, in the first decade of the twentieth century, were appearing before Victorian magistrates in huge numbers, often with as many as forty-four prior convictions.[14] In evidence heard by a Joint Parliamentary Committee of Inquiry into Habitual Drunkenness, in 1899 the statutory number of public houses in Greater Melbourne (1116) was exceeded by a wholly unregulated 153. There were forty-six *too many* pubs in Bourke Street alone, thirty too many in Lonsdale Street, and thirty-five too many in La Trobe Street, adding to an already huge number of licensed premises within easy staggering distance of the Maison Dorée in Swanston Street and The Chicago and Winter Garden in the Block Arcade.

Restaurants in Edwardian Melbourne had evolved rapidly from demotic, often dirty threepenny, fourpenny and sixpenny establishments providing a fixed-price *table d'hôte* service to a ballooning, often itinerant population. The modern idea of a restaurant or 'café' where respectable men and women dined together in public was slow to reach Britain and her Australian colonies. In Melbourne, 'shilling' restaurants served alcohol and reserved a separate room for ladies, but they were mostly still raffish and the food was terrible. Staff were not concerned with waiting tables so much as breaking up fights or expelling one sitting to make room for the next. Gentlemen, by contrast, tended to dine at their clubs. Hotels provided more adventurous meals, albeit of varying degrees of quality.

Comparatively few busy, sumptuously decorated restaurants along Parisian lines existed in Melbourne, but the Maison Dorée was certainly one of the first to succeed. To this extent it was at the vanguard of hospitality, even if the clientele tended not to be.[15] That Rubinstein should have secured a position working there, even for a little while, is further evidence of the indomitable spirit of enterprise with which she had already distinguished herself. It certainly helped that she had lived for a while in Vienna.

Eyewitnesses

In 1971, Patrick O'Higgins described in some detail encounters he witnessed in April 1957 between two visitors who paid separate impromptu calls upon Rubinstein in her suite at the old Menzies Hotel on the southeast corner of Bourke and William Streets. Rubinstein, aged eighty-four, was visiting Melbourne for the last time.[16] Both visitors claimed to have known her in the period 1903–07:

> When I was in Melbourne, staying at the Menzies Hotel with Madame in 1958 [sic], a shabby old man popped into her suite. As with her offices everywhere, the door was ajar. She liked unexpected visits.
>
> 'My name is Abel Isaacson,' he introduced himself. Madame heard him perfectly clearly. But she cupped an ear and, turning to me, dropped her voice, 'What the devil does he want? Money ... I suppose.'
>
> 'We first met sixty years ago! You were a waitress at the Café [sic] Doré ...' Mr Isaacson announced with no further preliminaries.

'He's gaga ... get him out of here!' Madame hissed. She seemed alarmed and shot into her bedroom, banging the door. Mr Isaacson sat down in Madame's empty chair.

'Hasn't changed a bit! High strung ... You her son?' he queried, rolling a cigarette. Since it was difficult to explain my exact functions I nodded vaguely. 'I've been in Australia since ninety-eight [sic]. Lived at one time in a boarding house outside Melbourne on Grey Street. Saint Kilda. Run by a woman called Mrs Stern. The Madame ...' he cocked a finger at the bedroom door, 'stayed there in 1904. She was one of Mrs Sensenberg's girls at the Café [sic] Doré. Used to give me two helpings of fish for the price of one. That was well before she rented a place in Collins Street and started selling them face creams. Some worker!'

Through the corner of my eye I saw the bedroom door open an inch. Madame Rubinstein was listening.

'Tell you something ... I'm eighty-four. She must be nearly as old!' Madame rattled the door. Mr Isaacson went on: 'Without Mr [Harry] Thomson [sic] – he was Manager of the Robur Tea Company – the Madame wouldn't have done what she did. He helped her ... He taught her ... He made her! Mark my words, he was the brains behind the little lady!' With that, stubbing his cigarette and pocketing the butt, he left.[17]

In several respects this passage conforms to O'Higgins's disloyal pattern of condescension, even hostility. He is at pains to portray Rubinstein in a thoroughly unattractive light – hissing, secretive, door-slamming (despite otherwise liking her doors left ajar) – but obviously he goes much further by using it to disclose information that he knew perfectly well she wanted to suppress. However, inasmuch as it carefully retrieves a number of flecks of historical detail with considerable deviousness and economy, one may safely conclude that O'Higgins's inquiries in Melbourne were a good deal more thorough than he implied.

Abel Isaacson is well documented. He was born in Australia, the fourth son of Mr S. Isaacson of Stawell in the Wimmera. In 1908, Abel Isaacson married Rose, the sister of the Reverend Jacob Danglow of the St Kilda congregation. She died at home in York Street, St Kilda, on 24 December 1915, having earlier been delivered of a stillborn son. As for the accommodations in St Kilda, Elizabeth Stern's boarding house was indeed at 29 and 30 Grey Street, but there is no other surviving evidence to place Rubinstein in those lodgings in 1904 or at any other time. We only have Isaacson's word for it. However, we can independently add Mr Harry Thompson, and in the same year.[18]

As for Rubinstein having been 'one of Mrs Sensenberg's girls at the Maison Doré', this is an erroneous conflation of two different establishments. The Maison Dorée in Swanston Street changed hands in 1900 upon the death of Madame Josephine Lacaton, *proprietaire*. Monsieur Charles Brezzo, sometime chef at the Menzies Hotel, took it over amid much fanfare in the Melbourne press.[19] Mr Isaacson's point about the helpings of fish would appear to relate to the Maison Dorée. 'Mrs Sensenberg', however, points separately to the Chicago and Winter Garden in the Block Arcade, Collins Street, which was named in honour of the World's Columbian Exposition held in Chicago in 1893 to mark the 400th anniversary of the arrival of Christopher Columbus in the New World.

The Misses *Siegenberg*, proprietresses, were the daughters of John Siegenberg, tobacco merchant of Swanston Street, and his wife Frances (Fanny, *née* Cohn).[20] Mrs Siegenberg had indeed been proprietress of the Chicago and Winter Garden, with a separate office on the second floor of the City of Melbourne building on the southeast corner of Elizabeth and Little Collins streets. However, in 1902 Mrs Siegenberg retired to Jackson Street, St Kilda, suffering there, according to a well-meaning but indelicate press report, from chronic bouts of constipation.[21] Miss Rose Siegenberg was still running the premises in the Block Arcade as late as 1940, by which time the name had been patriotically altered to the United Service Café.[22]

One would think that by then, indeed long before, the Siegenbergs might have found a way of hitching their caboose to the Helena Rubinstein express, but apparently not. Much more recently, however, in an ABC Radio interview, the late Professor John Mulvaney AO CMG, sometime doyen of Australian archaeology, recalled that his grandparents, John and Fanny Siegenberg, had engaged Rubinstein as a waitress in the Chicago and Winter Garden in the Block Arcade, c. 1901 or 1902.[23] According to John, Rubinstein sold pots of her signature Valaze from a table in that establishment even before she opened her first rooms in Elizabeth Street – but this may well have been, in John's recollection, an only partly reliable conflation of fact (waitress) and myth (Valaze).[24]

In 1905, the Siegenbergs undertook an eclectic Renaissance cum Moorish cum Japanese redecoration:

> The Winter Garden of the Chicago Tea Rooms, 'The Block' Arcade, have recently undergone a renovation, and are now amongst the most attractive in the city. The Winter Garden, with its three fine reception and dining rooms, has been entirely redecorated, and the handsome pillars dividing the different rooms have been ornamented in harmony with the surroundings. The arches have been decorated in the Renaissance style of fretwork, and have a very pretty effect. The centre room is Moorish in character, in shadings from rich Egyptian pink to faded rose tones. The friezes and dadoes are in copper and autumn tints, illustrative of quaint conventional designs. The reception rooms on each side are Japanese in character, and lighter and brighter in treatment. The artist, Mr Harry Grist, has also supplied a number of artistic scenes, including the sacred bridge over which the Mikado passes but once a year; a gateway with handsome iron lanterns leading to the temple, and a pretty Japanese landscape, with tall foliaged trees and flowering plum trees reflected in the lake below. Oval mirrors, hung with purple wisteria, coloured in Japanese pink, divide the different landscapes, and a dado of Jap. latticework in bright tones lends further brightness to these dainty wall pictures. The pillars are decorated with the sacred ibis and the bright-winged

Japanese cherry-pickers. The tout-ensemble is rich and effective. In a more material sense, the Chicago maintains its high repute for an excellent cuisine, good attendance and moderate tariff.[25]

Harry Grist, a painter of stage scenery, was connected with the Theatre Royal on the north side of Bourke Street between Swanston and Russell streets. Tom Roberts and Arthur Streeton had also done scene painting for the Royal, but by 1905 both were in England. Grist had four daughters, at least one of whom (Ethel) was an actress, while his son Frank was an actor and producer. To mark the Federation, Grist painted a 65 × 25-foot transparency for the Craig, Williamson & Co. building in Elizabeth Street. His presence alone would suggest that the Chicago and Winter Garden had strong links to the visual and performing arts.

But what about Harry Thompson? One can only speculate as to Patrick O'Higgins's motives for implanting and laying considerable emphasis upon that detail, which attributes Rubinstein's success to an older, relatively influential man – 'the brains' – and in doing so simultaneously impugns her independence, belittles her achievement and hints at something improper. If Mr Isaacson's testimony is to be believed, Thompson and Rubinstein dwelt (separately) for a while in the same boarding house, Mrs Stern's. However, Thompson was still lodging there when, on 19 December 1906, he married Isabella Grist, a divorcee residing in Kew.[26] It is also true that the Valaze advertorial with which the Melbourne press was awash from 1903 onwards runs eerily parallel in style and content with that of Robur Tea, and vice versa. In 1909–10, a widespread Robur Tea campaign took the form of a monologue, attributed to 'The Block Girl', that emphasised an unexpected benefit:

> I say, deah, isn't the weather something awful? It really isn't fit to be about – come let's go and have a cup of tea. What nonsense! Why it has been proved without a shadow of a doubt that women who drink tea have better complexions than those who don't – just look at the

English and the Russian girls, what lovely complexions they have, and they drink a frightful lot of tea, I'm told ... [27]

Drinking tea is good for the complexion. This message provides just about as blunt an alignment of two otherwise unrelated businesses as it was then possible to contrive, but perhaps the most persuasive piece of hard evidence is the otherwise inexplicable appearance of a skin-nurturing Robur Tea advertisement in Rubinstein's in-house beauty booklet, *Beauty in the Making*.[28] Harnessing, this time, the celebrity testimonial of the Viennese actress and Gaiety girl Grace Palotta, the accompanying copy ran: 'A great portion of any liquid you consume, comes away through the pores of your skin. You should therefore be at all times careful what you drink. Pure tea properly brewed materially helps to make a Complexion beautiful, it stimulates a healthy skin action, and acts soothingly on the nerve centres ...'[29]

Though this evidence is circumstantial, it now seems likely that there existed some sort of mutually advantageous business or even personal relationship between Rubinstein and Harry Thompson. However, the label design and copy contained in Rubinstein's first (1903) Valaze trademark application, which survives in the National Archives of Australia, was written in Polish. As we shall see, Valaze was hardly marketed to Polish-speaking women only. If indeed Thompson had a hand in Valaze publicity, there is no other firm evidence of this except that, crucially, at least £100 of Rubinstein's initial seeding capital of £250 in 1902 – the only money she ever borrowed – appears to have been supplied by him.[30] In 1965, Rubinstein claimed to have raised those £250 from a Miss Helen MacDonald whom she met on board the *Prinz-Regent Luitpold*. There is no record of any such person in the ship's manifest. Thompson is not a phantasm, but his business or personal relationship with Rubinstein has proven impossible to confirm or disprove or better elucidate in any way.

Apart from a few not especially helpful dribs and drabs, and the tantalising elision, stylistic affinities and close proximity of Robur Tea and Valaze publicity, the testimony of Abel Isaacson as transmitted by Patrick O'Higgins is all we have. At least Isaacson had the decency to lay particular emphasis

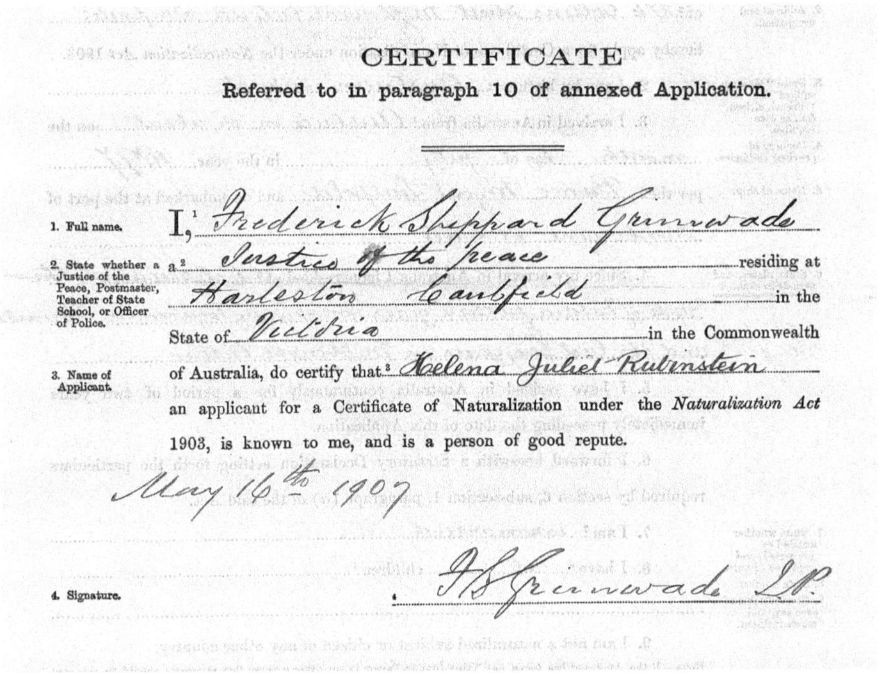

> **CERTIFICATE**
> Referred to in paragraph 10 of annexed Application.
>
> 1. Full name. I, *Frederick Sheppard Grimwade*
> 2. State whether a Justice of the Peace, Postmaster, Teacher of State School, or Officer of Police. a *Justice of the Peace* residing at *Harleston Caulfield* in the State of *Victoria* in the Commonwealth
> 3. Name of Applicant. of Australia, do certify that *Helena Juliet Rubinstein* an applicant for a Certificate of Naturalization under the *Naturalization Act* 1903, is known to me, and is a person of good repute.
>
> *May 16th 1907*
>
> 4. Signature. *F S Grimwade JP*

Figure 16. The signature of Frederick Sheppard Grimwade (1840–1910), who sponsored Helena Rubinstein's application for naturalisation as a British subject, May 1907.

upon Rubinstein's work ethic. Maddeningly, there is no surviving evidence in the vast Russell and Mab Grimwade Archives (incorporating the Felton Grimwade papers at the University of Melbourne) of the business association we know from oral tradition existed between Rubinstein and Frederick Sheppard Grimwade JP. The only firm documentation that exists is the latter's signature on Rubinstein's 1907 naturalisation papers (fig. 16). Gentlemen who stood sponsor needed to be able to vouch for applicants based on direct personal acquaintanceship (at least), or longstanding professional association.

The second 1957 visitor to the Menzies Hotel that O'Higgins went on to describe has proven far more elusive, and remains so. This was a lady who, according to O'Higgins, looked even older than Mr Abel Isaacson.

Bird of Paradise feathers decorated her hat. There was a cameo hanging from her neck and she twirled a white parasol in her hand although it was midwinter. 'I'm Mrs Dedman, dear.' Madame eyed her finery. '... Remember? I was your neighbour in Glen's Building on Collins Street when you first [sic] opened.' She turned to me. Her voice was genteel but precise. 'We were the only two real ladies in trade. There were twenty-four singing teachers besides us. Very trying ... That's how Dame Nellie Melba became one of her customers. After practice, she always popped in for a facial ... claimed it helped her high C's.' I longed to hear more, but Mrs Dedman fared no better than Mr Isaacson. Madame prodded her out of the door, and when she was safely out of hearing, said, 'Another nut ... Who cares about the past?'[31]

There is, here, some obviously fake embroidery. Dame Nellie Melba could only have consulted Rubinstein at the very end of her celebrated, amply documented visit to Melbourne between September 1902 and February 1903, and in the altogether less salubrious premises of O'Connor's Chambers at 138 Elizabeth Street, the ones to which Rubinstein never referred.[32] However, O'Higgins's account has again proven well worth checking in detail. Rubinstein's *third* premises at 274 Collins Street (from November 1905 onwards) were indeed in upstairs rooms in Messrs. W.H. Glen & Co.'s Music and Piano Warehouse, right next door to the Block Arcade. When she moved in, the music teachers numbered closer to fifty, at times even more. According to advertisements placed by many of them in *The Argus*, these taught either singing and voice production or pianoforte or both, or else pianoforte and violin – all except a Miss Fredman, who, deliciously, gave zither lessons 'according to Max Albert's normal system'.[33]

But what about Mrs Dedman? At first, I wondered about the suggestive similarity of the names of Dedman and Fredman, but at length (among various other Mrs Dedmans) I found one, Mrs W.H.J. Dedman, who advertised 'Dress-Cutting, Designing, and Fitting System, approved [by] London teachers. No charts. Evening class ... 1 Burchett Street, Brunswick,' which although the most promising of many other less likely candidates nevertheless didn't seem especially warm until I discovered the same Mrs W.H.J. Dedman two years later, this time lurking in the *Age* classifieds: 'Dress Making Classes. – Cutting, Fitting, Trimming, practical making, expert teacher. Mrs Dedman, 274 Collins Street, 2nd floor.'[34] There she is, right upstairs from Rubinstein and doing well enough the following year to be advertising from the same address for a 'skirt assistant, 3rd year, used to city work'.[35] One hears the thumping treadles of her sewing machines, the cacophony of music classes drifting up and down the stairwell from Glen's classroom studios, and the tinkling of a zither being played according to the Max Albert normal system. One sees a parasol in the hall stand, and, downstairs, the light rattan and bamboo furniture that Rubinstein herself painted green, white and gold.[36] There is also the thrum and zapping of Rubinstein's novel electrical depilatory and other equipment, which before too long brought her company an inconvenient civil action, to which we shall return.

The person who presented herself to Rubinstein in the Menzies Hotel in 1957 was either a clever invention by O'Higgins, or an impostor. This putative Mrs Dedman claimed to be the widow of William Hine James Dedman.[37] In April 1900 at Koroit, about seventeen kilometres northwest of Warrnambool, Mr Dedman married Anne Jean Baxter. The intriguing problem is that this Mrs W.H.J. Dedman died at Koroit of senile dementia, aged seventy-three, on 19 February 1933, more than twenty years before the lady with the cameo and the bird of paradise feathers and the parasol entered Rubinstein's suite.[38]

It seems there are only two possible explanations. Armed with some facts, either O'Higgins concocted this picturesque encounter to shoehorn Dame Nellie Melba into his account, or the encounter *did* occur. If so, this Mrs Dedman was an impostor, perhaps a former employee of the real Mrs Dedman, or, as Rubinstein suggests, 'a nut' – albeit some sort of nut with a purpose, probably gain. Patrick O'Higgins, meanwhile, has Mrs Dedman saying that there were only two ladies in business at 274 Collins Street, but there was definitely a third, and that one was the genuine article.

Mrs Ralph Ward, Madame Alexis and Nellie Stewart

When Rubinstein opened her rooms at Glen's in 1905, the following advertisement had been appearing regularly in *Melbourne Punch*:

> Artistic hairdressing, Shampooing, Face Massage, Manicure. Mrs Ralph Ward, 'The Salon Charmazelle,' 274 Collins Street (Glen's Basement), and at Woods' Chambers, Moore Street, Sydney.[39]

Rubinstein's and Mrs Ralph Ward's establishments at Glen's were separated by only one intervening floor. However, in that same year, these two businesswomen were keeping far more public company. Both were given extended entries, side-by-side on the same page, in the third volume of James Smith's commercial *Cyclopedia of Victoria*. Rubinstein's entry, to which we shall return, was unillustrated, but Alice Ward's was accompanied by a stately portrait photograph.[40] This alone implied that for the time being Ward's was the senior presence on the page, as it was at 274 Collins Street.

Although separated by more than fifty years, the photograph of Mrs Ralph Ward – Alice Ward never made herself known publicly by any other formulation – and Graham Sutherland's portrait of Rubinstein stand in fascinating counterpoint: two modern businesswomen committed to enterprises of direct relevance to women and, crucially, employing women. What, if anything, do the hitherto almost completely forgotten careers of Ward, and of several other well-established competitors at large in the City of Melbourne, tell us about the origins of Rubinstein's business?

The most basic point is that upon her arrival at Glen's in November 1905, Rubinstein could at least rely upon the fact that there was already, and had been for several years, a steady flow of female customers through the Gothic Revival front door. An initial challenge was therefore how to persuade them to mount the stairs instead of descending them to the basement or, according to the ancient principle of cluster marketing, to do both. There was nothing to prevent ladies who continued to seek the ministrations of

Alice Ward from also going home with a large jar of Rubinstein's Valaze, and perhaps several small ones for their daughters or friends.

Ward's entry in the *Cyclopedia of Victoria* laid emphasis on a number of key points. Her move in 1902 to 274 Collins Street was a consequence of steady expansion since 1898. 'The work carried on includes hair-dressing, manicuring, and face-steaming and massage. A staff of six girls, under the supervision of the principal, carry on this work with great deftness and skill.' She also sold special lines of skin food, including '"Creme Celine," an excellent complexion beautifier'. However, unlike Rubinstein, Ward was a painter by profession, 'and for ten years a member of and exhibitor with the Victorian Artists' Society'.[41]

Having been something of a fixture in the social pages through the 1890s, Ward first occupied premises in the City of Melbourne Building (City Chambers), 114 Elizabeth Street on the corner of Little Collins Street. Her rooms were right next to the office of Mrs Fanny Siegenberg, proprietor of the Chicago and Winter Garden in the Block Arcade. In 1899, *Melbourne Punch* ran a brief profile:

> Although dusty summer is the season when the female skin shows the ravages of the weather most, winter is the time for paving the way to that prevention which is better than cure, and now is the time when prudent beauty takes especial care of the complexion. Mrs Ralph Ward and Miss [Alice Emma] Monk, who have three pleasantly-lit parlours (no artificial light) in City Chambers, 114 Elizabeth Street, opposite James McEwan and Sons (famous for their phenomenal sale), have called their establishment 'The Salon Charmazelle.' These clever ladies have a skilled assistant, are kept busy at face and scalp massage, manicuring and hair-dressing, and have a large connection for each department. In the matter of improving the complexion Mrs Ralph Ward has been very successful, especially in the removal of freckles, and has received many grateful testimonials from well-known society ladies whom she has treated. Great attention is paid to

hairdressing, and as the charge is so reasonable – 2s for dressing, waving, etc. – there is no excuse for ladies appearing at balls or theatre with unsuitable or old-fashioned coiffure.[42]

Coincidence? Perhaps – indeed, with Mrs Siegenberg, an exceedingly tantalising proximity. That Rubinstein and Ward should have proceeded, however, to rent space *in the same building*, Glen's, from 1905 until the Salon Charmazelle suddenly diminished at the end of November 1912, might have been accidental, but the adjacency is undeniable and powerfully suggestive. What, then, was the relationship between the Rubinstein wonder-product Valaze and Ward's venture in freckle-removal, face massage and nutritious vapours, to say nothing of her 'Creme Celine', to which there is no other reference in the Melbourne press? Why did the former succeed, and the latter vanish almost without trace? We shall speculate, but it is possible that Rubinstein modelled her business on, or else crafted it in careful contrast to, Ward's not long but nevertheless well-established and successful prototype. And in doing so, Rubinstein exercised, neither for the first nor the last time, a high degree of confidence that enabled her to push against an obstacle while simultaneously drawing energy from it.

Beyond her entry in the *Cyclopedia of Victoria*, a long string of references, mostly in *Melbourne Punch* and Maurice Brodzky's society weekly *Table Talk*, spanning the decade of the 1890s – some brief, some relatively long – bring Alice Ward the *artist* into some focus, as do the printed records of the Victorian Artists' Society. For Ward and many other women, *Table Talk* and *Melbourne Punch* proved to be vital tools for engineering social visibility, and in many different, sometimes surprising contexts.

It would be wrong to conclude from her many appearances that Ward occupied any particularly lofty rank within Melbourne society. Most of her social engagements that were reported in the press were 'public' to the extent that the organisers of such events, usually but not always in aid of charities, advertised well in advance in those same social pages the catering arrangements, the musical and other offerings and, most importantly, the gowns. One bought tickets, and the organisers were urged to supply *Melbourne Punch* and *Table Talk* with two (gratis) to guarantee coverage. This system became Ward's main form of advertising. In any event, 1898 was the year in which Ward made the decisive shift from practising artist to woman of business, and it is important to grasp that in doing so, the one persona merged effectively with the other.

By the strongest possible contrast, when Rubinstein started her business three years later, she consigned all previous personas to permanent oblivion. She made no attempt to enter the busy social circle of Edwardian Melbourne. She never sought to align her business with it. If, as seems likely, Rubinstein was aware that she lacked an *entrée*, at the same time her ambition was unconstrained by any such impediment. Indeed, it relieved her of many time-consuming, often late-night obligations. The only company Rubinstein was interested in keeping was commercial; her primary focus was upon her business and, before too long, it would be operating on a national scale.

According to 'Lady Kitty', the Melbourne correspondent of the Adelaide *Critic*, writing in August 1898:

> Another massage and manicure salon (not saloon), is to be opened shortly in the Block neighbourhood by Mrs Ralph Ward a well-known Melb. artist, who is thoroughly qualified to take care of feminine complexions. She intends to undertake hairdressing as well, and when she opens the salon I shall be prepared by her to be photographed by Talma or Falk.[43]

Lady Kitty's point about Talma and Falk suggests that from its inception, Ward's business was conveniently aligned with the burgeoning world of Edwardian society portrait photography. So far as I am aware, Rubinstein never made any attempt to follow suit. With her new and exotically decorated 'Salon Charmazelle', Ward effectively merged all three of her spheres – the artistic, the social and the commercial.

Ward was entering no less competitive a field than the one Rubinstein joined three years later. In January 1898, 'Madame Alexis', whose Oriental Massage Company also occupied premises in 'Talma Buildings' at 119 Swanston Street:

> beautifies faces by honest hygienic methods only; cosmetics not tolerated. Pimples, blackheads, liver spots, acne, blotches, redness, eczema, freckles, tan, wrinkles, and loose, baggy, sallow skin, eradicated by Medicaments and Turkish Steam Massage Treatments. Consultations free. All Branches Ladies' Hairdressing – Dyeing, Cutting, &c.; also latest method of Manicuring. Hours 10 to 6.[44]

In a particularly batty piece of advertorial that appeared eighteen months later, 'Mona' wrote from Toorak:

> Dear Mamie, – Whatever you do, don't let your fancied disfigurement through sunburn and freckles prevent your coming down to the Cup festivities, as there is now in Melbourne a quite up-to-date Hygienic Turkish Steam Massage Establishment that will eradicate all such blemishes and make you quite too charming. This process is no secret, as you will meet the smartest people in Melbourne at these 'Parlours,' for during the season most society ladies go through a regular course of massage and toilet treatment at the hands of Madame Alexis and her skilled assistants.
>
> You might hint to Nina that she also might take a course of treatment with advantage, as one of Madame's specialities is the removal of those unsightly blemishes which trouble her so, viz., pimples and blackheads.
>
> I must not forget to mention that this establishment includes the latest up-to-date Pompadour hairdressing and manicuring amongst its many delightful benefits – in fact it will out us Sun-kissed Golf Girls beautiful for the Cup season, if not for ever. So take my word for

it, and bring along your most swagger gowns, and Cup week will find you quite your old charming self, sunburn and freckles a memory of the past.

In case I should not meet you on your arrival, I herewith inscribe Madame Alexis' address, viz., 119 Swanston Street (Talma Buildings).

In conclusion I would advise you to write and book appointment, as Madame is sure to be extremely busy at this season, and by so doing you will avoid disappointment. Ta, ta, till Cup. –

Yours, etc.

MONA[45]

Setting aside the liberal but indelicate airing of Nina and Mamie's country skin problems, Mona's metropolitan pitch on behalf of Madame Alexis frames what was a well-established business model. However, Alice Ward seems to have aligned herself with the branch of her new profession that laid particular emphasis on the artful and the 'artistic', neither of which could be achieved unaided or at home.

Ward's unusually evocative choice of name, the Salon Charmazelle, was inspired by a novel by Marie Corelli, *Ziska: The Problem of a Wicked Soul* (1897).[46] That source accounts for Ward's choice of Egyptian pink and peacock blue for 114 Elizabeth Street, because *Ziska* concerns the doomed character of Ziska-Charmazel, the most beautiful woman in Eighteenth-Dynasty Egypt, and the most captivating dancer at the court of the Pharaoh Amenhotep III. 'As an effort of imagination it is wonderful', sniffed the Adelaide *Evening Journal*. 'As a work destitute of the faintest approach to realism it is unique.'[47]

Operating her 'Salon Charmazelle' did not inhibit Alice Ward socially. On the contrary: she kept up her busy round. There were many society weddings and numerous other engagements that reinforce the impression that Ward was trading on social cachet. When Rubinstein moved into Glen's, *Melbourne Punch*, with which Alice Ward had long enjoyed a cosy relationship, reported in October 1902:

Mrs Ralph Ward, the proprietress of the now well-known Salon Charmazelle, and her partner, Miss Monk, owing to the increase of their business have been compelled to take larger and more centrally situated rooms. The entrance to the new salon adjoins Glen's music warehouse and is the same as the well-known Vandyck Studio. There is one large entrance hall which forms a kind of atrium for a number of dainty little boudoirs very prettily fixed up, the decorations of which are in restful tones of white and pale green. Face and head massage, American shampooing, cutting, singeing and the general care of the hair are all made a special study of by the firm. Hairdressing, in particular, in the latest styles, is still carried on at the Salon Charmazelle, for the very reasonable price of 3/6.[48]

The least conspicuous but most important point, here, is economic. Having previously charged 2s, Alice Ward was charging 3/6 for a service that was time-consuming, labour-intensive and laden with overheads – not least the maintenance of all those dainty little boudoirs. Rubinstein charged 3/6 for the smaller-sized jar of her single product, Valaze. Although she added various services, including face massage, her business thrived upon a steadily accelerating outward flow of jars of ready-made Valaze with a 620 per cent mark-up. All she had to do was operate the cash register and keep a careful eye on mail orders and her substantial investment in advertising, to which we shall return.

At the same time, Rubinstein was obviously aware of the need to create a certain ambiance in which to receive her customers. Ward's shift from the luxurious 'Oriental' flavour of Egyptian pink and peacock blue in Elizabeth Street to the dainty little boudoirs in 'restful tones of white and pale green' is particularly noteworthy, because Rubinstein's own decorating choices two floors above ran closely parallel. In 1905, Rubinstein chose white for the walls and curtains, and inexpensive bamboo and rattan furniture of the kind used in conservatories. 'I filled the three small rooms with these comfortable chairs', Helena Rubinstein later recalled, 'and covered the seats in bright calico ... By the time I was ready to open my first [sic] salon, the three rooms looked as light and friendly as I could make them.'[49] *Table Talk* went into greater, even more suggestive detail. Miss Rubinstein's upstairs rooms were:

> decorated in art green. Carpet and cosy corners are in the green tones, but the wicker table, couch and chairs are gilded, and at one side is a white enamelled cabinet. Here and there are some beautiful terra-cotta ornaments and other artistic novelties brought from Europe by the owner, and everywhere flowers. The effect of the whole is delightful.[50]

The similarities are undeniable, although Rubinstein seems not to have attempted to follow Ward's society path until later, exploiting instead from the beginning celebrity testimonial, above all that of the famous actress and singer Nellie Stewart.

In 1903, Stewart was forty-five years old, but she had lately had one of her greatest stage successes in the role of Nell Gwynne in Paul Kester's 'exquisite comedy drama' *Sweet Nell of Old Drury* (1900). At this high point in her long and varied career, Nellie Stewart became known as 'Sweet Nell' or 'Our Nell' or even 'Australia's idol', so the window of opportunity for exploiting her own celebrity testimonial was narrow but promising, and fortunately for her it lasted. She went on to enjoy a long season in San Francisco, until the catastrophic earthquake of 18 April 1906 destroyed all the sets and costumes. This prevented her company from proceeding thence to Broadway, but in 1911 Stewart starred in Raymond Longford's filmed version of *Sweet Nell of Old Drury*, which became one of the most popular Australian films of the silent era.

Rubinstein was therefore not necessarily lucky to secure the services of Nellie Stewart. Stewart showed herself more than willing to render them to whomsoever was willing to pay, for example to Mr W. Richards, proprietor in Sydney of Capilla Hair Tonic:

> Allow me to take the opportunity of my present visit to Sydney again to express my entire satisfaction with your wonderful Hair Tonic.

I am leaving for New Zealand shortly, and as I don't know whether I will be able to obtain it there, send me, please, six bottles to the hotel. Wishing 'Capilla' all the success it deserves,

    I am, dear Mr Richards,

        yours very faithfully,

        Nellie Stewart.[51]

There was also product placement. Hunter Brothers, jewellers 'on the Hill' in Wagga Wagga, offered 'the famous Nellie Stewart bangle', but so did Stewart Dawson & Co. in Sydney, and the Modern Art Jewellery Co. at 187 Pitt Street. Robur Tea issued a 1906 Nellie Stewart calendar, adorned with her portrait, which might suggest the involvement of Harry Thompson and is yet another tantalising example of Robur and Valaze proximity – except the Dunlop Rubber Company also issued a 'Beautiful Art Calendar for 1910 (Miss Nellie Stewart)'. Rubinstein was joining a relatively long queue of publicity-seeking businesses to whom Stewart was only too happy to lend her name, image and prestige. However, Rubinstein was amply willing to garner celebrity testimonial elsewhere, from the London actress Miss Alice Crawford and, in due course, on an almost industrial scale, from Grace Palotta, Sybil de Bray, Gladys Cooper, Maxine Elliott and many others, all of whom in due course headlined full-page Valaze publicity in the London theatre paper *Play Pictorial*.[52]

Rubinstein's expansion into the Sydney market had been heralded by advertisements in *The Bulletin* and elsewhere while she was still in the Fourth Victoria Building at 243 Collins Street, Melbourne. One appeared immediately above that of a competitor already established around the corner in Moore Street (and elsewhere), not even a stone's throw from Ward's Salon Charmazelle:

The Queen's Face Food
Old ladies made young. Young ladies made beautiful. No more wrinkles, pimples, or blackheads, but a beautiful, clear, peachlike complexion,

for those who use the QUEEN'S FACE FOOD. Manufactured by Dr Noel, the Queen's own beautifier. Thousands have derived the greatest benefit from it, and speak highly of it. Obtainable at Mr Brothwood's and all leading chemist's, and at Madame Olga's beautifying Boudoirs, Gov. Savings Bank Chambers, Moore Street, Sydney. 3s 6d, 6s.[53]

This bold alignment with the celebrated age-defying beauty of King Edward's consort Queen Alexandra appealed to patriotic sentiment. The queen's reputation for beauty was, for years before their coronation in 1902, much aided by the circulation of thousands of carefully doctored photographs. At this point, Rubinstein was going head-to-head with Madame Olga and 'the Queen's Face Food'. Their retail prices for small and large jars were identical: three shillings and sixpence (3/6), and six shillings (6s). That Ward should so soon afterwards establish herself in Woods Chambers, Moore Street, was even bolder. Not to be outdone, Rubinstein soon followed suit and became Alice Ward's near neighbour in Melbourne *and* in Sydney, just around the corner in Pitt Street.

H. Westall Guest

It is tempting to see Mr H. Westall Guest in relation to Alice Ward just as the fictitious Dr Josef Lykuski was to Helena Rubinstein – for lending the appearance of male 'expertise' to an otherwise feminine undertaking. However, unlike Dr Lykuski, H. Westall Guest was real. Indeed, at times Ward and he were mentioned in tandem, as in the following account of a Sydney dinner party:

> A unique dinner party was given at the residence of Mrs Levy, 'Cahors,' Macleay Street, Sydney, in honour of the coming of age of her grandson, Mr Leslie Cohen. The decorations were pink roses, surrounding miniature lakes, and the ladies all appeared with powdered hair and

patches. The most artistic dressing came from the Salon Charmazelle, Woods Chambers, Moore Street, Sydney (Mrs Ralph Ward).

All that the most exacting could require as regards a high-class Tooth Powder is filled by Mr H. Westall Guest's 'Sweet Nell Dentifrice'. The exquisite bouquet, the freshness it gives to the mouth and its pearly whitening effect upon the teeth all mark 'Sweet Nell' as being a decided advance upon any Dentifrice we have yet happened upon. Small wonder that Mr Guest is at his wits' end to meet the demand for his new venture. 'Sweet Nell' is in the form of a minutely-sifted powder, with exquisite bouquet, and has, we believe, a most beneficial effect upon the gums.'[54]

True, the only connection here is in the abutment but, crucially, it recurs elsewhere.[55] As well, Sweet Nell Dentrifice was named for Nellie Stewart, so there was by then a link to Rubinstein as well. However, with his 'Golden Key Pharmacy' at 229 Bourke Street, H. Westall Guest had established himself in Melbourne as a skin specialist and 'Beauty Doctor'. In many respects, he was closely comparable with, but years ahead of, not only Ward's Salon Charmazelle, but also Rubinstein's Valaze venture.[56] In March 1900, the Adelaide *Critic* ran a long interview, according to which Mr Guest:

first commenced face massage during the visit of Madame Sarah Bernhardt [in 1891], and since then his business has increased enormously. He has branches in Sydney, Auckland, Napier, Wellington, and Adelaide.

'The great difficulty I had at first,' said Mr Guest, 'was to educate the ladies of Melbourne to the necessity of face massage, and care of their complexions in a tropical climate like this. The dirt and dust that collects in a lady's face in one morning while she is in the city is appalling. And it was in face massage that I found a perfect remedy against the ravages of heat, dirt, and dust.'

Today in Australia we distinguish between the tropical climate of Far North Queensland and the subtropical and temperate climates the further south you travel. British Edwardians knew no such distinction. To them, the entire continent was tropical, and that concept therefore embraced the ravages of heat, dirt and dust. We have already heard Rubinstein making the bold claim that her intention in introducing Valaze to Australia was that it should subject her product to the supreme test of a 'tropical climate'. H. Westall Guest is making essentially the same point and reveals a similar posture with respect to cosmetic enhancement:

> 'But some people think,' said the interviewer, 'that face massage is a form of make-up intended chiefly for the theatrical profession.'
>
> 'Quite a mistake, I assure you. Face massage is merely a perfect method of keeping the face clean and preserving a good complexion. I have dozens of testimonials as to its efficacy from leading society women, including the Countess of Hopetoun, Lady Brassey, Lady Madden, and the rest of Melbourne society. Lady Brassey was particularly pleased with face massage as practiced by my assistants.'
>
> 'Your business includes also manicure, pedicure, head massage, and hair dressing?'
>
> 'I have specialists for each. Miss Rose is manageress; Miss Bertha Wade is the best and most expert manicurist in Australia, and she is also the pedicurist. Miss O'Connell is hairdresser and masseuse, and my daughter, Miss Olive Guest, who is an enthusiast in her work, as indeed are all my assistants, is an expert hairdresser, masseuse, and manicurist.'
>
> 'Then you can guarantee to make the average woman very beautiful, if, for instance, she is going to a very modish function?'
>
> 'We do our best,' said Mr Guest, with the modesty of a mere man.

Rubinstein's later strategic use of lengthy advertorials and celebrity testimonials echoed many of the points that flowed from the unctuous lips of

H. Westall Guest. However, closer to him in time, and occupying premises in the same building, Madame Alexis struck similar chords in *Melbourne Punch* on behalf of 'women not on the sunny side of forty'. Her toilet treatment was 'the same as that practiced by the most famous skin specialists of Paris'. Madame Alexis 'has had full training and great experience in her art – the art of making healthy and beautiful the "human face divine."' This last phrase, borrowed from John Milton's *Paradise Lost* (III. II. 44), effectively adds to Madame Alexis's art an unapologetically ambitious literary dimension.

Out of all this, we may observe a sort of commercial leapfrog. In 1906, 'Mr H. Westall Guest, toilet specialist, 229 Bourke Street, announces that in addition to his various toilet treatments, he has opened a hairdressing department for ladies. This branch is entirely in the expert hands of Miss Ida Lawrence (late with Mrs Ralph Ward, of Collins Street.)'[57] Alice Ward had also introduced significant modifications to the Guest model, such as appealing to clients on the ground of economy on the one hand and of the generally 'artistic' on the other, and by presenting herself as a well-known artist. Importantly, she also highlighted the availability of her own or 'in-house' preparations – as did Madame Alexis. To these we may add the relatively novel concept of an exotic 'brand' – The Salon Charmazelle – a brand, moreover, that was well supported by ads and advertorials in almost every issue of *Melbourne Punch*. Rubinstein would follow in 1903, but with far greater ambition and success.

No doubt one reason for that success was Rubinstein's startling headline, 'Beauty is Power', which was a genuinely novel and, as it turned out, prescient point of difference – until it became necessary, during World War I, to make the patriotic but undeniably strained adjustment to 'Beauty is a Duty'.[58] 'Beauty is Power' first appeared simultaneously in advertisements in Melbourne, Sydney and Brisbane in May and June 1904, followed by Perth at the end of August.[59] It seems to have had immediate resonance. An unsigned article, 'How to Become Beautiful', appeared in *The Express and Telegraph* at the end of July and concluded with this advice for the women of Adelaide: 'Don't forget that beauty is power. There is nothing more potent.

It is to a woman what capital is to a merchant. Its absence is a misfortune; its culture, wise and proper.'[60] Whether the author had picked up on the new and startling message conveyed by Rubinstein's headline in big, bold letters is impossible to say, although the dates are suggestive. Regardless, thenceforth 'Beauty is Power' became her most effective tocsin.

Another fundamental difference between Rubinstein and Ward was that the former concentrated on skin, and positively avoided hair. We would call this niche marketing, and it obviously worked. From what little we know about Alice Ward, it seems unlikely that an approach or marketing tactic as bold as 'Beauty is Power' would have sat comfortably with the nutritious vapours arising from the dainty, restful boudoirs in the Salon Charmazelle. It also seems doubtful whether the relatively long sequence from H. Westall Guest and Madame Alexis to Alice Ward and thence to Helena Rubinstein amounted to any sort of direct cause and effect – but the proximities are impossible to ignore and, most importantly, provide ample context for Helena Rubinstein's Valaze.

Alice Ward was every bit as modern as Helena Rubinstein, but so too were, in their different ways, H. Westall Guest, Madame Alexis and Madame Olga. In due course, however, there proved to be a crucial difference. None exhibited the elevated commercial metabolism with which, from the very beginning in February 1903, Helena Rubinstein sloughed quite so many skins.

PART II—*VICI*

I CONQUERED

I decided to go to London, then the world centre of thought, taste, money and beauty. From the other side of the globe it appeared the richest, the gayest, the most elegant capital in the world. It was, therefore, the city in which I most wanted to succeed ... London was then at the height of its Edwardian splendour.

Helena Rubinstein, New York, 1965

Figure 17. Helena Rubinstein while fact-finding in Vienna in 1905.

5

Valaze™

A photograph taken in the early 1930s in Paris by the Ukrainian-born Boris Lipnitzki captures Helena Rubinstein in glamorous middle age. This and many other publicity and portrait photographs are today in the special collections and archives of the Library of the Fashion Institute of Technology in New York. It shows Rubinstein hard at work in her Saint-Cloud laboratory and runs parallel with much earlier photographs of Marie Curie working in *her* chemical laboratory, which Rubinstein had visited. They shared Polish heritage and language, although Curie was born and initially educated in Russian-occupied Warsaw. The parallels are obvious. Whereas Curie won the 1911 Nobel Prize in Chemistry for her discovery of the elements polonium and radium, and her solemn portrait photograph shows her as an almost monastic servant of science, Rubinstein's work is obviously far more alchemical and, to be fair, she often referred playfully to working not in her laboratory but, rather, in her 'kitchen'.

In the Lipnitzki photograph, Rubinstein is dressed in crisp hygienic white. She carefully decants murky liquid from one beaker into another through a slender glass funnel. Her expression is one of serene concentration, with the hint of a smile. Shelves in the background are crowded with labelled bottles containing obscure unguents, while the bench in the foreground is crowded with test tubes, Bunsen burners, enormous gourd-shaped flasks, scales, and all the other appurtenances of a working scientific laboratory, exactly like Curie's but without the same solemnity and aureole of natural light. Indeed, the dramatic slanting fall of artificial light accentuates Rubinstein's flawless maquillage, coiffure and clear skin, almost certainly doctored for the photograph. Yet she looks as if she knows what she is doing, and the intriguing thing about this is that there is not much hard evidence to suggest that by then she *didn't* know at least some of what she was doing. There is no sign here of any other staff or assistants.

Figure 18. Helena Rubinstein's Saint-Cloud laboratory, c. 1958.

Later laboratory photographs up the ante with far bigger, loftier banks of bright fluorescent lights and attentive, white-coated male staff – all of which imply far more ambitious research, development and production (fig. 18).

Yet the Lipnitzki publicity photograph crafts and documents an elaborate performance upon which Rubinstein's booming business depended. It successfully conveyed the idea that Rubinstein formulated her products herself, and with clinical, even scientific, rigour. The origins of that performance lie with Valaze.

The first firmly documented act of Rubinstein's business career (apart from leasing her rooms in Elizabeth Street) was the lodging of her 'Application for Registration of Trade Mark' with the Patent Office in Melbourne on 23 February 1903.[1] This was a bold step: the cost of trademark registration was £5/6/– , roughly equal to two months' wages at the Chicago and Winter Garden. The label copy doubled as an ambitious description of her product, except that it lurked beneath the veil of the Polish language (fig. 19):

VALAZE
Usuwa zmarszczki piegi liszaje,
nadaje twarzy delikatną białość
przezroczystość

VALAZE
Removes wrinkles, freckles, blemishes
Gives the face a delicate whiteness
[and] limpidity [or transparency][2]

At the time of Federation, there was in the Australasian colonies a widespread obsession with freckles: their causes and consequences, their disfiguring effects, and natural and artificial methods of preventing and removing them. The press was awash with freckle treatments and remedies, ranging from simple lemon juice applied in various unpleasant ways to complicated recipes involving ingredients such as powdered borax.[3] A few lonely voices remarked upon the charm of freckles, for example in verses as bad as the first two wobbling stanzas of this widely syndicated anonymous 1902 Christmas poem entitled 'What Freckles Show':

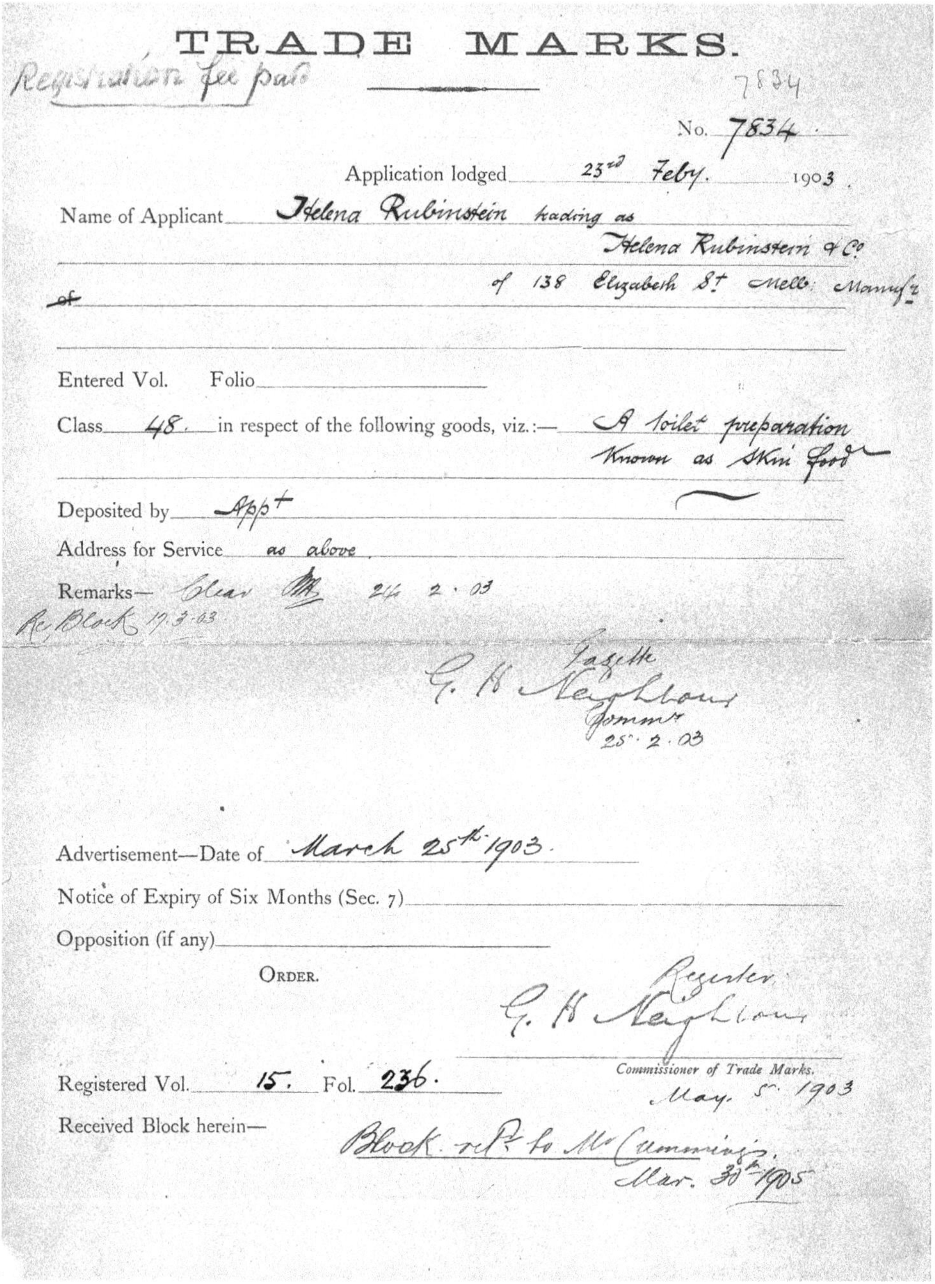

TRADE MARKS.

Registration fee paid

No. 7834

Application lodged 23rd Feby. 1903

Name of Applicant Helena Rubinstein trading as Helena Rubinstein & Co of 138 Elizabeth St. Melb. Manufr

Entered Vol. Folio
Class 48 in respect of the following goods, viz.:— A toilet preparation known as Skin Food
Deposited by Appt
Address for Service as above
Remarks— Clear M. 24. 2. 03
Re Block 19. 3. 03

G. H. Neighbour
Gazette
Commr
25. 2. 03

Advertisement—Date of March 25th 1903
Notice of Expiry of Six Months (Sec. 7)
Opposition (if any)

ORDER.

G. H. Neighbour
Register
Commissioner of Trade Marks.
May. 5. 1903

Registered Vol. 15. Fol. 236.
Received Block herein— Block. ret'd to Mr Cummings.
Mar. 30th 1905

Figure 19. Helena Rubinstein's 1903 application for registration as a trade mark of the distinctive label copy of Valaze.

Plates 1 and 2. Graham Sutherland, *Helena Rubinstein in a Red Brocade Balenciaga Gown* and *Helena Rubinstein* (overleaf), 1957. Rubinstein would later observe that Sutherland had portrayed her as 'an eagle-eyed matriarch'. 'At first I hated it,' she wrote. 'I had never seen myself in such a harsh light.' But she acquired the smaller of the two pictures (plate 1) for her personal collection, and conceded that over time, the portraits grew on her: 'Although I scarcely recognised myself through Sutherland's eyes, I had to admit that as paintings, they were indeed masterpieces.'

Plate 3. Silk evening ensemble, c. 1956, by Cristóbal Balenciaga of the House of Balenciaga. It was Graham Sutherland who suggested that Rubinstein wear the crimson brocade gown for her portrait sittings, declaring that it made her look 'like an empress'. (By the time this photograph was taken, the dress had been altered; it was a full-length gown when Rubinstein wore it.)

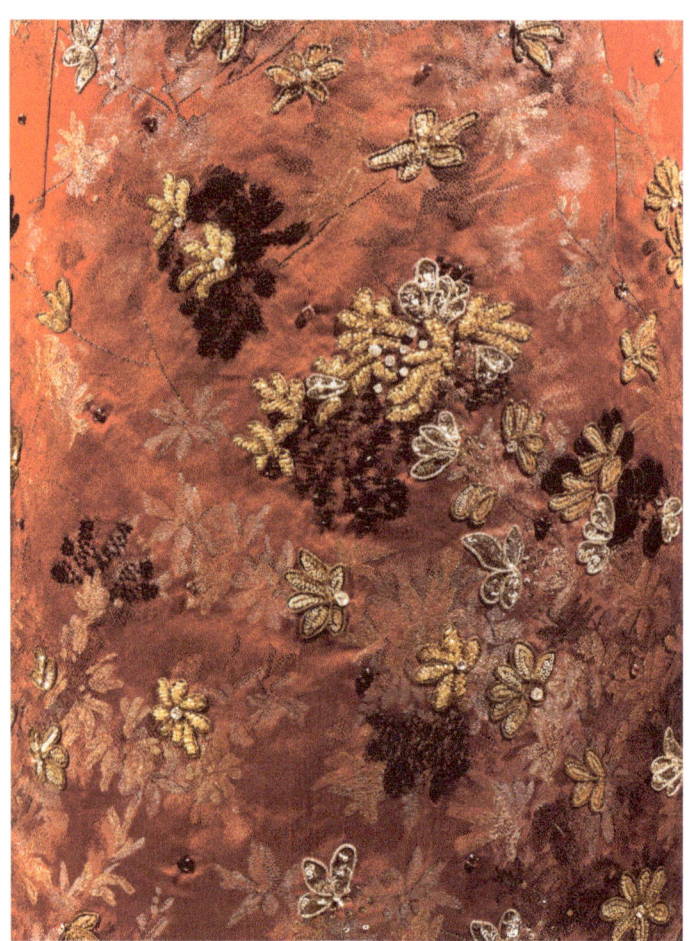

Plates 4 and 5. Details of the Balenciaga ensemble and of Graham Sutherland's *Helena Rubinstein in a Red Brocade Balenciaga Gown*. Sutherland captured the gown with superb fluency, brilliantly conveying its richness of texture and hue, the stiffness and weight of the fabric, and the complexity of the design.

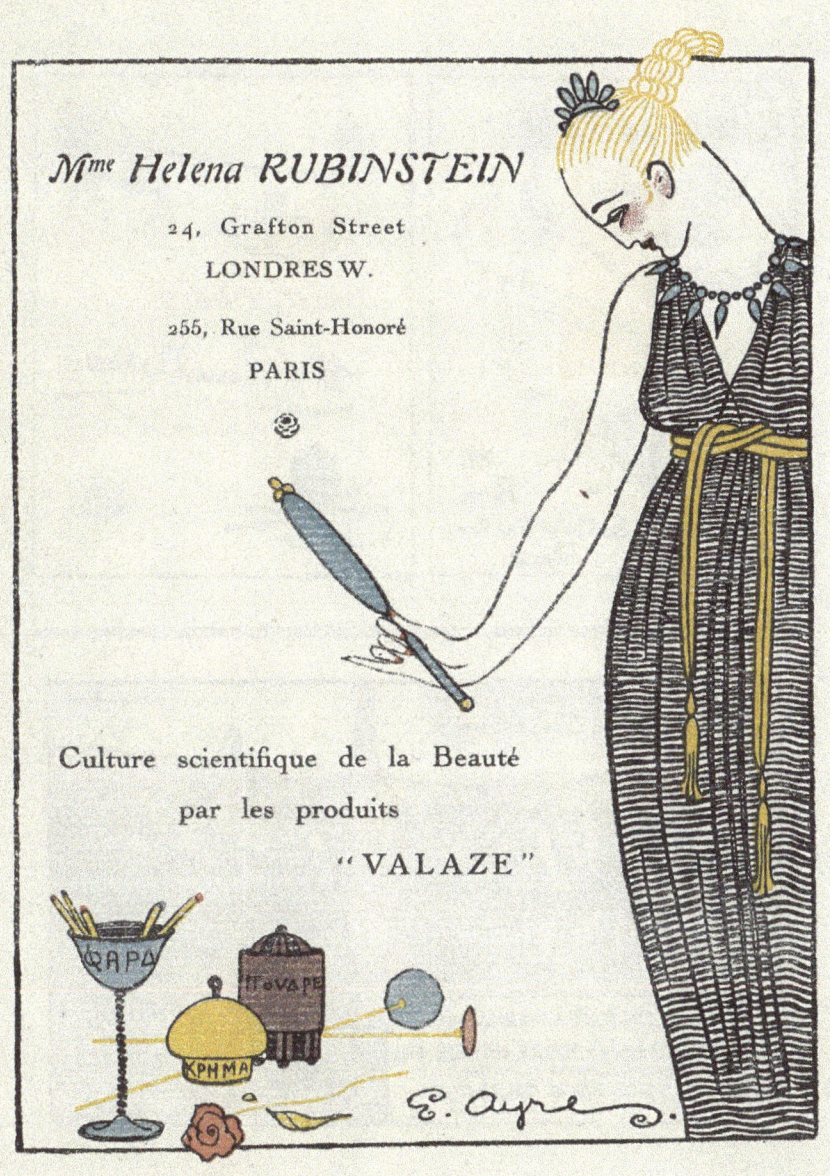

Plate 6. An advertisement for Helena Rubinstein's London and Paris salons, from *La Gazette du Bon Ton*, c. 1912–1914, illustrated by Emilio Ayres. Allusions to classical Greece and its imagined beauty standards became a regular feature of Rubinstein's advertising during these years, as she relaxed her professed opposition to cosmetics. The Greek labels on the jars and long-stemmed cup translate as 'cream', 'powder' and 'make-up'.

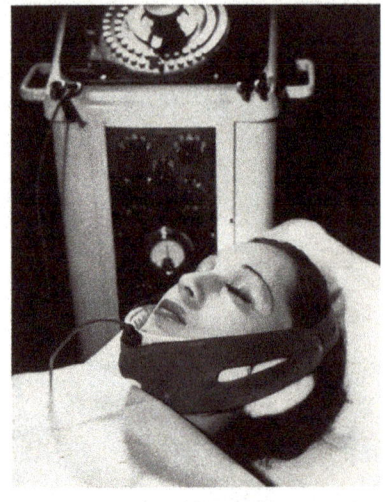

La Science rénove la Beauté

Le traitement électro-tonique de Helena Rubinstein.

La beauté, soumise ainsi que toute chose vivante à l'évolution naturelle, subit, en outre, des altérations artificielles : manque de soins, soins mal appropriés, dérèglement glandulaire dont les effets désastreux s'aggravent chez la femme à mesure qu'elle avance en âge.

Sans avoir recours aux moyens extrêmes de la chirurgie esthétique, la femme doit, sous peine de déchoir, employer des traitements plus énergiques, plus puissants, au premier rang desquels se place le nouveau traitement **électro-tonique** de **helena rubinstein**.

A quel moment doit-on recourir à ce traitement? Nous dirons que ce moment est venu lorsque l'épiderme perd de sa fermeté et de son élasticité. La peau n'a plus ses couleurs naturelles, et déjà les rides y apparaissent. Les tissus, en se relâchant, altèrent la courbe juvénile des profils, et creusent le pli naso-buccal. Les paupières se plissent, et des boursouflures se forment sous les yeux.

La femme avisée ne se trompe pas, qui s'examine avec soin chaque jour. Elle doit agir sans retard avant que ces symptômes ne deviennent de véritables dommages.

Grâce au **traitement électro-tonique que helena rubinstein** applique avec un succès grandissant dans ses cliniques de Paris, de New-York, d'Hollywood, de Londres, la jeunesse peut véritablement être retenue, la beauté recouvrée et le déclin ajourné.

•

HELENA RUBINSTEIN, avec son autorité indiscutable, recommande des soins quotidiens essentiels à chaque femme qui veut maintenir sa jeunesse et sa beauté, ou corriger des défectuosités causées souvent par la négligence.

La Crème Pasteurisée, qui nettoie profondément les pores, débarrasse l'épiderme de toute trace de maquillage, en le laissant souple, frais et velouté : 20 et 30 francs.

La Georgine Lactée, tonifie les muscles, leur rend toute leur fermeté. Corrige les contours fatigués du visage, les bajoues et le double menton : 30 et 55 francs.

Crème Perfection, indispensable pour nourrir les peaux sèches. Efface les rides, les petites lignes et assouplit considérablement : 30 francs.

L'extrait Valaze, lotion anti-rides, employé en compresses, délasse les yeux et résorbe les bouffissures. Il constitue un merveilleux tonique pour l'ensemble du visage : 40 francs. Pour celles dont le visage montre des signes de fatigue et un manque de vitalité, Helena Rubinstein a composé les **Crèmes Hormones**, de jour et de nuit, qui nourrissent, régénèrent les tissus appauvris, effacent les rides, grâce aux extraits de glandes qu'elles contiennent. Ces deux crèmes constituent un régime parfaitement équilibré. Les 2 crèmes, jour et nuit : 200 francs.

A la Clinique de Beauté, une séance comportant un nettoyage, un massage, maquillage : 50 francs.

I. Le masque électro-tonique active la circulation, resserre les tissus et raffermit la peau, dont il fait disparaître les plissements. Il redonne leur galbe aux contours du visage, en résorbant les bajoues et le double menton.

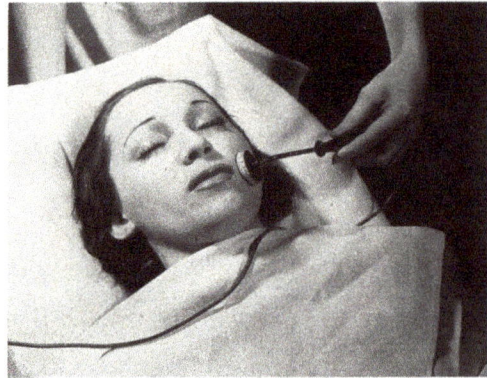

II. La gymnastique électro-passive lente et pénétrante, atteint en profondeur les muscles les plus ténus, tels que ceux, si délicats, des paupières. Elle tonifie et raffermit la charpente du visage.

III. Les rayons, sélectionnés pour leur action salutaire sur la peau, complètent le traitement, parachevé d'ailleurs par un massage sur les fameuses crèmes aux Hormones.

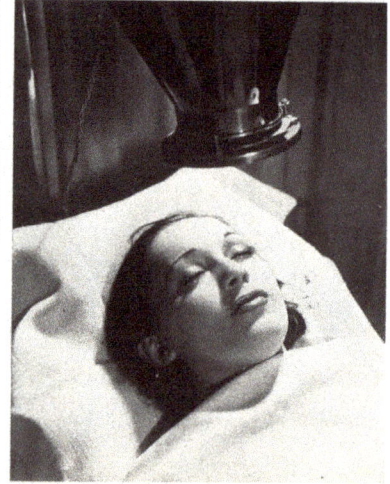

helena rubinstein
52, Faubourg Saint-Honoré, Paris. Anjou 47-50

Consultations gratuites à la clinique et examen de la peau au Dermalens. — Conseils par correspondance à titre gracieux.

Plate 7. 'Science restores beauty': a 1920s advertisement for 'electro-tonique' treatments at Rubinstein's Paris salon. Scientific claims had been central to Rubinstein's branding since the beginning. A 1905 advertisement for her first Melbourne salon promised that 'modern science has disclosed methods of making the human face more beautiful in all cases', and she was offering electronic treatments from as early as 1908.

Plate 8. *Portrait of Princess Artchil Gourielli (Helena Rubinstein)*, 1943, by Salvador Dalí. In 1942, Rubinstein had commissioned Dalí to paint three murals for her Park Avenue triplex, and the following year she agreed to let him paint her portrait. A reviewer for *The New York Sun* dismissively likened the painting to Mount Rushmore, which had been completed in 1941, but Rubinstein liked it enough to buy it for her personal collection.

Plate 9. *Helena Rubinstein* by William Dobell, 1957. During Rubinstein's final visit to Australia, she sat for Dobell in her Sydney hotel suite. Riveted by what he saw as a duality in her public and private personas, he made a number of drawings, five small studies in oil, and later no fewer than eight full-sized portraits. Rubinstein never saw any of Dobell's paintings other than in reproduction.

She's as sweet a little lass
As the clover in the grass
    And a group of saucy freckles mark her nose.

They are kisses of the sun,
And they stand out one by one
    Like the stamens mid the petals of the rose.

All the freckles on her face
Are an alphabet to trace
    Memoranda of vacation's wholesome play

In their dotted lines one reads
Tales of merry thoughts and deeds
    That long hours of school life shall not fade away ...[4]

Even here, while the thoughts and deeds were merry, and the play wholesome, the freckles themselves were 'saucy'. That the label copy of Rubinstein's Valaze singled out freckles for attack, on an equal footing to wrinkles and blemishes, is hardly surprising given the scale of contemporary condemnation of this natural phenomenon. The following critique was typical. There were thousands like it:

> The fact that freckles are the usual penalty exacted by nature for the bestowal of a delicate complexion in no way compensates any daughter of Eve for their unwelcome presence. The poetess may call them 'the kisses of Apollo,' but she prefers to dispense with the attentions of the sun god. Probably the least offensive and disfiguring of all skin blemishes, they are the most obstinate in resisting removal.[5]

An even lonelier voice was an anonymous Sydney woman who in June 1902 submitted the following satirical 'cure for freckles' to *The World's News*, one of the innumerable fragments and one-liners with which the papers rounded out their dense columns, the humour in them being so often difficult to retrieve from historical oblivion, although this one is plain enough: 'Remove the freckles with a putty knife, soak them in salt water overnight, then hang them up in a smokehouse in a good strong smoke made of sawdust and slippery elm bark for about a week. Freckles thus treated never fail to be thoroughly cured.'[6] One senses, here, the exasperation of a woman who correctly perceived that she faced an insuperable rampart of prejudice. However, hers was a lonely exception that proved the rule. More often than not, humour was deployed in the onslaught against freckles, as in this example from the same issue:

Didn't Want Freckles
SWEET GIRL (in photographic studio): 'I wish you wouldn't put that big camera so close to me.'
PHOTOGRAPHER: 'Don't you want the photo cabinet size?'
SWEET GIRL: 'Yes, but I don't want the freckles cabinet size.'[7]

Throughout Australasia, an almost universal barrage of public comment insisted that women needed to be saved from or cured of freckles, even with the aid of borax. Valaze was therefore aimed to satisfy a market with proven potential, and indeed to meet a pressing need.

Victoria and New South Wales, but not all the other Australian colonies, had trademark, patent and copyright systems before Federation in 1901, however all ceded their powers to the Commonwealth through placitum 51 (xviii) of the Constitution. This is why Rubinstein's application was lodged with the Commissioner of Trade Marks in Melbourne, but now slumbers peacefully in the National Archives of Australia in Canberra. Making that application to protect the 'distinctive label' of her one product was a significant step for Rubinstein, and one that was laden with risk. We have seen that there were plenty of other similar products and services in a burgeoning local market that enjoyed no such protection in what was a densely populated jungle of malfeasance and misrepresentation. This was for their various inventors, purveyors and distributors a different sort of gamble.

For Rubinstein, the risks were several. First, trademark protection was expensive (and relatively more expensive then than it is now). Patent protection was even more expensive. What was most expensive, however, was enforcement, should that ever become necessary. With trademark registration, therefore, came the risk of being obliged to enter into expensive, potentially ruinous, litigation. On the other hand, early Commonwealth control over imports gave remarkable benefit to a trademark holder, and without recourse to the courts. Until quite recently, customs officials would check all branded imports against the trademark register. If there was an Australian trademark holder who was not the importer, customs simply impounded the cargo. Rubinstein's position seems to have been that Valaze was well worth protecting by means of a trademark, but there may have been another reason for taking the decision to register.

It is possible that in reaching some sort of agreement with Felton Grimwade in Flinders Lane, Rubinstein was strongly urged by them to register her trademark because it was the gold standard for assuring acceptance by distributors. Any exclusive outlet might also expect such assurance as a condition of placing an order to protect against claims from others. This was even more probable when Rubinstein was busily concocting an exotic backstory that was intended for widespread publication: the great Russian skin specialist Dr Lykuski. Felton Grimwade's anxiety may have been that anything local (but sounding appealingly foreign) was just a rip-off of something genuinely foreign. A certificate from the Commonwealth that Rubinstein, 'manufacturer', was the registered owner of the trademark would provide much comfort in Flinders Lane.

Be all that as it may, under imperial copyright law, if you sought copyright in a colony, which before 1886 included registration of copyright, you obtained colonial copyright but not imperial copyright. This was an additional problem. The only way to gain imperial scope for your copyright was to publish first in England. This potential vulnerability was beyond the horizon of Rubinstein's ambition at the beginning of 1903, but it would gain relevance by 1904, when she is on record in print as having set her sights upon London and Paris. Others might have been wracked on the shores of their ambition, but Rubinstein was canny in opting for protection, even if that choice had not been urged upon her by Felton Grimwade. As Mark Williams points out, 'a trademark is not the brand. It is the sausage, and not the sizzle. Without the sausage in all its intestinal, gristly and fatty technicality, the sizzle is but ephemeral.'[8]

*   *   *

Helena Rubinstein's entry in James Smith's commercial *Cyclopedia of Victoria* (1905) is longer and more elaborately worded than Alice Ward's adjacent entry and, although it lacks a photograph and misspells Rubinstein's surname, the content rests entirely on the foundation of Valaze, the skin-nurturing face cream that purported to contain rare herbs found only in the Carpathian Mountains, together with essence of almonds and the bark of an evergreen tree:

> Miss HELENA RUBENSTEIN [*sic*], 243 Collins Street, Melbourne. – Modern science has disclosed methods of making the human face more beautiful in all cases, and less unbeautiful in numberless instances, without having recourse to artificial agencies, which are always palpable to the eye and unpleasing to the aesthetic perceptions of the beholder. No cosmetic that was ever invented could rival the delicate whiteness and transparent bloom of a beautiful female complexion, notwithstanding all that has been said and written about the powders and pomades which are alleged to have enabled Ninon de Lenchos [*sic*] to preserve her youthful loveliness until she was upwards of sixty years of age, and the cosmetics which are reputed to have rendered Madame de Pompadour so fascinating that she retained at forty all the charms that had made her so irresistible at twenty.

As exempla of cosmetic enhancement that can never rival a beautiful natural complexion, these two French women are noteworthy choices. Ninon de l'Enclos (or de Lenclos or de Lanclos) was a famous courtesan in seventeenth-century France, as famous for wit and independent wealth as for her beauty. Queen Christina of Sweden admired her, and the youthful Voltaire was one of her legatees. Jeanne Antoinette Poisson, Marquise de Pompadour, meanwhile, was official mistress to King Louis XV in the 1740s and remained a favourite at the court of Versailles until she died. Both women embodied that curious combination of intellect, social cachet, independence of mind and sexual intrigue that is associated with the greatest salons of the *ancien régime*, a world with which the Edwardians were fascinated, in Melbourne no less than in London. However, the point being made slightly laboriously here is that in order to create in old age the melancholy illusion of lost youth both women resorted to artifice, to which there is a further ground of complaint:

> But apart from other objections to the use of such palpable deceptions, they are to be deprecated upon hygienic grounds. They are almost invariably perfumed, and there are few perfumes devoid of poisonous ingredients. These are absorbed through the pores of the skin, and their effect upon the system is often deadly. This was the case with Mlle Mars, the great French actress, who died suddenly from the presence of some toxic element in the hair dye she was using.

Here we shift into the world of Anne Françoise Hyppolyte Boutet Salvetat, known as Mademoiselle Mars, whose distinguished career in the *Comédie Française* lasted from the glory years of Napoleon all the way down to the July Monarchy, the world of Balzac, with which the Edwardians were also entranced. These references to French milieux with such pungent literary and artistic associations suggest that this piece was composed with the aid of a fairly sophisticated literary mind:

> Now the mode of treatment recommended by Miss Helena Rubenstein [*sic*], in connection with the Russian 'Valaze,' which is not a cosmetic, but a skin food and epidermic tonic, possesses the three recommendations of being simple, natural, and efficacious. Its foundation principle is cleanliness, and a recognition of the fact that, as experience has shown, pure water is the very best cosmetic.

What is so striking about this last point is that it demonstrates how Rubinstein managed successfully to steer her company from an initially defining mindset in which 'pure water is the very best cosmetic' through several relatively cautious stages to the diametrically opposite, a mindset in which by the 1920s Rubinstein's own products were the best and most beautiful cosmetics in the world. Those products had by then been transformed into an arsenal with which modern women defended a new kind of independence and personal autonomy. 'Beauty is power' began its life as a strong appeal to the idea of natural beauty – but gradually, within twenty years, Rubinstein adapted it to the idea of cosmetic enhancement: rouge, kohl and lipstick; fuchsia, cyclamen, magenta and the rest.

In 1905, however, Valaze was invisible, and to be made more effective by the action of the fingertips:

> Then by a process of what may be called digital massage of a gentle nature, assisted by the 'Valaze,' any lady, by following the directions given, can efface wrinkles, remove freckles and other superficial blemishes of the skin, communicate firmness and roundness to the flesh, impart vitality to the sebacious glands, which have such important functions to fulfil with regard to both transpiration and respiration, and, it is claimed, acquire and preserve 'a healthy, clear and natural complexion,' which is admittedly one of the first requisites of female beauty.

The concentration here upon the simplicity, naturalness, cleanliness, purity and efficacy of a product that furthermore had the virtue of not being a potentially dangerous cosmetic appears to have characterised Rubinstein's principal business strategy in the first five Australasian years. The liberal use of dignifying phrases such as 'modern science', 'epidermic tonic', 'mode of treatment', 'sebaceous glands' and 'transpiration and respiration' already created the mirage of healthy clinical practice that reached its apogee with Boris Lipnitzki thirty years later. These elements, together with carefully harvested celebrity testimonials and the inspired 'Beauty is power' headline brought Rubinstein immediate success, keeping in mind that this document was published barely two years after she introduced Valaze into an unsuspecting Melbourne market. For the time being, 'digital massage' of the face was to be done by the customer herself, in accordance with Rubinstein's instructions.

It was not long after her arrival in London and Paris that Rubinstein's firm posture in opposition to cosmetics of any kind gave way to, at first, cautious dalliance, with a concentration upon subtle pallor and classical 'Greek' effects, including that of Helena Rubinstein's own signature chignon, and subsequently, soon after the Great War, a frenzy of expansion into every conceivable cosmetic line. An intermediate step in this process of transformation demonstrates Rubinstein's preparedness to adapt and revise her own narratives. In an article entitled 'Beauty – A Real Definition' that appeared in *Arts and Decoration* in 1923, she wrote:

> Cosmetics really call for a study of art. To understand the matching of tones and to get a clear conception of the great artists' ideals of beauty, I made a long tour through Europe's most famous picture galleries. Without this, I don't think I should ever have realised how subtle is the matter of colouring, and what a variety is needed in all that beautifies.[9]

Here, to the scientific principles is added a sound knowledge of art, Old Masters and Moderns, with which to help sanitise the idea of cosmetics. However, for as long as she operated only in Australia and New Zealand, Rubinstein placed most of her eggs in the single basket of Valaze, her nourishing 'skin food'. True, she offered a handful of other products, but these were pressed upon her customers as complements to Valaze. It was, yet again, as will by now be familiar and obvious, a strategy overladen with risk – and a level of risk of which Helena Rubinstein was entirely tolerant.

*   *   *

Rubinstein created her business in a commercial environment almost entirely devoid of regulation. It was an environment, moreover, wholly reliant upon print media for advertising and publicity. The general principle of *caveat emptor* (let the buyer beware), together with the English common law tradition, meant that in Melbourne at the time of Federation the content of advertising was almost completely unfettered unless it strayed into the territory of criminal libel. True, the Parliament of Victoria had in February 1896 enacted legislation the purpose of which was more or less to replicate the British *Sale of Goods Act 1893*. This did little more than codify the common law, but it did make progress in the areas of conditions and warranties of title, 'sale by description', quality and 'fitness for purpose' implied in contracts of sale. Nevertheless, there is little evidence of the Victorian *Sale of Goods Act* having been anything more than a toothless tiger, wandering moreover in that densely populated jungle of malfeasance and misrepresentation. Not only were most products and services not held to any particularly stringent standard, there were hardly any standards whatsoever, neither in law nor in practice. Litigation was then, as now, expensive and mostly inaccessible to working people, who were also handicapped by virtue of class, implicit trust in the authority of the printed word – indeed in every kind of authority – and a degree of whole-of-population gullibility that created a pressing need for documents such as Henry Labouchère's *'Truth' Cautionary List for 1910*.[10]

This useful publication was designed above all to arm servant girls, young widows and inexperienced and/or unassisted executrixes against the predatory activities of 'thieves, blackmailers, swindlers, rogues, imposters, and other dishonest persons'. Running to 715 carefully drafted entries spread over 128 dense pages, the *'Truth' Cautionary List for 1910* is a fascinating compendium of Edwardian scams specifically and cruelly directed towards the poor, the ignorant and the credulous. These included, but were by no means limited to, fake religious subscription-hunters and charity-mongers; fraudulent begging-letter writers and medical, dental and ophthalmological quacks. There were fake premium bond peddlers; fake insurers; fake mediums; fake cancer-curers; fake debt-collectors; fake biographical dictionary compilers, and offerers of fake legal aid – fake everything. It is a desolate vista of criminal imposture, and a vast expansion of the criminal underworld of Charles Dickens into the era of mass media.

It would be naïve to overlook the fact that the proprietors of *Truth* profited handsomely from the price of one shilling and 1½*d* per copy, and from the revenue from the sale of many advertisements scattered through its pages. Still, the *Cautionary List for 1910* obviously filled a social need, because the scale of fraud and exploitation was far beyond the capacity of Scotland Yard or the Director of Public Prosecutions in the Home Office, or the fledgling Commonwealth or state authorities to crush it on their own. Indeed, many of the schemes *Truth* identified are depressingly familiar to us in the current form of disembodied spam. Unlike those, however, which lurk behind an impregnable façade of anonymity, *Truth* named names, disentangled aliases, furnished addresses, described in plain language the exact nature of the fraud or racket, and in several cases successfully defended its detailed allegations in English courts of law. It is important to remember that 112 years ago the burgeoning tabloid press was a genuine white knight, often galloping to the defence of the completely defenceless – although they often failed in the effort.

All this is why Rubinstein could so easily get away with her various bogus claims about the Russian origins and exotic ingredients of Valaze, the 'skin food' that was not, repeat *not*, a make-up or cosmetic. Indeed, compared with *thousands* of other far less scrupulous advertisers with whom she shared column inches in Australasian newspapers through the first raucous decade of the twentieth century, Rubinstein was positively respectable. For as long as Valaze did no discernible harm, and even if, as we shall see, occasionally it did, Rubinstein was entirely free to market it in whatever way she wished. What is so remarkable is that although she was cavalier with the facts, from the outset she seems to have fully grasped that her product needed to work and was justified in asserting with vigour that mostly it did. For this, she should be given credit. She was emboldened by the fact that she had long used Valaze herself and had the fresh clear complexion to prove it. It was not until 1938, when President Franklin D. Roosevelt's United States Food and Drug Administration came into being, that Rubinstein was obliged to desist from using the beguilingly simple phrase 'skin food', something she hotly resented for the ensuing twenty-five years.[11]

We do not yet know anything about the origin of the name Valaze. Thanks to Binny Lum's 1957 radio interview with Rubinstein, which survives in the collection of the National Film and Sound Archive in Canberra, however, we do know that the correct original pronunciation of Valaze rhymes with *malaise*, not *galahs* (and likewise with emphasis upon the second syllable) – this from Rubinstein's own unimpeachably authoritative lips. Rubinstein often implied that, like the product, the provenance of its name was Russian or Polish. This is at best doubtful. A careful search of Polish, Russian and Ukrainian vocabulary, experimenting with different Slavic vowel sounds from the Cyrillic alphabet, results in little success. The only even remotely closest words are the noun валіза (*valiza*, derived from the French *valise*), which means a small suitcase; or the verb вилазить (*vylazyt*), meaning to crawl or climb out of – neither of which holds any promise.[12] Rubinstein may simply have invented the name of Valaze, but such inventions often arise from some exotic association or referent, any traces of which have alas long been forgotten. The quest for even more abstract associations rolling off an English tongue, meanwhile – value, valour, valiant; phase, craze, blaze like a torch of victory – must vanish into the whirlpool of doomed conjecture. O'Higgins once asked Rubinstein outright:

> 'What was the meaning of the word 'Valaze'?' I asked Madame, hopeful that she might come up with a glorious anecdote.

'Nothing. Just a good word ... easy to remember.'
'But who thought of it?'
'Someone who was probably paid too much!'[13]

Harry Thompson was credited with the naming of the Robur Tea Company, but that name was used earlier in Britain for a type of tonic and derived from the Latin noun *Robur,* meaning, literally, an oak tree, but also physical strength more generally. This resonated with Englishmen. Whether Thompson played a part in dreaming up Valaze has so far been impossible to determine. What is clear, however, is that Valaze, by name as well as in substance, ran closely parallel with Dr Lykuski, and both the brand and the medical phantasm served Rubinstein extremely well for decades. Lykuski, incidentally, is close to закуски (*zakuski* or *zakąski*), a generous assortment of *hors d'oeuvres* in Russian and Polish gastronomy, so it is possible that humour played a part.

According to her own account, Rubinstein first opened her salon at 274 Collins Street, and subsequently moved to 243 *Little* Collins Street.[14] However, we now know from press advertisements appearing in large numbers from February 1903 that in fact Rubinstein first established her business at O'Connor's Buildings (or O'Connor's Chambers) at 138 Elizabeth Street, right next door to J.K. Smith's Sports Emporium at number 136.[15] Rubinstein's trademark application gives as the applicant 'Helena Rubinstein trading as Helena Rubinstein & Co. of 138 Elizabeth St., Melbourne, *Manufacturer*' (my italics). The earliest advertorial, 'What is Valaze?', appeared in *Table Talk* only three days later, on Thursday 26 February 1903, which close proximity must have entailed a good deal of strategic planning in advance:

> A recently introduced and most delightful preparation for the skin is creating quite a little mild sensation among Melbourne society women, many of whom have already discovered the great improvement which quickly results from its use.

This introductory point about Valaze having lately caused a sensation among Melbourne society women cleverly implied that the business had already been operating for some considerable time, which was not true. It is also contradicted by the admirable self-sacrifice with which Rubinstein goes on to claim that she sought to avoid 'exclusiveness', and to make Valaze available to 'all classes':

> 'Valaze' is really a skin food, which is prepared by the most celebrated of all the European skin specialists, Dr. Lykuski, from herbs which grow in the Carpathian Mountains, the dividing range between Galicia and Hungary. It is in no sense a 'make-up'; in fact it is not visible upon the skin in any way. It is in the truest sense of the word a 'skin food.'

This idea of 'skin food' may have been inspired by a model that thrived through the years immediately preceding Rubinstein's sojourn in Australia, and indeed during it: that of 'lung food'. The basic no-nonsense term 'food' was, in any case, used for a vast range of products and medicaments such as Benger's Food and Neave's Food. Both products were intended for infants, invalids and the aged. Dr Morse's Indian Root Pills were described as 'brain food', while Allenbury's Foods were also pressed upon infants. However, 'lung food' was the commonest formulation.

In a period when opportunities for travel and leisure were rapidly expanding, access to seaside destinations in Australia was seen, more often than not, in therapeutic terms. The purely hedonistic joys of sun worship and bathing in the ocean were yet to take hold of the national character. Strolling fully dressed or sitting and reading on pristine ocean or estuarine beaches, as in Charles Conder's *A Holiday at Mentone* (1888, Art Gallery of South Australia, Adelaide), the late Victorian and Edwardian holidaymaker or daytripper could breathe deeply off the ocean spray and benefit from the health-giving properties of that natural lung food, 'ozone'. However, numerous products were also pressed upon people with weak lungs under the same rubric of lung food, for example Dr Williams' Pink Pills for Pale People, 'an immediate, unmistakable lung food and nerve tonic'. This and various other forms of lung food and Rubinstein's skin food had in common the combined benefits of subcutaneous nourishment, the maintenance of already healthy organs, and, if needed, active improvement and healing. Thus, Valaze:

> When rubbed into the skin it is absorbed into the pores, and creates a perfectly healthy condition ... It removes freckles, that bane of the Australian girl, blackheads and all such minor disfigurements, and gives to the skin that soft, firm, transparent appearance which is so noticeable in a healthy child, but is so seldom seen after childhood in Australia. It is imported by Helena Rubinstein and Company, whose rooms are at present situated in O'Connor's Buildings, 138 Elizabeth Street. Miss Rubinstein herself is the strongest advocate 'Valaze' can have, for although she has lived for some years both in Victoria and Queensland, her skin is exquisite, of that clear, soft transparency which charms above all things, and she admits having used the preparation for some years. The price puts the preparation within the reach of everyone, for, although Miss Rubinstein has been advised to charge much more for it, presumably to keep 'Valaze' exclusive, the firm prefers to make a smaller profit, and to introduce it widely among all classes. It is sold in attractive [white] porcelain jars, is obtainable in two sizes, the prices being 3/6 and 5/6 respectively. Other toilet preparations by the same medical man are also imported, including a delightful soap, a face powder and skin lotion, and a splendid hair tonic. These of course are intended for use in conjunction with 'Valaze' where necessary, and are all as good and efficacious in their way as the 'skin food.' Neither is in any way a 'make-up,' but are the preparations of clever medical authority, who caters for the Russian ladies, celebrated for their beautiful complexions...[16]

Already we see points of emphasis that recur again and again in Rubinstein's publicity: that she herself was living proof of Valaze's efficacy; 'clever medical authority'; importation from Russia; and the fact that Valaze was in no way any sort of cosmetic. In any event, by the end of February 1903 Rubinstein's business was well under way; supplies of Valaze were already to hand, and premises made ready for customers. Given that she had departed from 138 Elizabeth Street by 1 October 1903, and if she had signed a year's lease, she may even have been *en poste* by September or October 1902. The other tenants in O'Connor's Buildings point to a decidedly middling, not entirely satisfactory mixture, at times raffish. Mr Edward F. Gay, 'merchant', was on Friday 13 May 1904 fined £10 by the police magistrate for importing 'into the Commonwealth certain Swiss watches containing indecent pictures'.[17]

By 1 October 1903, Rubinstein had moved to the Fourth Victoria Building at 243 Collins Street, almost directly opposite the Block Arcade.[18] She may have taken over premises previously occupied by 'Mrs Wilmer, fashionable masseuse. Salon … next Rocke & Co. First Floor. Take Lift.' There, she joined several well-known architects, including I.G. Beaver; the 'Parisian School of Dress-Making'; the offices of two building societies (including the eponymous Fourth Victoria); the Hepburn Alluvial Mining Company; and the Automobile Club of Victoria.[19] It was clearly a step up, and Rubinstein remained there for not quite two years. *Table Talk* caught up with her there in August 1904:

> One day, while chatting with Miss Rubinstein in her pretty rooms, 243 Collins-street, the query is put –
>
> 'What made you first think of setting up in business,' and then it is learned that the idea first dawned in a very simple way. Miss Rubinstein has a beautiful clear complexion which seems impervious to any changes of climate, even the most severe. Naturally, wherever she went this was the envy of her acquaintances, who all sought to learn what special cream or salve she used. No secret was made of the fact that it had been her custom for some years to use a simple skin food,

very well-known in Warsaw, called 'Valaze,' prepared by a very clever skin specialist.

The business idea seized her – she introduced 'Valaze' to Melbourne. Miss Nellie Stewart wrote, when once she used it: 'It is the most wonderful preparation I have ever had,' and with every order from her since comes fresh appreciations of the skin food.

'Of course I knew "Valaze" was good,' Miss Rubinstein says, 'or I should never have introduced it, for I would not like to recommend anything I was not sure about.

'I could make much more by having a locally manufactured article, but that would never do. People are under the impression I am making my fortune now, but with cost, freight and duty, there is not much profit on each pot of "Valaze." I am told I should have asked a bigger price for it, but my idea was to place it within reach of everybody, instead of only those with ample means.'

One imagines, here, Frederick Sheppard Grimwade sitting in the coffee room at the Melbourne Club, with his copy of *Table Talk*, quietly chuckling to himself.

'I knew, you see, from personal experience, that once it is used it is always used. For instance, I never worry about my skin now, nor take precautions [...] against sunburn, for I know that a little "Valaze" rubbed in at night will set everything right.

'Yes, I have other preparations; among them some splendid herbs to infuse for steaming the face. They are so cleansing that they are particularly good.

'I much prefer people to come and see me at least once when they first buy "Valaze," for skins vary so and need different treatment. Therefore I like to see each one and advise her to the best of my ability. "Valaze" nourishes the skin, it really is a skin food, not at all a make-up in any respect.

'It is my intention to go to Europe shortly, to personally learn all I can about the skin and its treatment from the foremost European specialists in each country. Then I shall return to Melbourne and establish myself in a larger way.

'Of course already the business is large; my only difficulty is I cannot obtain big enough supplies, for Dr. Lykuski is most particular that "Valaze" shall be manufactured under his supervision, and, as you know, it is made from special herbs found only in the Carpathian Mountains. I take as much as he can supply me with, but even yet it is not enough. I must see what I can do to remedy this when I go 'home.'

'Imitation may be the sincerest form of flattery, but I must confess I have not appreciated it. In fact, I have been rather worried and annoyed by the way some local manufacturers have been got up to resemble "Valaze." My advertisements even have been copied, and in every way it has been made to resemble Dr. Lykuski's preparation as closely as possible. It is very annoying, but time will prove which is the most worthy. In my opinion, such things cannot be satisfactorily prepared, except by a thorough skin specialist.'[20]

This is deft orchestration. Rubinstein speaks about money. She emphasises her democratising vision for Valaze – that it should be placed within reach of everybody. She was prepared to live with a smaller profit margin in order to achieve this worthy aim. This was not true, and, besides, any such effort was bound to be relative, limited in this instance to the circle of readers of *Table Talk*. Given that this piece purported to be an interview, Rubinstein must have cultivated a particularly convenient and friendly relationship with *Table Talk*. Most of the other elements are there: living proof; Dr Lykuski's Russian or Polish medical credentials; rare herbs that exist only in the Carpathian Mountains; not by any means a cosmetic. The announcement of her travel plans, the purpose of which were to engage with European skin specialists, amplifies the narrative of clinical consultation and treatment.

The move to 243 Collins Street represented growth and acceleration. In November 1903, we find 'Mddle Rubinstein, complexion specialist, announces that she will be in Ballarat on 4th, 5th and 7th December, and may be consulted from 10 a.m. to 6 p.m. at Miss Jones' rooms, 10 and 11 Camp Hill Chambers'.[21] After she returned with Ceska Rubinstein and cousin Lola Beckmann from her fact-finding mission to Europe in September 1905, Rubinstein traded at Glen's, 274 Collins Street, another step up and into the far more 'artistic' *milieu* of those many respectable music teachers, dressmakers, and Alice Ward's concomitant Salon Charmazelle.[22] All three establishments were a virtual stone's throw from the Block Arcade, where Rubinstein had previously worked at the Siegenbergs' Chicago and Winter Garden, but by the middle of 1905 Rubinstein had added to her headquarters at Glen's, '158A Pitt Street, Sydney', and less than two years later '9 Brandon Street, Wellington, New Zealand'.[23] Her great, unstoppable expansion had begun, and for the time being it continued to rely almost entirely upon the strong forward propulsion attained by Valaze.

Rubinstein had a genius for business. She seems to have instinctively grasped from the outset that her products needed to be comparatively expensive – the unit cost of a pot of Valaze was 10*d*; at first she sold the larger size for 5/6, then soon afterwards for 6*s*, a mark-up of nearly 620%. She sensed that working women thirsted for luxury and were prepared to pay for it. So much for her claim to have sacrificed profit upon the altar of availability to all Australasian women, not merely those with ample means. As we have seen, hers were not the only skin nostrums available in Melbourne and elsewhere, but they were among the first anywhere to be aggressively and unapologetically marketed as a luxury that was, at the same time, based on scientific or clinical expertise, beneficial to the skin, and capable of removing blemishes, wrinkles and freckles,[24] none of which, thirty years later, were permitted to mar Rubinstein's own appearance in Boris Lipnitzki's photograph in the Saint-Cloud laboratory, where she is shown painstakingly continuing to formulate ever more efficacious products and treatments, the first of which was for a long time the only one: Valaze.

6

To Europe and Back

At the beginning of February 1905, Helena Rubinstein sailed from Melbourne aboard the Norddeutscher Lloyd steamer *Rhein*. Her destination was Bremen. This was a long and carefully thought-out mission to acquire knowledge, new products and equipment with which to strengthen the Melbourne business and to fuel an ambitious expansion that Rubinstein had already embarked upon prior to her departure. In late March 1905, the Melbourne correspondent of the Launceston *Daily Telegraph* paid a visit to 243 Collins Street:

> I saw in her pretty rooms last week some colossal orders being carried out against time. Two men feverishly packed, nailed, and hammered immense cases while the girls enveloped the herbal soap in wrappings with astounding celerity, and Miss Rubinstein herself endeavoured to see a steady procession of ladies, while her two rooms were filled with others waiting with orders, and telegraph boys were waiting for reply wires. The scene was confusing. It is like that, I believe, every day in the week.[1]

A shrewdly orchestrated press campaign added to the confusion, because *Table Talk* (among others) had by then also called for a detailed briefing:

Miss Helena Rubinstein leaves for Europe at the end of this month. Her trip will, however, scarcely be one of pleasure, but business solely. As is well known, Miss Rubinstein is the sole agent and importer of that very excellent skin food, 'Valaze,' and of other preparations of the celebrated Russian skin specialist, Dr. Lykuski. So convincingly has the splendid and lasting qualities of the 'marvellous skin food, Valaze,' as Miss Nellie Stewart calls it, been recognised, that the demand for it all over Australia has become prodigious, and Miss Rubinstein has had the greatest difficulty to supply the demand.

Rubinstein had dilated upon the theme of demand outstripping supply for some time and, as we shall see, would continue to do so for years. It was necessary for her to furnish an explanation that would, at the same time, reinforce the unique qualities of her single product, which was scarce; however, its scarcity was an asset as well as a problem. Dr Lykuski proved to be useful: his methods, and his circuitous route of exportation:

Although huge cases of the Valaze in its attractive white jars seem always coming to hand, yet it is distributed so quickly that the supply is not nearly sufficient. For some time past it has seemed that Miss Rubinstein has always been short of something, for as soon as a goodly stock of, say, Valaze, was to hand, the soap became short, or the wonderful herbs gave out. Frantic cabling has been quite common but as Miss Rubinstein explains, this mode is not only too expensive, but it is not satisfactory, and the goods take longer in coming, for they are sent first to Antwerp, thence to Southampton, and so shipped here. This, the exporters declare, is the most expeditious way of sending them.

Miss Rubinstein has thought the matter out, and has come to the conclusion that the best way is to go home and try and make better all-round arrangements, for a larger and regular supply of Valaze, etc., and for a more direct route. The one trouble is that the output is somewhat limited, as the curative herbs from which Valaze is made are found only in the Carpathian Mountains, and to insure its purity and excellence, every batch of it is manufactured only under Dr. Lykuski's direct supervision, and in but the one place.

Rubinstein was careful not to specify *which* place. An additional risk was that she could not be sure that some nimble competitor in Melbourne might not attempt to seek out Dr Lykuski so as to secure from him a supply of Valaze in violation of what she characterised as her exclusive agency and importation arrangement. In the absence of a real Dr Lykuski, this was not of any great concern except that, in the attempt, her competitors might expose the far more prosaic reality of Felton Grimwade in Flinders Lane. The supply of Valaze from that source might even have been delayed or disrupted by something as basic as Rubinstein's cash flow. She had overheads. She had staff. No doubt she had slow months and/or unexpected bills to pay. Still, it was necessary to improvise; to underline her friendship with Dr Lykuski so as to ward off competition, and to proffer more verifiable business reasons for travelling to Europe:

> At the same time, Miss Rubinstein is going to consult the foremost skin specialists of Europe as to the best treatment for the skin, hair, etc., and will spare no expense in making herself au courant not only with the treatments, but with all the leading preparations which are manufactured by authorised skin specialists, and bear genuine testimonials of excellence. Anything else she will not consider as it is useless to touch anything she cannot conscientiously recommend, and for which the demand would be only for the time being and by no means permanent.
>
> Meantime Miss Rubinstein has been overwhelmed with orders, since her intention of being absent from Australia for a time has been known. There has been a decided disposition shown to lay in a reserve of stock of the goods she imports, although, of course, the business will be carried on as usual at her rooms, 243 Collins Street.[2]

Rubinstein's aim appears to have been to engage with European dermatologists, specifically Frau Doktor Emmie List, or Litz, of Vienna, who is said to have developed shortly before 1905 the first 'chemical peel' treatment, and scientists more generally, above all the famous organic and physical chemist Marcellin Berthelot of Paris, who in 1889 succeeded Louis Pasteur as permanent secretary of the Académie Française des Sciences and had lately been elected to the Académie de France (1901).

The problem of fact and fiction is never greater than when pursuing Rubinstein back and forth across continental Europe in 1905. Dr Berthelot was indeed a famous and distinguished man. Much of his work was built on the foundation of a brilliant early study of the chemical composition of fats, and the synthesis of new fats. In theory, Rubinstein could have met him in Paris, but it now seems unlikely that someone as eminent would have received her without a sufficiently persuasive or influential formal introduction. He and his work were well known in Australia, but it is hard to gauge the plausibility or otherwise of Rubinstein's claim to have consulted and even worked with him.

Wherever she went, she also took some time and trouble to test the waters of other commercially available skin products and salon treatments. She was also careful to observe and critique the premises in which they were offered to customers. Based on her observations she bought a good deal of furniture and decorative objects, some of them quite substantial, with which to improve her new rooms in 274 Collins Street. However, for the purposes of her publicity it was important to emphasise the specialist clinical dimension.

Already by 1905, Rubinstein grasped that her products needed to be seen as 'scientifically formulated in the laboratory'. With the aid of her European contacts, she adapted her products to various skin 'types': dry, normal and oily. She understood the need to emphasise the use of 'natural ingredients', even though she was an aggressive user of bleach and other synthetic agents. At the same time, she was prescient in maintaining that prolonged exposure to the sun was harmful to the skin.

She was back in Melbourne the following September, having sailed aboard the *Karlsruhe*. *Table Talk* proved, once again, to be a pliable mouthpiece:

> A Beauty Institute.
> Such a charming artistic room is invaded one day, when a rumour of the wonderful new 'Beauty Institute' arouses a desire to investigate. After a little delay, Mdlle Rubinstein comes to be questioned as to the real facts about the matter. 'Is it true you are prepared to treat all manner of blemishes?' and 'Have you brought two experts from Vienna out with you?'
> Answering 'Yes' to each query, Mademoiselle sits down and prepares to satisfy curiosity.

The expertise Helena Rubinstein here conferred upon Ceska Rubinstein and Lola Beckmann, and their Viennese provenance, were more or less impossible to verify or disprove in Melbourne, but it is entirely characteristic that she was careful, as always, not to overstretch the boundaries of credibility. Hence:

> She is called away several times, for, although there are quite a number of assistants, there seems a great deal of business which needs her personal supervision.
> The moments of her absence are devoted to admiring the room. It is large and airy, over-looking the busiest part of Collins-street, for it is situated over Glen's, to be exact, and is decorated in art green … It is not to admire the room, however, but to gain information, we are there. Naturally the culture of beauty is uppermost in the mind, and thoughts of how the Greeks valued it and cultivated it arise, probably induced by the contemplation of the beautiful terra-cottas.[3]

This is to my knowledge the first time Rubinstein ever alluded specifically to the character of Classical Greek beauty, which became for some years an important additional pillar with which to uplift Valaze and to relax, cautiously at first, her firm posture in opposition to cosmetics, but only after she moved to London and Paris.

This is neatly reflected in the design for a Valaze *pochoir*, a kind of four-colour stencil on fine-quality laid paper, by the Brazilian artist Emilio Ayres. (plate 6) This *pochoir* was originally published in Paris in Lucien Vogel's small, new but influential *La Gazette du bon ton* no later than 1914. The figure wears a long, chiton-like dress. Her profile is Grecian. She has the chignon, and a delicate pink blush to the cheeks, ears and lips, as well as red varnish on her fingernails. The jars are inscribed with Greek letters: KRHMA *crema*, cream) and POUDRE (*poudre*, powder). The long-stemmed cup is likewise inscribed FARD (*fard*, make-up). A rose and two redundant hat pins complete this otherwise classicising illustration of '*Culture scientifique de la Beauté par les produits "VALAZE"*', all to be found with Mme Helena Rubinstein at 24 Grafton Street, London, and 255 rue Saint-Honoré. However, at the end of 1905 and for the time being, the classical prompt was secondary, and merely to be evoked by the contemplation of those beautiful imported terracottas. It was the clinical dimension that remained Rubinstein's principal focus:

> Then comes the reflection, how for years past the foremost scientists have been seeking the ways and means of improving poor skins, and of removing all blemishes and disfigurements. The results of their investigations have been astonishing, and we have read marvellous tales of wonders that have been achieved, how positive ugliness has been turned almost to beauty, and of many cases where real youthful charm and freshness have been retained long after middle age; Sarah Bernhardt, for instance.
>
> The establishment here in Melbourne of a Beauty Institute thoroughly and completely equipped with the very latest and best system and appliances, and in charge of thoroughly trained experts, is an important event.

A Beauty Institute, no less – and not long afterwards the Valaze Institute. Between the beginning of September and the end of December 1905, we find many references in the Melbourne press to institutes of every description, but apart from the Temperance and Seamen's institutes, the majority are professional, technical, medical, scientific or charitable, a formidable aggregation. This is not even to take into consideration the many Mechanics' Institutes that thrived all over Australia and made such an important contribution to late nineteenth- and early twentieth-century technical and vocational training. Rubinstein's choice of name was strategic, and its institutional pretension contrasts sharply with Alice Ward's Salon Charmazelle two floors below, a pretension, moreover, that was national in scope:

> Mddle. Rubinstein introduced the marvellous 'Valaze' skin food to *Australia*, and it was through the experience gained while dealing with it that the idea formulated of going to Europe and making a special study of the skin and its treatment under the very best skin specialists.
>
> To resolve is to do with Mdlle Rubinstein, for she is nothing if not energetic, and at the very first moment possible she set out to accomplish her purpose, and, as it will be seen, she has spared neither trouble, work nor expense to attain it. Her friendship with Dr. Lykuski stood her in good stead, and also her connection with some of the leading European medical men, for without the influential introductions obtained from them she could never have gained experience as a student to the hospitals of the big skin specialists.
>
> 'I wasted pounds,' Mddle. Rubinstein tells, 'in trying every method I heard of, and hundreds of preparations. It was in London I was most amazed, for I underwent a course of treatment at all the leading beauty parlours, and really there was absolutely no improvement whatever; in fact in some instances my skin looked worse afterwards.
>
> The people there are very easily pleased, much more so than the Australians; they would never pay here as they do in England for skin preparation or treatment.

Those spare pounds were not entirely wasted, for mixed results convinced Rubinstein that an opportunity existed for her:

> Why I could make a fortune in London in a very little time. I have introduced 'Valaze' there, for I have found nothing of its kind to equal it, and I have tested and analysed very many preparations since I have been away. It was difficult for me to obtain permission to study with the best skin specialists, for on the Continent the women do not dream of going to a woman for skin treatment, they would not trust their complexions to any but a medical man, who was a noted skin specialist. So they had to use subterfuges to enable me to be present at the various operations and treatments, especially in Paris, and to tell a story and say I was a Russian lady doctor, who was studying for a skin specialist. I had to pay very big fees, for I had to learn much in such a short time, but I did not care what I paid so long as I gained the knowledge.

To the costs of travel and accommodation; the investment in treatments and new equipment, is now added 'very big fees'.

> I worked under Dr. Pashki, of Vienna, whose reputation as a skin specialist is known all over Europe; under Professor Lasaar, of Berlin, quite as well-known in his way; with Dr Pokitonoff, a Russian [sic] doctor established in Paris, where he [sic] enjoys the largest practice, and with Dr Una, in Hamburg, for the peeling cure. Some of these doctors, I am sure, must be known to medical men and chemists here through their own skin preparations and their researches.

Rubinstein's gambit here is a clever one. The medical men of Melbourne were well aware of the existence of Marcellin Berthelot. If, as seems likely, they may never have heard of Dr Una, Dr Pokitonoff, Dr Pashki or Professor Lasaar, that could be made to reflect badly upon them. However, if one or two were known by reputation, even if that reputation had not been talked up by Rubinstein alone, so much the better. Even so, there was no guarantee that a public question mark might not be hoisted over one or more of Helena Rubinstein's distinguished continental consultants. It was also important to underline her own work ethic:

> While at the various hospitals I worked fifteen to sixteen hours a day, so was able to gain a great deal of experience and practice, and also my certificate. It is most interesting work, and it is wonderful to see the improvement growing under your hands. You know the Russian and Viennese ladies are noted all the world over for their skins, and these are the best patrons of skin specialists.
>
> As for face massage, while the doctors all agreed that hand massage is very good when properly and scientifically applied, they saw it is so seldom that it is properly done that now in general cases they always recommend the rollers out with me; these are they, and it is wonderful the improvement they work in a very short time. Of course, there are cases where hand massage is necessary, and we then use it. But doctors discourage it generally, because unless properly applied it really does more harm than good.

The idea that mechanical rollers could do a better job of face massage than the work of human fingers, even when 'properly and scientifically applied', may belong to the age of Thomas Edison, or even Heath Robinson, but it served as a launch pad in Melbourne for the novel equipment and electrical contraptions that Rubinstein brought home from Europe and took with her to Sydney, Brisbane and New Zealand.

Through the last three decades of the nineteenth century, the advent of a reliable supply of electricity, as well as battery storage, furnished a convenient method of enhancing and glamorising all kinds of existing products, and devising entirely new ones, such as the Sydney sexologist Dr Towle's 1895 'Hercules Life Renewer', a type of battery belt with suspensory attachment with which to stimulate the genitals. There were electric corsets, electric hairbrushes, W.C. Crump's 'Electro-Voltaic Shield', a type of wobbling girdle to help with weight loss, and any number of other quack remedies that relied upon the allure of electricity and/or batteries. Electricity was novel, exciting and, for the time being, the equivalent of what would no doubt be pressed upon us now as 'cutting-edge' or 'advanced' technology. In this respect, Rubinstein's electrical gadgets brought her business into an already crowded and rapidly expanding field, even if they could go badly wrong.[4]

It is hardly surprising that Rubinstein made no reference in *My Life for Beauty* to her first brush with litigation. According to an article headed, mockingly, 'An Illuminative Nose – Suffers from Electrocution', the *Northern Miner* (Charters Towers, Queensland), reported on Tuesday 1 December 1908:

> An unusual action was called on in the County Court, Melbourne, last week, before Judge [John Burnett] Box. Plaintiff was Walter Thornton, who described himself as a fire engineer, of Bourke Street, Melbourne, and defendant was Helena Rubinstein & Co., of the Valaze Institute, Collins Street. The statement of claim showed that plaintiff demanded £150 in damages because of alleged negligent treatment. On 12th September plaintiff had his nose treated by certain electrical appliances with the view of reducing the redness; but, according to his contention, the instruments were in a septic state, and a suppurative condition followed.[5]

The matter was adjourned owing to the absence in Western Australia of Dr Kent Hughes, a material witness. Similar reports, the purpose of which were to hold the plaintiff up to ridicule, appeared in the Perth *Daily News* and the Hobart *Mercury*. The case was dismissed due to Mr Thornton's failure to pay temporary costs, but it demonstrates the degree to which the Valaze Institute embraced unusual treatments. However, there were even more radical therapies. Rubinstein continued:

'The peeling process is wonderful; the skin is removed wholly, not by any violent means of course, and you would be astonished to see how youthful and creaseless the face looks afterwards. It takes five days to do, and you must not go out during that time. Nearly all the doctors have a private hospital, and patients are treated there. No, I have not started that, but we would attend to patients at their home. In Paris, when I first went there, was a Russian countess in the hospital; she had then had several skins removed. I went through my course and left, but when I went back months afterwards she was still there, and I must own there was a vast difference in her skin, it was beautiful then. She meant to stay six months, and did not care what it cost; she seemed to be enjoying it, too,' Mdlle Rubinstein adds with a smile.

'It is surprising what they will spend in Paris for complexion preparations. A woman will come in, looking not particularly prosperous, perhaps to buy something which costs a few cents, and before she goes out she will have spent thirty or forty francs. They think far more of the complexion and the skin than we do in Australia.'

No doubt Rubinstein's outlay in francs was comparable, if only to take the measure of competing products, but the overall impression one gains from her account is that her European journey constituted a substantial investment, even in items of décor, but it was an investment from which she had no certain prospects.

Just then there happens to be a moment's lull with patients, and the large operating-room is visited. It is daintily upholstered in cool, green tones, and is divided into several apartments by large movable screens. The wonderful appliances are examined and briefly described, as well as some of the delicate instruments.

'This is a special machine for curing unduly flushed skins, or those disfigured by blotches; this is specially for curing double chins; this again is for the electric treatment. We can cure red noses now by electricity, you know. This is for warts, as she fingers a fascinating-looking little thing; this we use for the very latest method of removing superfluous hair. It is quicker and less painful than electricity. Oh, yes, it is efficacious, as it kills the root at once. I could not recommend anything I did not feel sure about myself, and I can never feel enthusiastic about anything unless I have seen for myself that it is really good and what is pretended. This is for the paraffin treatment to fill up wrinkles and hollows in the face or neck; it is something quite new, and is only needed in extreme cases.'

Curing red noses with electricity; non-electric root killer (less painful than electricity); paraffin wax filler for extreme cases: Rubinstein was creating the daunting impression of a wide range of treatments, and for some fairly radical purposes, although it is hard to think of any piece of equipment that might reasonably be expected to cure double chins.

'This, again, is for removing wrinkles', explains Mdlle Rubinstein, picking up a little cup-shaped thing on the end of a tube and applying it to her own smooth skin, in such a manner that is apparent that some method of suction is the power.
The two experts, both dressed in red, look smilingly on, and show the working of the appliances, but do not attempt much conversation, as they have not yet quite mastered English. One has previously studied medicine. They are both enthusiastic and very much interested in their work.

At this time, Ceska Rubinstein and Lola Beckmann spoke almost no English at all, which may at least have had the virtue of preventing their claim to medical expertise being inconveniently tested.

'Did you find any good toilette preparations?'
'Yes, I have brought out some very good ones – plenty of "Valaze,"

of course, for there is absolutely nothing to equal it. The new things include a preparation called "Voskpasta," to be used in conjunction with "Valaze" soap, which will wonderfully improve the skin and help to fill out hollows and impart new life to the complexion. Another is a cream to use when going out by day or evening, which is most soothing, prevents any brownness through sunburn, and is altogether cooling and refreshing. It was used by the beautiful Comtesse Potocka, a Russian who was famed for her complexion, and is named after her. Then I have a splendid blackhead cure, prepared by Dr Lykuski.'

Countess Emanuela Pignatelli Potocka was Italian and her husband was a Pole. She was a celebrated *salonnière* in Paris.

'I have proved, as I have always said, any skin, however bad, can be improved, but what will suit one skin will not do at all for another, so each one has to be specially studied and treated accordingly,' are Mdlle Rubinstein's last words.[6]

Numerous points of emphasis in this feature article reflect the buoyant sense of forward propulsion with which Rubinstein returned from Europe to Melbourne towards the end of 1905. Even if she was careful not to overstretch, she was plainly willing to stretch the boundaries of credibility almost to breaking point. Once again, we encounter the problem of fact and fiction.

Between the middle of March, when she arrived in Bremen – if, as usual at this date, the voyage took approximately six weeks – and the end of July or early August when she set sail from Genoa, a period of only a little more than four months, she claimed to have worked those sixteen-hour days with Professor Lasaar in Berlin, a visit initially planned for a fortnight but which apparently spread into eight weeks.[7] She spent time with Dr Pashki in Vienna, who seems to have taken the place of chemical face-peel Frau Dr Emmie List, or Litz, who is instead turned into Dr Una in Hamburg, just as to the famous

Marcellin Berthelot has been added the German Dr Mathilde Pokitonoff, for whom in her Paris clinic Rubinstein was obliged to masquerade without a passport or visa as a 'Russian lady doctor'.

James Bennett's painstaking research has led him correctly to identify Pashki with the Viennese pharmacologist and librarian Dr Heinrich Paschkis; Lasaar with the Hamburg dermatologist Professor Oskar Lassar; Pokitonoff with the paediatric dermatologist Dr Mathilde von Wulfert Pokitonoff, and Una with the Hamburg dermatologist and dermatopathologist Dr Paul Gerson Unna. Whether during her European tour Rubinstein actually met all or even any of these doctors, who varied in degrees of eminence, is an open question; perhaps a few of them, quite possibly none at all. Bennett also makes the point that Rubinstein could have studied certain of their publications, thereby satisfying herself that these were ample grounds for the claim that she had indeed 'consulted' them.[8] It is possible that Heinrich Paschkis's *Kosmetik für Ärzte* (*Cosmetics for Doctors*), Paul Gerson Unna's *Allgemeine Therapie der Hautkrankleiten* (*General Therapy for Skin Diseases*), but perhaps not so much Oskar Lassar's *Zur Therapie der Hautkrebse* (*On Therapy for Skin Cancer*) had much to offer Rubinstein, as did Marcellin Berthelot's *Les Origines de l'alchimie* (*The Origins of Alchemy*), but, crucially, she could have read and comprehended all of them.[9] The question is therefore not whether Berthelot, Paschkis, Unna, Lassar and Pokitonoff existed, so much as whether Rubinstein's claim to have consulted and even worked with them, even if she had actually done so, acquired and held sufficient weight in Australia and New Zealand. If so, Valaze might take on considerable intellectual ballast. If not, the risk was that Valaze could be shown to lack any such thing.

On top of her extensive consultations, Rubinstein threw in a fairly thorough scouting visit to London – a market which showed her much promise, and into which she claimed to have taken the opportunity to introduce Valaze. She must have visited Kraków too, to gather up Ceska Rubinstein and Lola Beckmann, and to pay what turned out to be a final visit to her parents. Rubinstein also let it be known that there was business to transact with Dr Lykuski, wherever he might have been. The problem is simply one of available time, the more so if we take into account her various long journeys by steam train.

In the decade before the outbreak of World War I, it took eight and a half hours to travel from the Gare du Nord in Paris to London's Charing Cross via Calais and Dover. Depending on the weather, the English Channel crossing could take up to three additional hours, sometimes a lot longer if rough conditions caused any delay. It took nearly fifteen hours to go from Vienna to Berlin, and twenty-two hours to go from Paris to Vienna on the famous Orient Express. There was a 36-hour *Argo* steamship service that ran between London and Bremen; however, the overland Nord Express from Berlin to London Charing Cross covered much of the same distance and took only twenty-one reasonably comfortable hours. Alas, it has proven impossible to reconstruct Rubinstein's 1905 continental itinerary in its proper sequence, but it must have involved at least some of these journeys, or others of comparable duration. The final leg of her journey was probably from London or Paris to Genoa to rendezvous with Ceska and Lola aboard the *Karslruhe* (up to thirty-two hours, if going from London), or else from Vienna to Genoa (twenty-six hours), the same journey she had made in August 1896.[10]

Communications en route benefited from an excellent international wireless telegraph and telegram service. In 1905, Rubinstein was absent from Melbourne for seven months (three of them at sea), and the only way she could keep tabs on whoever she had left in charge of 243 Collins Street and her new venture at 158A Pitt Street in Sydney was by sending and receiving many telegrams. A not entirely satisfactory rule in the telegraphic system was that the sender of a telegram also paid for any reply. We have already seen, back in April, several post office telegraph boys patiently waiting for Rubinstein to reply to wires that they had delivered to her only minutes before. It was assumed that the purpose of a telegram was to elicit a quick response, sometimes within twenty-four hours, but correspondents couldn't be sure that the person replying would keep it as brief as they did.

The easiest way around this problem was for the travelling proprietor to arrange for her office at home to send her the telegrams, upon some agreed schedule, to which she could reply gratis and at whatever length was necessary wherever she happened to be. The charges would be paid by her business in Melbourne.[11]

In 1905, Rubinstein was approaching her thirty-third birthday. She had not been back to Europe for nearly nine years. Most of her destinations were novel, but Kraków was steeped in her experience of childhood, adolescence and early adulthood. All of her sisters still lived there, as did most of her mother's extended Silberfeld family. Despite the absence of Helena and Liebisch Splitter, imperial Vienna was also for her an old stamping ground. Had she been swept up by a wave of homesickness, Rubinstein would have been forgiven for changing her plans and electing to stay in Europe. Those plans had been spelled out in great detail in the Melbourne press, so it would have been hard to modify or even abandon them without cutting her losses and relinquishing her Australian business altogether.

Keeping up that business by remote control was, at this stage, more or less viable in the short term, but impossible in the medium to long. However tempting it might have been to realise her ambition to tackle the London and Paris markets, or to start from scratch – something she had done several times before – in 1905 she resisted any such temptation to abandon Australia. Instead, she returned as she said she would, and with renewed energy, ambition and focus. In this respect, Rubinstein's determination to board the *Prinz-Regent Luitpold* in 1896 was only exceeded in boldness by her decision to embark on the *Karlsruhe* nearly ten years later.

The professional 'certificate' to which Rubinstein soon afterwards referred in *Table Talk*'s feature article 'A Beauty Institute' was a nice touch, but to the clinical consulting and her testing of courses of treatment here and there we should add a good deal of shopping for wholesale electrical equipment, rollers for face massage, one or two new products and decorations for 243 then 274 Collins Street. She turned her consulting room into an 'operating room', while at the same time it was 'a charming artistic room' decorated in cool shades of art green. She turned her business into an 'Institute'. Fortunately, perhaps, Rubinstein seems to have been willing to discuss and describe the scarifying chemical face peel process – 'the skin is removed wholly, not by any violent means of course' – but without having any intention of putting it into practice. Her tolerance of risk was high, but not infinite. All of these things Rubinstein directed towards turning her business into 'a Beauty Institute thoroughly and completely equipped with the very latest and best system and appliances, and in charge of thoroughly trained experts'. And it worked.

* * *

In the middle of October 1904, Rubinstein spent a little more than a fortnight in Brisbane, consulting from a room over Messrs William A. McGuffie & Co., Chemists, 289–291 Queen Street.[12] This was a mission by train that she added to her first consulting stint in Sydney at Washington H. Soul Pattinson's, the chemists in Phoenix Chambers, Pitt Street, between Moore and Hunter Streets. Wherever she traded, Rubinstein had a keen eye for advantageous retail and consulting premises, even when they were only temporary, as in the case of her trial runs in Sydney and Brisbane.

When she first tested the commercial waters of Sydney in 1904, barely eighteen months after she started her business in Melbourne, it was most unusual for a sole trader to operate in both places. We have seen, however, that Rubinstein shared this distinction with Alice Ward and her Salon Charmazelle. Although the conditions for retail commerce in Melbourne and Sydney were in many respects similar – much the same population density, reliable supplies of electricity, excellent postal and telegraph communications, comparable shopping districts served by electric or cable trams, and so forth – yet they retained, even celebrated, many differences.

None of this necessarily mattered to Helena Rubinstein, but it helps to underline the fact that in 1904 she had resolved to do business in two places that revelled in their differences. The press was awash with disagreements between the two largest cities, everything from which one of them should be the spot where the Duke and Duchess of Cornwall and York first made landfall on their official visit to open the first Commonwealth Parliament in May 1901 down to Sydney's poor opinion of Melbourne's weather: 'We don't want to insinuate that it's ever very warm in Melbourne', quipped the *Sydney Stock and Station Journal* in 1900, 'but the last time we were there, though, it was a bit – well, let's say a bit trying!' Melburnians, meanwhile, enjoyed referring to Sydney rain as 'monsoonal'.[13]

Given this pervasive atmosphere of mutual disregard, any impression Rubinstein created that she was shifting her attention or lifting her ambitions to Pitt Street at the expense of Collins Street would therefore be dangerous in Melbourne. Equally, any impression she created that Pitt Street was merely an adjunct to Collins Street might ruin her prospects in Sydney even before she started there. Handling this required tact. It needed care. That from 1904 onwards Rubinstein managed successfully to navigate between the two cities, and prosper in both, is the more impressive.

At the beginning of 1903, Rubinstein's only mercantile springboard was from O'Connor's slightly raffish Chambers at 138 Elizabeth Street, Melbourne. By 1904 she had one foot planted in the far more salubrious Block neighbourhood of Collins Street and the other was testing out an equally prominent stretch of Pitt Street. However, in that year an ambitious and ingenious part of her strategy was coming to the conclusion that if she were prepared to tackle Sydney, she might as well attack Brisbane as well – both of them in quick succession. The benefits were potentially double, but so was the risk of failure, especially because at the same time Rubinstein was proposing to absent herself from Australia for another seven long months soon after she returned to Melbourne.

Queen Street, Brisbane, formed the civic and commercial spine of the city.[14] The location of McGuffie & Co. was attractive and busy. However, she also needed some helpful publicity. In the 'Social Gossip' column of *The Queenslander*, right in the middle of her Brisbane sojourn, Valaze was given the following encomium:

'Cynthia,' writing in the Melbourne 'Leader,' says: – 'I have just happened on something which I feel it no less than my duty to commend to your notice. Several of our mutual friends have been appearing lately with new faces. Mary, who is developing into a golf maniac, came to see me yesterday, with her complexion so presentable that manners were thrown to the winds. I demanded the reason of her facial rescue from a weather-beaten appearance that was nothing short of lamentable. I was prepared for the answer, and I got it in the word "Valaze."'

The manners, here, that were thrown to the winds were obviously Cynthia's, for demanding to know how poor weather-beaten Mary had exchanged the lamentable state of her appearance for one of presentability, despite her developing golf mania – a mania which had spread throughout the British Empire through the last decade of the nineteenth century largely thanks to the influence of the Prince of Wales.[15]

Skin after skin have I recently seen responding to the influence of this preparation. It is really a skin food prepared by the great Dr Lykuski from herbs which grow on the Carpathian Mountains, and has been introduced to Melbourne by Miss Helena Rubinstein. It removes tan and freckles, and by toning up the skin does very much towards eradicating wrinkles. It is reasonable in price, which is a great consideration for the average woman, who does not feel justified in 'buying a complexion at a guinea a pot.' It is applied at night, like any other cream, and is, of course, in no sense of the word, a make-up. In the course of a visit to Miss Rubinstein the other day, she showed me quite a formidable pile of letters. From these she sifted out half a dozen notes from well-known actresses who have used 'Valaze' for some time. Two at least of these women appear lately to have been absolutely defying time, and if 'Valaze' is, as I have every reason to believe, at the bottom of this attitude, women have something to be thankful for by reason of its introduction to Melbourne.[16]

Rubinstein must have done quite a bit of leg work in advance of her visit to Brisbane so that this vision of Melbourne fashionability could be implanted in *The Queenslander* long before she arrived there. This was neither the first nor the last time when Melbourne was pressed upon smaller Australasian cities as the *fons et origo* of new fashions and exciting developments. The earliest of Rubinstein's many Brisbane advertisements, 'Would You Like a Fresh, Beautiful Complexion?' appeared in *The Queenslander* on Saturday 16 January 1904 and, through the ensuing nearly nine months before she arrived in town, forty-eight more ads were printed in the same paper and in *The Brisbane Courier*, on average one per week in each paper.[17]

In the first decade of Federation, charges for advertising in the Australian press were not excessive, but they were not insignificant either. For 'casual' or one-off ads, or ads placed in twos, threes or fours, a charge of 4s per column inch plus 1/6 for each additional inch or fraction of an inch was pretty standard.[18] Ads with larger heads, fancy borders, graphic material or spreading over two or more columns were more expensive, while quarterly orders for 'standing' weekly or fortnightly ads triggered a 'liberal discount' – the larger the order, the bigger the discount. However, you paid in full in advance and those batches of standing ads could not be withdrawn before the expiration of the quarter in which notice of cancellation was given by the advertiser.

By 1906, Rubinstein was placing many such standing orders, often in two or more newspapers in every Australasian city. Her ads often belonged in the fancy category, extending to four or five inches or more. The extra charges for fancy ads were partly offset by the discount for a quarterly standing order; they more or less cancelled each other out. Therefore, assuming each fancy standing ad cost about 6s, which strikes me as conservative, not three years after she started from scratch in Melbourne, Rubinstein was paying about £70 *per quarter* for newspaper advertising throughout Australia and New Zealand, probably more, to which we may add the costs of obtaining testimonial matter and lengthier advertorial based on obscure arrangements with *Table Talk* and other friendly organs. Given that her quarterly sales of Valaze were then hovering at around £510, Rubinstein was placing much faith in her investment in advertising. However, she could gauge its effectiveness by keeping a close and critical eye on the number of mail orders she was receiving from all corners of both countries. Judging from the continuation of her investment, she must have concluded that it was well worth the outlay.

Rubinstein's brief initial foray into the Brisbane market gave rise to one of only few explicitly hostile notices in the press, albeit a predictable one. Writing in *The Worker*, 'Comrade Mary' went straight to the point:

> There is a new beauty doctor in town, Helena Rubinstein, and the first result of her special treatment on the face is that a rash appears on the skin. Patrons are advised to take no notice of this little outbreak, but persevere with the treatment and the ugly duckling will, of course suddenly change to a lovely swan. The case of an English beauty who scarred her face so badly with skin foods that she has not been seen outside her house for fifteen years is now going the rounds in the English papers.[19] After all, there's nothing like a plain face; it lasts a lifetime.[20]

Whether or not this 'rash' arose from some tropical adulteration of the Valaze formula, or some other cause, and whether or not this unwelcome publicity played a part in her decision, Rubinstein beat a relatively hasty retreat. However, she must have done well enough to justify in her own mind a return visit to Brisbane in 1906, this time offering novel electrical treatments she had picked up in continental Europe the previous year. A plucky piece of advertorial appeared in, once again, *The Queenslander*:

> Not content with the fame and ever increasing popularity of Valaze, Mdlle Rubinstein toured Europe last year for a more beneficial beautifier. But she searched in vain. Nothing in all the scientific and medical centres of Europe furnished a better skin-nourisher and beautifier.

Valaze stands unrivalled. Its healthful effect on the skin and its miraculous complexion-making properties distinguishes the Russian skin-food from all others on the market. But Mdlle Rubinstein made one important discovery – electrical massage, with all the electrical treatments for curing red noses, disfiguring veins, double chins, and all the ills the skin is heir to. She saw the tremendous value of this scientific branch of the beauty cult. She entered the laboratories and worked under the greatest specialists of Paris and Vienna. The enterprising young Viennese selected two students for Australian purposes. They are now established at The Beauty Institute, 274 Collins Street, Melbourne, where massage rollers and instruments are used in the development of the arms, necks, shoulders, and also in the elimination of double-chin and those bulging parts that destroy the line of the face and neck. In fact, at Mdlle Rubinstein's charming establishment is everything of value and help to appearance, from Valaze and blackhead cure to all the great electrical massage instruments. Mdlle Rubinstein has just arrived in Brisbane, and will stay here until the end of the month. Her consulting rooms are first floor, MacDonnell Chambers, next McGuffie and Co., chemists.[21]

Although she stopped short of establishing any permanent premises in Brisbane, Rubinstein must have enjoyed at least a little success on this relatively brief second visit in 1906, despite Comrade Mary's earlier counterblast in *The Worker*. McGuffie's provided continuity and a steady supply of Valaze between Rubinstein's consulting stints, and she kept up her run of ads. Crucially, she was remembered in Brisbane, and more than two years later: 'It will interest a number of the friends of Miss Helena Rubinstein to hear of her marriage', reported *The Brisbane Courier* in October 1908, 'which has recently taken place [in London]. The bridegroom, Mr Titus, has been a notable traveller, and is a very clever linguist.'[22] Moreover, she continued to be remembered. In late February 1909, *The Darling Downs Gazette*'s Melbourne correspondent reported:

My dear Beatrice,

... At the Melbourne Races last Saturday (writes a friend) two particularly smart and up-to-date women were Mrs Gilbert Wilson and Mrs Titus (Miss Helena Rubinstein, of Valaze fame). They were both recent arrivals from Europe, and naturally aired the latest Paris fashions, both wearing the dark Directoire coat over a light skirt and waistcoat, upon which has been set the hall-mark of Parisian approval ... Mrs Titus wore a rich black Ottoman silk Directoire coat, trimmed in the regulation way, with froggings of cord, cavalier cuffs, and handsome buttons, and the large pocket flaps over a pleated skirt of fine ivory cloth. Her large hat was of black satin, with a number of uncurled white ostrich feathers caught together by a large round embroidered ornament, and laid flat across the crown ...

Yours affectionately,

Pansy.[23]

Rubinstein's visibility in the press between 1903 and 1907 was almost entirely confined to her business. She is conspicuous by her absence from the social pages. Indeed, she only appears to have made her debut as late as 1906 – a notable one, for she was mentioned in the same sentence as Phelia, Mrs Norton Grimwade, Frederick Sheppard Grimwade's daughter-in-law – at a 'special entertainment at Menzies' Hotel in aid of the memorial fund for Australian soldiers who fell in the South African war'.[24] This may well constitute the first of Rubinstein's many subsequent acts of reputation-enhancing philanthropy.

Coming on the eve of her departure for London, this may suggest a shift in strategy, and a prudent one. It is perhaps ironic that it was not until she set her sights on London that Rubinstein turned her attention to the Australian social round. Her marriage to Edward Titus soon followed, and it is no accident that upon her triumphant return visit to Melbourne in 1909 we find her so fashionably attired – smart and 'up-to-date' – at the races.

However, there was also an important piece of business to transact in Melbourne, because the following September Helena Rubinstein Pty Ltd was incorporated in Victoria under the *Companies Act* 1890 and 1896.[25] The legal matters were handled, once again, by Rubinstein's Queen Street solicitors Cleverdon and Fay.[26] Upon her departure from Melbourne, therefore, Rubinstein was well on her way to becoming the owner of her first public company.

When in early 1903 she launched her business at 138 Elizabeth Street, Melbourne, Rubinstein used three methods of operating on a national scale. First, her headquarters in Melbourne and, later, Sydney, provided a not always reliable source of Valaze for local customers and by mail order. Second, she resolved, when and where possible, to travel elsewhere for brief periods of consultation. Whether 'at home' or on the road, Rubinstein relied upon an expensive national advertising blitz. Although she never went there before 1938, the ladies of Adelaide were at first urged in the pages of *The Critic* to seek Valaze from headquarters at 243 Collins Street, but soon afterwards to obtain it locally from Mr J.W. Clayton, chemist, 28 Hindley Street. Within a year this had expanded to Mr Clayton 'and all leading chemists'.[27] Rubinstein began her attack on the Tasmanian market with blanket advertisements in the Launceston *Examiner*, which from November 1904 stated that Valaze was 'obtainable at all leading chemists', and later 'all leading chemists in Tasmania'. Readers of *The Mercury* in Hobart were soon enjoined to 'ask your chemist to write to Mlle H. Rubinstein & Co., 274 Collins Street, Melbourne. Mention this paper and receive *Guide to Beauty* free'.

She neither crossed Bass Strait nor sailed to Western Australia; nevertheless, she put herself about in Perth and Kalgoorlie in essentially the same ways, eventually recruiting the services of Mrs Buscombe, Campbell Street, Kalgoorlie, as her Western Australian agent, and 'Madame Helen', 18 Newcastle Chambers, Murray Street, for her Perth 'depot'.[28] In this way, almost from the beginning, Rubinstein was reaching into all six states of the Commonwealth. However, all that was about to change.

7

New Zealand

The year following her return from Europe in September 1905 was a busy one for Helena Rubinstein. In February and March 1906, leaving Ceska Rubinstein and Lola Beckmann in charge of Melbourne, she made her first extended visit to five New Zealand cities, to which we shall turn presently. Beforehand, however, Helena Rubinstein made the move from the Fourth Victoria Building to 274 Collins Street. She also leased, decorated, equipped and opened a new salon in Pitt Street, Sydney, and proceeded thence to Brisbane for a second stint consulting alongside McGuffie's the chemist in Queen Street. The Sydney venture, known as the Valaze Massage Institute, was in a suite of rooms in Washington H. Soul Pattinson's Phoenix Chambers at 158A Pitt Street. On Friday 31 August 1906, Rubinstein held an invitation-only afternoon-tea *vernissage* in her new Sydney premises.

Establishing premises in Sydney so soon after having moved from old to new ones in Melbourne, and somehow compiling a list of no fewer than 120 carefully selected Sydney guests, while at the same time keeping tabs on Melbourne and Brisbane – all this took considerable planning and investment. However, Rubinstein's first foray into the New Zealand market was perhaps her riskiest to date. So far as we know, she did not know anybody in Auckland, Wanganui (Whanganui), Wellington, Christchurch or Dunedin. On 26 February 1907, *The New Zealand Times* mentioned that Rubinstein carried 'sheafs of flattering introductions', which is possible, but she had never been to New Zealand before.[1]

In the circumstances, it was prudent to treat the first New Zealand venture in February and March 1906, exactly as Rubinstein had approached Brisbane for the first time eighteen months earlier – as a series of relatively brief periods of consultation to test the waters, establish contacts and make an initial assessment of future prospects. As in Brisbane, Rubinstein needed advance publicity:

> Mlle Rubinstein, of Valaze fame, who returned to Melbourne recently from an extended trip to Europe, is about to visit New Zealand, to give ladies an opportunity of interviewing her on complexion matters, and to further introduce the many Valaze beauty-giving preparations, which have already such a wide sale in Australia and are also so well known in New Zealand. Her New Zealand tour will include all the large cities, and the leading chemists will be able to advise where she may be consulted. It is interesting to know that Mlle Rubinstein's visit to the Old World convinced her after careful and indefatigable inquiry, that Valaze stands supreme and alone as a skin food, a conclusion gratifying to herself and to her ever-increasing Australasian clientele. It is certainly a most exquisite herbal preparation for removing wrinkles, freckles, tan, and all such facial disfigurements. Among the new preparations secured in Europe are – a blackhead and open pores cure, a crema promenade for use before concerts, outdoor entertainments, etc., and a delightful preparation called Voskpasta. A result of Miss Rubinstein's visit to Europe is the establishment of a massage beauty institute in Melbourne, and it is intended to open branches in all the capitals of Australasia. New Zealand ladies are advised to make a point of seeing Mlle Rubinstein during her tour through New Zealand.[2]

This was the first salvo in an onslaught, a barrage, of advance publicity that appeared in the last week of January and through the first half of February

1906, and in newspapers all over the country, often in the 'medical' column, and mostly under the heading of 'Beauty for New Zealand Women': 'Ladies are advised to await Mlle Rubinstein's arrival.'[3]

We may discern a clear pattern that seems to have worked for Rubinstein. In the outermost of her markets, she targeted chemists, as she had always done, beginning with Miss Jones in Ballarat in November 1903. It is noteworthy, however, that Rubinstein never aligned herself with any chemist or chemists in Melbourne. Continuing in 1904 with Washington H. Soul Pattinson in Sydney and McGuffie's in Brisbane, she proceeded to follow the same strategy in New Zealand. Her advance publicity stated firmly that Valaze was available from *all* chemists, but failing them by direct mail order from 274 Collins Street, Melbourne. However, Rubinstein had no choice but to be far more selective.

It is not hard to imagine. She arrived in a new city or town. She sought out the right location and, within the space of a busy day or two, made her pitch to the most prominent chemist in the best and most commercially attractive street. Edwardian chemists were, like ours today, purveyors of many products, not all of them pharmaceutical. Throwing in your lot with a completely unknown newcomer 'consultant' was, for the chemist, a gamble worth making, especially because it might last only a few days. But if the product sold, and if the product kept selling, they had an opportunity to gain significant advantage in an already crowded and highly competitive market. If Valaze took off, a steady supply could apparently be obtained from 274 Collins Street or 158A Pitt Street, and on an ongoing basis. Rubinstein could, at every new point of consultation, rely upon ample advance press coverage, and report in her next destination impressive results accumulated in the space of only a few weeks.

And that is exactly what she did. Her itinerary was ambitious. Rubinstein arrived in Auckland on or shortly before 11 February 1906, and from the thirteenth to the twenty-fourth offered consultations free of charge on the first floor of Legal Chambers, 143 Queen Street *and* at Woollams' Chemist nearby. It was evidently a slow start, because on 19 February we find her setting out on an overnight excursion to Rotorua, which destination must have interested her enough to warrant a return visit on her way from Auckland to Wanganui on 1 March. Auckland was the only destination on this initial foray where Rubinstein rented her own space. In all subsequent New Zealand cities she instead took advantage of the hospitality of a chosen chemist. She must have concluded either that dedicated consulting rooms were an unnecessary expense, or that it was counterproductive to put herself in the position of being needed in two places at once.

From 3 to 8 March in Wanganui, where it was emphasised that this was her only destination outside the four principal cities, Rubinstein offered consultations at the Davies Pharmacy, Victoria Avenue. She proceeded thence to Wellington, consulting at Mr Salek, Chemist, 17 Willis Street. Christchurch followed (15–19 March) at Mr Bonnington's Chemist, High Street, and, finally, Dunedin for several days beginning on 21 March, consulting at Mr Wilkinson's, Chemist, in Princes Street. Rubinstein's days were tied to consultation and sales, but the sheer volume of advertising and advertorial in more than ten New Zealand newspapers has her conducting a solo media blitz of astounding proportions, planned well in advance, but adjusted from time to time midstream.

There are signs of overexcitement. We find her, for example, confiding to the ladies of New Zealand that the great Dr Lykuski lived *in* the Carpathian Mountains, and that while it was he who first discovered the miraculous properties of those rare herbs that grow there and nowhere else, it was Rubinstein, his compatriot, who had lately realised the discovery's full therapeutic potential. This was, at best, inconsistent with the earlier narrative, according to which Dr Lykuski's direct supervision of the Valaze formulation in Russia was key to its high quality and efficacy.[4]

The media blitz did not end when Rubinstein sailed away from Dunedin. It continued, and the final element of her touring pattern was, after she departed, to have set in place some sort of loose agency arrangement with each chemist. The Davies Pharmacy went so far as to place numerous advertisements warmly thanking the ladies of Wanganui for the enthusiasm with which they had taken up Valaze – thanks, somewhat shrill in their cheerfulness, that persisted for weeks in the pages of the *Wanganui Chronicle* and the *Wanganui Herald*. Despite her slow start in Auckland, Rubinstein left New Zealand with every reason to look upon this first sweep of the country as a resounding success.

She returned a little less than one year later, in February 1907. By then, the ladies of Christchurch could obtain Valaze from a Mrs Fletcher, 62 Lichfield Street, 'and all leading chemists'.[5] Woollams' in Auckland and Wilkinson's in Dunedin remained the local points of delivery in those cities, but on her second visit to New Zealand Rubinstein straightaway let, furnished, decorated and opened her 'Valaze Massage Institute' at 9 Brandon Street, Wellington, 'next D.I.C.' D.I.C. was a sizeable department store, the Drapery and General Importing Company of New Zealand Ltd, on the corner of Lambton Quay. At the same time, Rubinstein was advertising for a 'Young Lady Pupil'.[6] A week later, she added to the young lady pupil a 'useful Girl (young)'. Repeatedly, she underlined the fact that her Valaze Massage Institute was established in Wellington on a scale closely comparable with 274 Collins Street and 158A Pitt Street, but that, equally, the ladies of New Zealand could order direct from both Australian cities free of any charge for return postage.

Having established this local hub in Wellington, Rubinstein proceeded to consult, as before, in Christchurch and Dunedin. Upon her departure in April, she had successfully established a permanent presence in New Zealand, and she had settled upon her lady pupil. Thenceforth she placed her Valaze Massage Institute at 9 Brandon Street, Wellington, in the hands of a 'responsible representative', Miss Ward Gillespie.[7] The following January and February 1908, Miss Ward Gillespie undertook her own ambitious Valaze tour of New Zealand, but concentrating her energies, which were considerable, on the North Island. Miss Ward Gillespie was in Auckland, consulting with Mrs Collins, City Chambers, Queen Street. She was in Wanganui, consulting with Davies' Pharmacy, Victoria Avenue. She was in Palmerston North, consulting with Leary's Pharmacy. She was in Christchurch, consulting, as Rubinstein had done, with the same Mrs Fletcher, but at the new address of 12 Chancery Lane. In each case, the press heralded her advent with the exciting news that Miss Ward Gillespie's supply of Valaze had been personally despatched from Vienna and/or Paris by Rubinstein herself, and to her sole [*sic*] Australasian representative.[8] In New Zealand, we sense an extremely swift, well-controlled consolidation, and steady acceleration. In the space of not two years, Rubinstein rose from being a kind of itinerant merchant and emissary from Melbourne onto the altogether higher plateau of oracle and Maecenas enthroned in Paris and Vienna.

* * *

A long profile piece by 'Dorothy C.' was carried simultaneously by *The Sydney Morning Herald* and four other papers at the end of January 1909, beneath the headline 'An Australian Favourite's Splendid Triumph' and the subhead 'How She Conquered the World's Metropolis'.[9] This was about eighteen months after Rubinstein had taken up 24 Grafton Street, London. The interview is noteworthy also for carrying what is thought to be the earliest commissioned portrait of Rubinstein, by the minor London-based graphic artist Otto Hagborg.[10] However, its tone and content represent something of a declaration of conquest, and a model for most if not all later Rubinstein publicity.

> Walking down George Street the other day, I met Mlle. Rubinstein, smiling, alert, unembarrassed, fresh from her triumph oversea[s].
>
> I had heard from an old friend in London of the marvellous success that had fallen to the share of this woman whose name is known so well all over Australasia. My friend wrote, 'How interesting she is, how attractive, how charming, how piquant is the constant appeal she makes to one's native curiosity! How unerringly she has stirred, fascinated, and compelled the interest of the grandes dames of this mighty London! I had heard all this, and marvelled; hearing more fully, I marvelled more.'

The curiosity of Dorothy C.'s friend in London, to which Rubinstein's appeal was so piquant, may well have been genuine, but her claim that in less than two years Rubinstein had stirred and compelled the interest of the *grandes dames* of London strains at the boundaries of plausibility. Still, she had obviously made some headway at 24 Grafton Street:

> I was not surprised at my friend's enthusiasm. Right into the heart and core of the great Mecca of fashion and feminine allurement stepped our enterprising Viennese [*sic*]. Right there she opened an establishment so refined, so complete, so altogether remarkable, that no other European capital has known its like.
>
> Here, in short, was a woman whose success was deeply based in scientific principles. A close and shrewd student of history, literature, philosophy, Mademoiselle knew how indelible and lasting was the impression made by feminine beauty on the whole page of human character.

This is new. To date, Rubinstein's most important claim was that the efficacy of Valaze was the result of clinical expertise. Here, however, to scientific principles and a sound knowledge of art are added history, literature and philosophy and, as we shall soon see, an entirely justifiable claim to business acumen, such that the feminine beauty either maintained or restored by using Valaze was not only skin deep, purely a matter of appearance, but was, as well, written on the very page of human character. Beauty was not only power. It was also a matter of the soul. Hence:

> She knew, in fact, just what beauty was worth to women. And she set herself to learn, in laboratories and hospitals – in Vienna, Berlin, Paris, St Petersburg, and elsewhere – how chemistry and hygienics could be most surely and safely enlisted in Beauty's service. With unremitting industry she combined remarkable business acumen. She could do no other than succeed.

On the whole, then, it was a very notable woman I met that warmish afternoon in George Street. She took me to her hotel, and with a reassuring gesture sat down to hear me talk.

'Mademoiselle,' I said, plunging, 'you are a very wonderful woman.'

'Ah, don't!' said she. 'There is nothing more distasteful to me than speaking of myself.'

Obviously managing to suppress this admirable instinct and withstanding, thus far, Dorothy C.'s hard-hitting conflict journalism, Rubinstein continued:

'But no! – Let me tell you, rather, how very glad I am to revisit Australasia, where I made my first success, where everyone was so ver' kind. I would far sooner –'

I interrupted. I told her that she was not there to be evasive. I said my visit was essentially professional. I said friendship was all very well; but I wanted to know things.

'Since you insist, then,' said she dubiously, 'I shall talk what you call shop. I have followed with all scruples the adage – "Be sure you are right, and then go ahead." That is why I succeed. Years ago, when I secured sole control of the Valaze Complexion Treatments, I knew I had a good thing – oh, but the best! Since then, Valaze is known to women of refinement through all the world. I knew that these Valaze specialties were of no obscure origin, but the fine fruit of the best thought and experience of scientists whose names are almost sacred in enlightened medical practice! I left home – straight from Vienna [*sic*] to Melbourne – and began. Why in Australia? you say. Because I wanted to put Valaze to the most difficult and searching test – the test of a tropical climate. Hot winds and aridity try the complexion; and I knew that Valaze would be best justified by the most trying conditions. If its worth were proved in Australia, its worth would be proved indeed. It was proved beyond cavil. From Melbourne the little jars of

Valaze set off in all directions across the world, as the demand grew – to New Zealand, to every nook and corner of this great Australia, to Fiji, to India, to Africa, to Turkey, to Italy, and – yes, to London and to Paris. So was the way paved for me to London, to the hub of all things. My success in London was partly made, you see, before I ever opened there.'

In her long interview for *Table Talk* in December 1905, Rubinstein had claimed to have introduced Valaze to London on her visit to the hub of all things in 1905, so this point may well have been true.

'At first, I thought of only a depot in London. But I soon found that that would not do. London was swarming with beauty specialists. They were in every street. They were practising this method and that. Some knew a little, and some knew nothing. They were selling compounds of all descriptions, nostrums of every kind – none possessing any special virtue, many causing positive harm. Then, London being only a few hours removed from Paris, there were scores of beauty doctors there. Discouraged? Ah, no. Here was the opportunity I sought.'

This is also new: opportunity. So far as I am aware, Rubinstein had never before explicitly couched her ambitions for Valaze in terms of seizing opportunity, although this is what she had been doing at least since the beginning of 1903.

'Here, also, should Valaze be tested severely, but this time by the hard test of competition. Only a good thing could compete successfully, and because Valaze was the best thing of all, I was quite confident from the start. Valaze had won with flying colours, despite the most extraordinary handicaps: I was all right. I was quite content to fling my fortunes into that mighty vortex. I did not fear the opposing armies of the other beauty specialists. Would victory be mine? I knew it must. It was not because I was reckless or optimistic; but only because I knew. I had lived with Valaze years enough. The battle began: diminutive Valaze, unheralded, against the serried hosts of charlatanism. In a month, Valaze had won all along the line. The noblest names of Great Britain were arrayed on my side. The most famous English actresses sent me letters of appreciation and thanks. My great establishment at 24 Grafton Street, in the fashionable West of London – twenty-three spacious lofty rooms, the Maison de Beauté Valaze – was thronged daily by the loveliest and most exclusive women in England.

'But there! why should I say more? Letters? Oh, I have lots of them. Here is one from [Gertrude,] Mrs Maesmore Morris, recently one of the greatest of Australian stage favourites, whose classic beauty is now proverbial throughout the length and breadth of England. She says, "I am so delighted to see that you have started a depot in London. For three years now I have been sending to Australia for Valaze, and it's joyful to think that I can obtain it here. I hope you will have all the success your truly wonderful crème deserves. I wouldn't be without it for the world, and my skin is not a bad advertisement, as you know."

'I show you that letter as evidence of what my expatriated Australian friends think of my Valaze when they are away from Australia, and have all of Europe's best preparations to choose from. I get scores of similar letters every day.'

And not another word would Mademoiselle say. But she showed me autograph letters from prominent women of every nationality – letters from Christiania [Oslo], from Constantinople, from Rio de Janeiro, from Paris, from New York – letters from every corner of Great Britain, from nearly every corner of the world – letters with crests, letters with coronets, letters bearing Royal arms – letters asking for appointments, ordering preparations, expressing thanks.

Setting aside her sizeable portmanteau of coronetted correspondence, Helena Rubinstein goes on (at comparable length) to outline her intention, prior to returning to London for the season, to visit New Zealand again; to revisit her establishments; to receive old and new clients; to introduce new preparations and treatments, such as 'a Russian balsam impregnation', and to alert women to the availability and usefulness of her new in-house booklet, *Beauty in the Making*.

The sheer flamboyance of most of Rubinstein's claims, here – valiantly made despite such strong and creditable reluctance – fail to clear an even modest hurdle of plausibility. Once again, the problem is one of time. In less than two years, from her arrival in London; the establishment of 24 Grafton Street; having made her even more fateful entrée to Paris; and taking into account her marriage to Edward Titus and their rocky honeymoon in the South of France, Rubinstein would have us believe that she had conquered the globe; lured even royalties into the warmth of her Grafton Street embrace, and reached as far as Constantinople and Rio de Janeiro. All that would come, or perhaps was already starting to come, but the truth at this date must have been far more prosaic. The myth she imparted with such thoroughness to Dorothy C. was intended solely for consumption in Australia and New Zealand, a shrewd and successful effort to compensate for her experimental foray into the Brisbane market, and to add momentum to 274 Collins Street, 158A Pitt Street and 9 Brandon Street, Wellington.

In 1906 there was nothing more to prevent Rubinstein from taking the measure of retail in Auckland, Wanganui, Wellington, Christchurch and Dunedin than had inhibited her expansion into the heart of Sydney barely a year earlier. Indeed, it was the similarity of New Zealand markets to those in which she had first established herself in Australia that must have persuaded her to straddle the Tasman Sea.

The view that mattered most to Rubinstein, on both sides of the Tasman, was the view at street level – the view of shops. That view was remarkably consistent whether she was standing in Collins Street, Melbourne; Pitt Street, Sydney; Queen Street, Brisbane; Brandon Street, Wellington; Chancery Lane,

Christchurch; or Princes Street in Dunedin. All but one of these thoroughfares were served by cable or electric trams. Prior to her departure for London in 1907, Rubinstein's business footprint, though rapidly expanding, was confined to shops or, at least, 'retail premises'.

Anyone who has ever worked in a shop will know the curiously hybrid experience of working at close quarters alongside neighbouring competitors, and at street level (or close to it). The shop forms part of the life of the street or strip or arcade, and depends upon it for delivering customers through the front door. Equally, however, the shopping street relies upon individual shops to drive, in concert, its commercial engine and to animate it. You cannot go window-shopping without shop windows to look into; and until recently you couldn't go shopping other than in shops.

Shopkeepers are often alone in their shop, but at the same time they form part of a relatively crowded mercantile community. That community feeds into the life of the street, but, viewed at intervals all day every day from behind the counter or cash register, the life of the street is both ever-changing and perennially the same. The passers-by may be many and different, but their various habits are more or less identical. Neighbouring shopkeepers also have certain shared interests and experience: the upkeep of contiguous premises or coordinating large separate deliveries when space is at a premium, or guarding against, ideally apprehending, the local thieves, grifters and vandals. The closeness and adjacency of shops can forge close bonds, during times of natural disaster, when confronted with a common nuisance, or in plain hard times.

Shopkeepers can also be bitter rivals. The closeness and adjacency that can hold shops and shopkeepers together can also, at the same time, amplify or escalate tensions that already exist between them, or make mountains out of mole hills, no doubt occasionally exacerbated by the gloom or anxiety arising from meagre takings, especially when the rent is due. All of this was doubly true of Edwardian shops and businesses, in or above many of which sole traders and their families also dwelt.

For the first five years, Rubinstein lived in this world, as she had during her childhood in Kazimierz, and later in Coleraine, Victoria. She thrived on its pressure-cooker intensity. We do not know if, in her consulting rooms at Glen's, the tinkling of a zither being played according to Max Albert's normal system, or the aroma of nutritious vapours arising from Alice Ward's basement (or the ringing of her telephone), or the drum-beat treadling of Mrs Dedman's sewing machines upstairs, or the more discordant of the many pianoforte or singing lessons being given simultaneously, ever got on Rubinstein's nerves. It would be surprising if they never did. However, she soon rose above the enclosed working world of the Edwardian shop simply by keeping premises in different Australasian cities and employing staff to keep shop *in loco* while she shuttled between them.

It is not hard to grasp the degree of skill and flexibility she needed to keep control of that enterprise and to maintain an increasingly complicated chain of supply, when communications between Melbourne, Sydney and Wellington were confined to the postal system and the wireless or cable telegraph, and while banking arrangements were fragmented. There were clients to cultivate, consultations to arrange, publicity to devise and propagate, celebrity testimonial to solicit and pay for. Rubinstein cannot have done all this on both sides of the Tasman Sea completely unaided, but the available evidence nevertheless suggests that the bulk of it she did by herself.

At length, in 1907, having set her sights on London since at least 1904, Rubinstein established herself in 24 Grafton Street, Mayfair – an elegant five-storied eighteenth-century townhouse facing Hay Hill, a stone's throw from Berkeley Square, once the private residence of the prime minister, Lord Salisbury. However, in making that move she had to be satisfied that she was leaving the Australasian company in a trusted pair of safe hands, those of her sister Ceska. Yet again, this entailed a considerable degree of risk. We have already seen that Ceska Rubinstein spoke little English at the end of 1905. Although she and Lola Beckmann must have made good progress in the meantime, upon her departure from Melbourne Helena Rubinstein needed an ongoing source of comfort. She may well have entrusted the task of monitoring her Australasian business to her Queen

Street solicitors, Cleverdon and Fay, or to a firm of chartered accountants who corresponded with them. In the years that followed, however, Ceska Rubinstein proved her worth.

When in 1914 Helena Rubinstein moved with her husband and two small children from London to New York, she put Ceska in charge of 24 Grafton Street and another sister, Pauline, in charge of 255 rue Saint-Honoré. Stella Rubinstein (later Stella Oscestowicz), the fifth sister, was drafted from Kazimierz to take Ceska's place in Melbourne. Much later, Stella succeeded Pauline in Paris.

Helena Rubinstein had planned her rapid expansion into Sydney, Brisbane and New Zealand even before her departure for Europe in February 1905, and she came back to Australia having already framed a plan ultimately to attack the London and Paris markets, and to do so fairly soon. From August 1904 at the latest, Rubinstein saw her eventual expansion into New South Wales, Queensland and New Zealand as part of a single strategy that had as its highly ambitious objective the twin lodestars of London and Paris.[11] She needed to grow the business fast. She needed adequate capital with which to finance 24 Grafton Street and 255 rue Saint-Honoré, which meant doing whatever she could to increase her revenues. In order to settle in London, she needed to become a British subject. She needed her Australasian footprint to remain profitable, indeed to become more and more profitable, and for all practicalities to elide as much as possible with what would become for a while her London headquarters.

Melbourne was a springboard, and on its own it might well have been a springboard into the heart of Mayfair. However, it made better sense to exploit that springboard in a number of preliminary, intermediate and mutually sustaining stages, and in rapid succession: first to Sydney, then Brisbane, Auckland, Wanganui, Wellington, Christchurch and Dunedin. It did not necessarily matter that the New Zealand economy was in 1906 so much smaller than the Australian, because, as we have seen, there was at this date a limit to Rubinstein's capacity to meet demand, such that even supplying Valaze to the ladies of Brisbane, Wanganui or Dunedin stretched her resources. But working in this way, on a manageable scale, stoked her ambition. If at this stage Rubinstein had contemplated much bigger targets such as San Francisco, Shanghai or Calcutta (Kolkata), she would have rightly concluded that she ran the risk of biting off far more than she could chew.

The New Zealand market, and thus a fully Australasian market, suited her because when the time came to make her move upon London, Rubinstein would do so with far greater momentum than if all she had to rely upon was 274 Collins Street alone. The promise of success in London did not necessarily depend upon being in possession of Helena Rubinstein Pty Ltd, a fully Australasian public company incorporated in the State of Victoria, but it definitely helped, if only because fledgling Australian and New Zealand corporation law was in lockstep with legislation enacted at Westminster.

Prior to her departure for London, Rubinstein gave one final interview to *Table Talk*. It amounts to an Australasian swansong:[12]

> 'Off again, Mademoiselle? Why, you have only just returned to Melbourne. What a bird of passage you are growing.'
>
> 'Yes, I must go at once,' the lady assures us in her most earnest manner, 'to arrange for bigger supplies of "Valaze." Why, I could not possibly fulfil a large order just now, no matter what I was offered.' She looks so bright and blithe and care-free as she says it, with her beautiful glowing complexion, that it is hard to realise she has fought the battle and established a business, turning over thousands of pounds in a few years.

Rubinstein had spoken to *Table Talk* about money on several previous occasions, but this last claim is on a different scale. If it was true that her turnover amounted to thousands of pounds, and that her most recent year's sales clocked in at a rough total of, let us say, £2000, based on the price of 5/6 or 6s per unit, she was selling roughly 7000 white porcelain jars of Valaze per annum, about 583 each month, and on average 135 every week, or

£40 worth. If we return to labour market figures published in December 1900 in *The Queenslander*, these weekly takings work out at almost twice the weekly wages of a male cook, or a little less than the upper estimate of the *annual* salary of a governess.[13] It was not a colossal turnover, but it was healthy – the more so because hers was a single-product concern. Rubinstein goes on to speak of Valaze having lately been in short supply, and this strong, steady and growing demand might well explain why. On the other hand, it seems likely that, however well she was doing, Rubinstein was talking up the numbers. For once, *Table Talk* may have agreed:

> An ultra-smart member of society she might be guessed, but a successful business woman, no. Still it is this wonderful energy of hers which has done the trick, and her invariable custom of never recommending anything she has not tested, and saying neither more nor less of a thing than it deserves. She is enthusiastic about 'Valaze', because she has known and used it from her schooldays and so have the ladies of her family. She explains: 'Russian and Polish women do not wait till their skin is bad or their complexion is going before they use a skin-food, but they begin early, so as to preserve it', and mainly to this fact she attributes their renowned complexions, for the climate is so severe that they really need something to keep the skin smooth and fresh.

Do not wait. Begin early. This brings to mind certain recent trends in cosmetic surgery, some procedures having been controversially urged upon younger and younger, mostly American, women on the basis that they will heal better and more quickly, and that the effects will last longer before needing readjustment or augmentation. Rubinstein was advocating essentially the same pre-emptive principle, but obviously without unnecessary surgical intervention. She was also able to exploit both extremes of severe climate: Valaze protected Russian and Polish women from the ill-effects of prolonged exposure to bitterly cold winds that blew off the Arctic or

Siberian tundra, and Australasian women from the severely ill effects of a 'tropical' climate, with its extremes of heat and dust and dirt. And demand was strong:

> 'I must go and arrange that the short supply of "Valaze" does not occur again. I have been writing and cabling to hurry it forward, and the last few mails have brought letters of explanation from the doctor. It sounds like a fairy tale, and I suppose it will scarcely be believed out here.'

It *was* a fairy tale, but it *was* believed. Perhaps this emboldened Rubinstein to provide further particulars about the good doctor and his present difficulties:

> 'The fact is,' he writes, 'the railways have been blocked by snow for months; thousands of soldiers have been employed clearing the line, but no goods trains at all were allowed to pass, only passenger traffic. In consequence there was almost a famine in many of the villages, and the poor peasants were perishing with cold and hunger for the want of food supplies. You can scarcely understand such a state of things here, but they do happen in Russia where the winters are so severe.' It is certainly little wonder, then, that the huge cases of 'Valaze' were held back, but it is a queer illustration of cause and effect, for fancy a series of train blockages in distant Russia affecting the wants of the women in Australia.

Yes, fancy. This news bulletin from Russia is something of a rarity, because Rubinstein was mostly content to allow Dr Lykuski to hover quietly in the background or, even when in the foreground, only as a named medical practitioner. Imposture is more likely to succeed the less concrete detail is permitted to flow from it. Here, however, she has Dr Lykuski writing from St Petersburg (not from the Carpathian Mountains), giving an account of the disruption of freight due to the severe Russian winter of 1906–07, and the lingering unrest that followed the revolution of 1905. Rubinstein proffers this as her explanation for the recent shortage of Valaze. Whatever the reason – demand outstripping supply, or else some production hiccough or bottleneck at Felton Grimwade around the corner in Flinders Lane – *any* shortage of Valaze posed a real danger to Rubinstein's company. And this was not the first time her supply chain had let her down. She regretted something similar in January 1905.

> 'There is another thing, too,' Mdlle Rubinstein adds. 'You must know I have been in constant communication ever since my last visit to Europe with seven of the most celebrated skin specialists and complexion experts in Europe.'

Orchestration and repetition: Rubinstein was careful to conclude by underlining the same point that she had made again and again in her publicity, with a dogged cheerfulness and consistency that modern marketing would describe as positive reinforcement: Valaze was the product of clinical expertise.

*   *   *

There is a dearth of pictorial material relating to Rubinstein's Australasian years. Almost all we have is the bright young woman in a straw hat who was photographed in Vienna at around the time of her departure for Melbourne in 1896. Dating from soon after 1909, however, a pair of nearly identical photographs herald an entirely new approach to her business, and to herself (figs. 20, 21). This was when Rubinstein first established herself in Paris, at 255 rue Saint-Honoré – at first an adjunct to Grafton Street in London. Newly married, Mrs Edward Titus posed in an exquisitely embroidered gown designed by Gaston-Lucien or Jean-Philippe Worth, with bold dark orchid motifs scattered across a complex lower register of pale floriate embroidery. The decoration of the bodice, rising from a tiny, cinched waist consisting of fine horizontal satin pleats, has something of the *Wiener*

Figures 20 & 21. Helena Rubinstein dressed by the House of Worth, Paris, c. 1909.

Sezession about it. Her bulky coiffure is upswept, and she wears a pearl necklace from which is suspended a large bejewelled pendant, in the then fashionable 'Renaissance' taste. Delicate pearl-drop earrings and a substantial pair of gold bangles on her left wrist complete the ensemble. She is photographed twice, with and without a complementary three-quarter-length cape, similarly embroidered. To date, the Fashion Institute of Technology in New York has been satisfied to describe both photographs as 'Helena Rubinstein, aged 18.' She was in fact thirty-six and a half. However, the interesting part is that there is an intentness to her calm facial expression and, I think, a self-possession that anticipates by almost fifty years the 'contained energy burning away behind her stillness' that Graham Sutherland observed in Rubinstein towards the end of her life. With the cape,

Rubinstein's eyes are cast down, but without the cape she looks straight ahead, and with disarming boldness. There is not a hint of coyness or show or self-satisfaction that might have arisen from the novel experience of being expensively dressed by the famous House of Worth in Paris.

When in 1913 Alice Ward sailed out of Sydney Harbour for the last time aboard Harland and Wolff's 'Jubilee Class' White Star liner the SS *Suevic*, she was sailing into a long, modest but comfortable retirement in Barnstaple, Devon. Six years earlier, and for the fourth time in eleven years, Helena Rubinstein sailed halfway around the world with radically different ambitions. She never contemplated retirement.

8

Business as Art

If Graham Sutherland's portrait of Helena Rubinstein would constitute a far more memorable encounter between a fine draughtsman, an exacting artist and his superb subject, paradoxically her greatest portrait was the one that never happened. When *My Life for Beauty* was published in London in 1965, Rubinstein was still expecting to take delivery of her portrait by Pablo Picasso. By 1955 she had known Picasso for more than forty years, and owned a number of distinguished early oil paintings, gouaches and a large *point de Beauvais* tapestry that hung in her 625 Park Avenue drawing room.[1] In 1938, Rubinstein described Picasso as 'the most interesting man I have ever met ... He writes well too and his conversation, when you can persuade him to talk, is witty and clever.'[2]

On two separate occasions, 16 August and 27 November 1955, the latter only six days after Artchil Gourielli-Tchkonia died in Paris and shortly before her eighty-third birthday Rubinstein sat for Picasso in his villa, *La Californie*, outside Cannes. One cannot help thinking of a comparable encounter some fifty years earlier between Picasso and a no less powerful woman, Gertrude Stein (1905–06, Metropolitan Museum of Art, New York). Rubinstein had known Gertrude Stein and Alice B. Toklas in Paris through the avant-garde publishing activities of Edward Titus.

By the 1950s, however, a decidedly unequal power relationship frequently existed between the universally lionised, by then enormously successful Picasso and his often much younger female subjects, women such as Marie-Thérèse Walter, Françoise Gilot and Jacqueline Roque – unequal, and steeped in undisguised sexual tension. Each for a while attained the dubious status of artist's muse, but according to Gilot it was not long before she went from being a goddess to a doormat.[3] Although on those occasions at *La Californie*, Picasso produced an impressive suite of drawings of Rubinstein, he seems to have been unwilling, even unable, to tackle her on anything like an equal footing. With Stein, the power dynamic had flowed in the opposite direction, from influential subject to youthful artist, on the rise but still emerging. Fifty years later, Picasso was temperamentally incapable of taking Rubinstein quite so seriously. The latter recalled part of their conversation:

'First, how old are you?' he asked.

'Older than you,' I replied, and this seemed to delight him. He then looked at me long and carefully.

'You have large ears,' he said. 'They are large as mine. Elephants also have large ears. They live for ever. We will too!' Then he put down his pencil and looked at me still more closely.

'The distance between your ears and your eyes is exactly the same as mine,' he shouted gleefully.

'What does that mean?'

'It means that you are a genius – just like me!'[4]

Whether or not Picasso was aware that he had met his match in Rubinstein is impossible to determine. He was certainly conscious that their friendship, often wary, extended far back into nearly forgotten territory, but whether he was intimidated by her wealth and power or by the fact that Rubinstein was in no way intimidated by Pablo Picasso – these are likewise difficult to gauge. As Keith Roberts described the encounter, 'at last, Greek met Greek' (fig. 22).[5]

Figure 22. Helena Rubinstein and Pablo Picasso at his Villa La Californie, Cannes, 1955, by an unknown photographer, possibly Patrick O'Higgins.

Rubinstein dressed for both occasions. In the first and second numbered studies in the sequence, her full pleated skirt is decorated with large seashells, perfect for the Riviera. According to O'Higgins, however – and far more suitable for November – 'under an opera coat quilted in shades of orange and lemon with calla lilies and sprigs of mimosa, Madame wore a medieval tunic of acid green velvet'. Over lunch, Picasso remarked: 'You look like a marvellous transvestite – '*un travesti*' – dressed for the *Bal des Quat-z-arts*.' 'I dressed especially for you. When do we start?' was Rubinstein's superb reply.[6]

When Picasso showed it to him, John Richardson thought that his dossier of quickly executed pencil and charcoal drawings was remarkable. However, nowhere in the group is there a drawing of the whole woman that might plausibly have anticipated his ideas for a full or three-quarter or half-length composition. It seems likely that Picasso had no intention of proceeding from his suite of drawings to canvas. He never painted the portrait. Yet the carefully numbered and dated sequence (with declarative Roman numerals), reveals a fascinating mixture of degrees to which Picasso engaged with but, at times, also eviscerated and even evacuated his subject. Most of them reflect a completely different approach from Sutherland's, playful certainly, but harsh, reductive and, as we have seen, verging on crudeness. (figs. 26, 27, 28)

Figure 23. *Portrait of Helena Rubinstein XIX* by Pablo Picasso, 1955.

We may agree that Picasso's Rubinstein folio exhibits a brilliance of characterisation that relies almost entirely upon sheer command over crisp authoritative line, and superb economy. The troublesome part, however, is the use to which Picasso put that brilliance of technique and characterisation. In XIV (27 November), for example, with fewer than five supremely confident fluid lines beginning with the ramus of her jaw, Picasso renders in silhouette a simple map of Rubinstein's head, coiffure, neck and three-quarter profile, but apart from her ear (and large earring) there are no facial features whatsoever. Her face is a blank. Picasso literally declined to face her. No doubt he would have insisted that in 1955 he was telling the truth about his octogenarian subject, and that he was not in the business of flattery. However, his truth was complicated and Rubinstein had no choice but to submit to its harshness. It is to her credit that she was more than prepared to do so. On his side, Picasso showed no such willingness to pay any such respect to Rubinstein, despite his glib words over lunch – from one genius to another.

* * *

The later years in which Rubinstein built up her global corporation, at first in London and Paris and then in New York, fall beyond the scope of this volume. Other biographers, above all Lindy Woodhead, have covered them exhaustively and well. Nevertheless, it is necessary at least to sketch the basic outline of her onward, upward trajectory so as to place Rubinstein's Australian years in proper context, and to bridge the fifty years that separate her arrival in London in 1907 from Sutherland's portraits and Rubinstein's final visit to Australia and New Zealand. After 1909, when her company was first incorporated in the state of Victoria, Rubinstein visited Australasia at not quite twenty-year intervals: in 1938, for a sort of extended working honeymoon following her marriage to Artchil Gourielli-Tchkonia, and in 1957.

In 1909, according to a single trifling notice by Pansy in *The Darling Downs Gazette*, Rubinstein had been seen at the races at Flemington, dressed in 'a rich black Ottoman silk Directoire coat, trimmed in the regulation way, with froggings of cord, cavalier cuffs, and handsome buttons, and the large pocket flaps over a pleated skirt of fine ivory cloth'. In 1938, however, from the moment the trans-Pacific *Monterey* docked at Circular Quay on Monday 31 October and Rubinstein disembarked, the local press coverage was blanket. That day she wore 'a Schiaparelli black cloth costume with four heavy gold buttons with Egyptian figures on them. Her black velour Suzy hat was finished with a narrow cyclamen ribbon.'[7] (Madame Suzy's boutique in the rue de la Paix was one of the most exclusive in Paris, and patronised by the newly married Princess Marina, Duchess of Kent, among other royals.[8]) Rubinstein took a suite at the Hotel Australia. Much of that press was enlivened with interest arising from Artchil Gourielli-Tchkonia's aristocratic credentials. In many respects, this was his debut. Did he play polo?[9]

Otherwise, however, the press was almost entirely preoccupied with Rubinstein's wardrobe, which was by then astounding in scale and scope:

> Madame Rubinstein is bringing with her to Australia a wardrobe planned and designed by Schiaparelli, Suzy, Molyneux, and Agnès. Her day and evening frocks will show her new mode for elegance and femininity with a strong Louis XIV influence, and will be of numerous metallic cloques, moirés, and the softest of woollens in ostrich greys, sleek blacks, port wines, russet, and seaweed greens.[10]

The Louis XIV influence did not preclude from the fertile imagination of Elsa Schiaparelli 'a short Patou pink evening coat reminiscent of the circus. Playful elephants stood upright on drums while trapeze artists swung gracefully from mid-air around the hem.'[11]

The ensuing busy social round suggests that Rubinstein had gone to some lengths to maintain, nurture and revive her Australasian contacts in the long meantime. In fact, there was a good deal of careful groundwork with press publicity even before her arrival, and during her extended visit. There are various references to the comings and goings of secretaries and publicity men in her hotel suite, the clattering of a typewriter and a constant flow of inbound telegrams from Europe, America and elsewhere.[12] The purpose of the visit was to stimulate or revitalise the Australasian business, and at a particularly uncertain time. Neville Chamberlain had extracted from Hitler the Munich agreement only a little more than a month earlier, and while for the time being the hopes of many nations were pinned on this promise of 'peace in our time', the international situation was nevertheless fearfully unstable.

A long and lavishly illustrated feature article appeared in *The Sydney Morning Herald* the Thursday before Rubinstein arrived in Sydney. She is shown working in her laboratory: the Lipnitzki photograph. There are also photographs of the interiors of the quai de Béthune, and a particularly strong focus upon her immense collection of jewels.[13] On the day of her arrival, *The Labor Daily* described Rubinstein as 'one of the most famous beauty specialists in the world', and reported that she was, in addition to being an art connoisseur, interior decorator and collector, 'a gastronomic expert'.[14] They explained that she had been 'a student from the University of Zurich', which claim the *Newcastle Morning Herald and Miners' Advocate* upgraded to 'graduate in chemistry' from the same university.[15] During a 'candid interview' by Helen Seager and A.F.D. Rodie in *Smith's Weekly*, Rubinstein let it be known that most of her 3000 employees were women, and that her annual turnover by then amounted to between £2 and £2.5 million.[16]

Rubinstein arrived in Melbourne on Thursday 3 November. She took a suite at the Stanhope in South Yarra, and 'spent a busy day seeing the Oaks Day races and greeting friends'.[17] The following evening, supported by Artchil Gourielli-Tchkonia, she hosted a cocktail party at the Menzies Hotel. 'She received her guests wearing, with her deep cyclamen lace tailored suit, a bougainvillea rolled felt toque, which had a chou of violets at the back, and her famous pearls and emeralds.'[18] One can only begin to imagine the startling effect that pearls and emeralds worn with deep cyclamen and violets must have had on the southeast corner of Bourke and William streets, Melbourne, in 1938.

Rubinstein paid an overnight visit to Adelaide on Wednesday 28 November, and over afternoon tea at the South Australian Hotel lost no time in providing to the Adelaide *Advertiser* 'some interesting cameos of her work and experiences', for 'talking anything but "shop" with anyone possessing such an extensive knowledge of the cult of beauty as the Princess is a waste of time'.[19] Rubinstein would have agreed.

Figure 24. Helena Rubinstein's Grafton Street salon, designed by Ernő Goldfinger, photographed in 1926.

Already before Rubinstein left Melbourne and Australia for good in 1907, she had turned what had previously been shops in Elizabeth Street and at 243 Collins Street into something different. 274 Collins Street became an 'institute', a place of consultation and treatment in elegant art-green surroundings. Pitt and Brandon Streets followed the same formula. That strategy, relatively modest at first, developed rapidly after Rubinstein moved to London and Paris. Thereafter, she insisted upon maintaining comfortably furnished, opulently appointed, well-staffed flagship salons (*'instituts' de beauté* Valaze) – to which access was perforce eventually restricted to the grand, the rich, the famous and the well-connected, so as to create widespread fascination with her products. There she adapted the by now familiar white-coated theatre of 'consultation', 'diagnosis' and 'treatment' to an atmosphere of pampered luxury within a design framework of sleek, chrome, up-to-the-minute hard-edged Modernism, a beguiling combination, albeit with a generous nod towards not entirely Modernist chandelier, sconce and velvet-plush sumptuousness. (figs. 29, 30) In fact, in later years the vast bulk of her products were sold through department stores, so the flagship salons worked mostly as an important tool for marketing and promotion, forming picture windows into a world of beauty to which Rubinstein's products promised relatively easy access.[20]

Figure 25. *Heroic Noon* and *Evening*, murals for 625 Park Avenue by Salvador Dalí, 1942.

We have seen *Table Talk* in May 1907 guessing that she could have been mistaken for 'an ultra-smart member of society', but as we have seen, this was in Australasia a late-breaking development. However, like her ultra-smart salons, Rubinstein's own smartness, social and sartorial, increased rapidly. It seems in Paris in the early 1920s, she was taken up by the celebrated Polish pianist and hostess Misia Sert, whom the writer Paul Morand once described as a 'collector of geniuses, all of them in love with her'. Those artistic and literary connections that Rubinstein had not already made through her marriage to Edward Titus duly came through the Pygmalion-like guidance of Sert in the charged atmosphere of her Bohemian Paris salon, as they would for Coco Chanel not long afterwards – or so it has been asserted.[21] This may be giving Sert entirely too much credit, however two of the famous men Rubinstein certainly did encounter through her (on separate occasions) were Marcel Proust and Salvador Dalí. Not long before he died, Proust quizzed Rubinstein at length about how she thought a duchess would apply her make-up. Much later, in 1942, Rubinstein commissioned Dalí to paint three murals for a room in her triplex at 625 Park Avenue (fig. 25). Then, in 1943, she agreed to let him paint her portrait for an unabashedly commercial exhibition of mostly 'society' portraits at Knoedler's. (plate 8) Cut off from Europe, Dalí needed the money.

Dalí seems to have formed the impression that there was in Rubinstein and her surroundings a good deal of surrealism at play. In his book *The Unspeakable Confessions of Salvador Dalí* (1977), Dalí claimed that by 1942 Rubinstein was worth $100 million, and 'plastered more than 50 percent of the feminine sex in a carapace of illusions that remade their faces as well as their souls'. We have much earlier encountered Roderick Cameron employing that same term, a *carapace* (of, in that case, 'glitter'), in connection with the Beaverbrook version of Sutherland's portrait of Rubinstein. Referring to the armature of a tortoise, crustacean or arachnid, 'carapace' implies hardness and protection or defence. In her bedroom at 625 Park Avenue, where Dalí claimed Rubinstein received him, 'she nestled like the minotaur in the heart of the labyrinth and waited for her prey in an immense transparent bed, the legs and incurved half-canopy of which were fluorescent'. That much was true. The lucite sleigh bed was famous, a bespoke piece of furniture that was designed by the Hungarian artist and theatrical set designer Ladislas Medgyes and built for Rubinstein in the late 1930s by the chemical firm of Röhm & Haas, manufacturers of Plexiglass acrylic for aircraft.[22] However, Dalí's description of Rubinstein lurking in her bed waiting for 'prey' is distinctly hostile.

Dalí also claimed he had never heard anyone talk so much about money: how much she had by then accumulated, and how much more she intended to make. He also noted Rubinstein's rich cargo of jewels, and the dubious fact that she wiped her nose on the satin sheets. He claimed she described Proust as 'a little Jew in a fur coat smelling of mothballs'. Much if not all of this may be taken with a pinch of salt, or filed away with Cecil Beaton, except that the relevant pages of *Unspeakable Confessions* demonstrate the degree to which Dalí, living mostly in Monterey, California, throughout World War II, separated from all the other surrealists, nevertheless appears to have derived much refreshment and fascination from Rubinstein. Unfortunately, the critical reception of Dalí's exhibition at Knoedler's, in which his portrait, entitled *Princess Artchil Gourielli* (*Helena Rubinstein*), hung prominently, was negative. The critic of *The New York Sun* went so far as to write:

> There is no exhilaration in the portrayals. Nothing but plodding, plodding, plodding workmanship and an infinity of detail. So much for so much. Even the attempts to laugh off the money go for nothing ... Princess Gourielli's face is carved upon a mountainside like the [John] Gutzon Borglum monstrosities out west [a reference to the monumental granite sculptures on the side of Mount Rushmore in Pennington County, South Dakota, 1927–41]. It's not at all interesting ... One's sympathies are all with the artist. So much effort is worthy of better direction.[23]

To be more accurate, Rubinstein's immaculately groomed but disembodied head is not carved so much as effectively mounted onto a steep rocky coastal promontory and, at a strange tilted angle, fastened there, Andromeda-like, by inescapable chains of her own emeralds.[24] She wears an expression of pristine cosmetic serenity verging on blankness, and towers thus over an attenuated flanking cliff-high female nude figure, while two further minuscule figures, some sort of combination of nymph and Cupidon, gambol on the rocks in the ocean shallows far below. It is a terrible picture, but Rubinstein liked it enough to buy it for 625 Park Avenue. It remained in the collection of the Helena Rubinstein Foundation until it wound up operations in 2011.

*   *   *

We have already spent a little time with Helena Rubinstein and Patrick O'Higgins in her suite at the Menzies Hotel in Melbourne in the early southern autumn of 1957, but it was in Sydney soon afterwards that she agreed to sit for the Australian painter William Dobell. Unlike Graham Sutherland, whose eminence as a portrait painter was undisputed in England (other than at Chartwell in Kent), by the late 1940s and 1950s Dobell felt himself backed into the corner of 'society' and boardroom portraitist. Whereas in 1956, Sutherland had not yet painted a major portrait of any female subject, in the southern autumn of 1957 Bill Dobell approached Rubinstein hard on the heels of having laboured for nearly two years on his portrait of another elderly female subject every bit as formidable, possibly even more so. Dobell's portrait of the pioneering feminist, journalist, writer, poet and radical Dame Mary Gilmore (Art Gallery of New South Wales, Sydney), was commissioned by the Australian Book Society to mark Dame Mary's ninetieth birthday.[25] If Dame Mary Gilmore tested Dobell, in due course he became obsessed by Rubinstein. Having made a number of drawings in her Sydney hotel suite, at sittings apparently spread over several days, Dobell rushed home to Wangi Wangi and immediately produced five small studies in oil on board. Through the years that followed, he created no fewer than eight full-sized portraits, of which the best known is the version acquired in 1964 by the National Gallery of Victoria in Melbourne, appropriately through the Felton Bequest, because in 1867 its wealthy Maecenas, Alfred Felton, had gone into partnership with Frederick Sheppard Grimwade to create the firm of Felton Grimwade (plate 9).

Like Sutherland, Dobell was riveted by a certain duality he immediately perceived in Rubinstein's character. She was, as usual, shy and diffident in private, and physically tiny – by her own account, even wearing high heels, she stood at not quite four feet ten.[26] However, obviously by sheer force of personality and hard work she was a powerhouse in the business setting. In public, Dobell thought Rubinstein seemed literally to grow in stature.[27] His assessment goes against many other observations, according to which Rubinstein was diffident and reserved in public, and equally withdrawn in private. In retrospect, however, Dobell's impression of his subject was far less awestruck than Sutherland's. One could argue, I think, that her flamboyant appearance made far better sense in the gilded environment of Claridge's and Grafton Street and the quai de Béthune than in Sydney, although Dobell had known London during the worst of the Depression, when he was 'really broke', and was far less easily captivated than Sutherland was by Rubinstein's form of transatlantic metropolitan glamour. No doubt we may read between the lines of Hal Missingham's introduction to the catalogue of Dobell's retrospective exhibition at the Art Gallery of New South Wales in 1964, namely: 'He is Australian in his utter disregard of the hierarchy of persons. Uncomfortable in the presence of those supposedly superior, he maintains a wonderful egalitarianism where the human and not the badge of office is the more important.'[28] Indeed, Dobell's post hoc recollection of his encounter with Rubinstein was, predictably therefore, quite different from Sutherland's:

> She was a very sad woman for all her millions. She still liked to show off her things as though she'd just been given them.
> For instance, every now and then she'd disappear and come out with another dress: 'Would you like to paint me in this?' – all over her arm. And honestly, over the arms of such an old woman it looked like

a scene in a gypsy fair. They were all frou-frou, although they were done by Dior and people like that.

She was pathetic when I first saw her in a Dior dress. It looked like an Australian man's dressing gown, and there's nothing worse than [an] Australian-made man's dressing gown. They're meant for comfort aren't they? Well, it just looked like that.

She said to me one day – she was asking me about travelling and reading – she mentioned several books and she said, 'Oh, but there are so many things still to read and I don't think there's much time left!'

This was Helena Rubinstein. She realised she was old and all her millions couldn't save her.[29]

It is safe to say that this all boils down to the difference in outlook between William Dobell and Graham Sutherland, not any inconsistency on the part of Helena Rubinstein. Yet there were also certain similarities between the encounters, Sutherland's in London and Paris and Dobell's in Sydney. When they first met their subject not more than a year apart, Sutherland and Dobell were roughly the same age, in their mid- to late fifties, as I am now. Each drew Rubinstein in the artificial, intimidating atmosphere of an extravagantly decorated hotel suite, before taking up the subject later in the privacy of their respective studios, and in her absence. The costume and jewels are strikingly similar in hue and texture and overall effect, even though those effects are in each case achieved by radically different means. The garment in Dobell's series is not Rubinstein's Balenciaga gown, but it *is* crimson and rich in texture and design.

In his small studies, Dobell seems to try out different combinations of jewels, in which the 35-carat square-cut emerald and diamond ring is clearly visible in the small Melbourne sketch, as well as the cabochon emerald drop earrings in the sketch at TarraWarra.[30] He settled upon these and a suite of accompanying emerald-encrusted bracelets, although one feels that for Dobell they were neither magnificent nor even sumptuous, but instead the occasion of a type of *Verfremdungseffekt* that runs parallel with a degree of antipathy towards her wealth and the sadness with which he associated it.

Following her departure from Australia for the last time, Rubinstein never saw any of Dobell's paintings other than in reproduction, after the Felton version won the artist the 1957 *Women's Weekly* Portrait Prize. The picture was reproduced in *The Studio* (London) in April 1958. We do not know what she thought of it, but I think she would have been even less pleased than she was when first confronted by Sutherland's portraits at Hecht's in the King's Road. Having reacted so strongly against the latter the previous August, and having for many years been especially self-conscious about her weight,[31] it seems likely that Dobell's exaggeration of the principal forms would not have gone down at all well. Nor, by any measure, is the likeness as faithful and precise as Sutherland's.

When in the summer of 1977, the Helena Rubinstein Foundation collaborated with the National Portrait Gallery in London on an exhibition of her portraits, it is hardly surprising that none of Dobell's portraits were included. Apart from the Canberra Sutherland, which then still formed part of the Foundation's collection in New York, the other portraits in the exhibition give a slightly unfortunate impression of thinness.[32] It is, at best, a mixed bag, but taken together the contents cover a long period: two portraits from before World War I, three from the 1920s, eight from the 1930s, three from the 1940s, three from the 1950s and a final one from 1960. Not surprisingly, the full sequence tends to map Rubinstein's evolving fashion choices, but a degree of flattery holds back the passage of time and ensures that in almost every case the likeness served Rubinstein's business interests – all, I should say, except for Graham Sutherland's.

* * *

In 1957, Rubinstein was everywhere. She was in New York, London and Paris, before she travelled to Australia and New Zealand for the last time in March and April. Accompanied, as usual, by O'Higgins, she went via Hong Kong and Japan, and it was there, apparently in Kyoto, that the young Andy Warhol,

Figure 26. 'Madame Rubinstein in Kyoto, Japan, drawn by Andy Warhol', 1957.

not yet twenty-nine years of age and halfway through an extended round-the-world adventure, encountered Rubinstein and drew her (fig. 26). Their meeting may have taken place through the good offices of Cecil Beaton, who, with Truman Capote, was also in Kyoto. Warhol was then still essentially a commercial artist and illustrator living in New York. Thus far, his graphic work was largely devoted to magazines, advertising and the design of shoes.

Coinciding with the Sutherland and Dobell portraits, and coming less than two years after Picasso's folio of pencil and charcoal drawings, Warhol's three surviving drawings are slight. The first, executed in ink on paper using his 'blotted line' technique, is a portrait of Rubinstein in a sort of Egyptological profile with, on the left, two formulaic geisha in full kimono, the foremost proffering Madame a teacup. A prominent, undulating longhand inscription with curlicues reads, 'Madame Rubinstein in Kyoto, Japan, drawn by Andy Warhol.' His subject's jet-black, inked-in coiffure elides rather obviously with those of the two geisha.

The other two drawings, one of which came up for auction at Phillips' in

2017, are done with ballpoint pen, and must have been executed on the same occasion as the first because Rubinstein is wearing the same dress and combination of jewels, including the famous pearls. In all three, Warhol lingers over her lips, eyebrows and eyelashes, but apart from laying emphasis upon her strong chin he does not appear to be in any way concerned with capturing an accurate or faithful likeness. Much like certain of Cecil Beaton's more heavily doctored portrait photographs, Warhol's drawings carve two or three decades off the precipice of his octogenarian subject's true appearance and great age. Still, whichever way you look at it, this constitutes a memorable encounter in the cultural and commercial life of the twentieth century.

Rubinstein's earliest commissioned portraits in about 1908 had all been for the purposes of publicity, all destined for publication. One was a fine graphic work by Paul César Helleu (fig. 27). Nearly fifty years later, Rubinstein was here playfully observed by an ambitious young man who would within a few years turn the world of contemporary American art, and soon

Figure 27. *Portrait of Helena Rubinstein*, 1912, by Paul César Helleu, originally reproduced in the May 1912 issue of *Le Théâtre*.

art everywhere, upside down. I have heard it said, and am inclined to agree, that for good or ill there is art before Andy Warhol, and art since. The same could be said about Rubinstein and cosmetics. As *The New York Times*' critic Karen Rosenberg observed when in 2014 the geisha drawing was last shown at the Jewish Museum in New York, 'It's a little moment of mutual admiration between two titans of art-as-business and business-as-art.'[33]

Mutual admiration may be going a little further than the drawings themselves permit. However, there can be no question that, when provided with pliant assistance, in old age Helena Rubinstein gladly shrank from that same precipice of true appearance. Being already alert to the fusion of art with business, and of business with art, one also senses that Andy Warhol – always a fast learner and, however briefly, seated alone at her knee – fully grasped in Kyoto the genius with which Rubinstein had for decades attained both of those satisfactory goals.

Epilogue

I began this book by considering the portrait in the Western tradition as a kind of paradox, the product of a real encounter between artist and sitter that took place in a room somewhere, and at a particular date or over a certain brief period. Yet from the moment it leaves the artist's studio, the finished portrait goes on a long and restless journey through hills of memory and valleys of forgetfulness. Graham Sutherland and Helena Rubinstein are in many respects themselves paradoxical. The sometime surrealist painter and printmaker, who after World War II was absorbed by the artistic challenge of capturing accurate likenesses, as he did with Rubinstein: the commercial titan who, creating and maintaining a startlingly flamboyant public persona, so often exhibited at the same time much reserve and diffidence. The bold singlemindedness with which she did business seems at odds with the scatter-gun eclecticism of her taste in art, furniture, design, fashion and jewels. Sutherland's larger than life-size portraits of Rubinstein are paradoxical too: especially, I think, the seated version in Canberra. The taut self-discipline and rigorous geometry with which the artist worked up such a relatively thin smooth paint film belies the gorgeousness of its effects of texture and colour and characterisation – richness wrought from thinness, and luminosity out of dryness.

In 1965, Rubinstein spoke of having at first hated the pictures. She had never seen herself in such a harsh light, but her perception of harshness belies the high-keyed clarity and superb colourism with which Sutherland conjured such sculptural effects out of his otherwise restrained flatness of technique – effects that Cecil Beaton noted at the time: 'depth and vitality and solidity'. Rubinstein saw herself as savage, 'a witch', yet she retained the Canberra version for 625 Park Avenue. A heavily doctored photographic montage, in which Rubinstein poses in front of a wall that is crowded with portraits of herself, portraits that she owned, includes the Sutherland painting (fig. 28). However, it is radically reduced in scale in order to accommodate all the others, merely for the benefit of the photograph – suggesting that whoever choreographed this arrangement, with Rubinstein's approval, had little regard for Sutherland's achievement.

The separate trajectories of Rubinstein and Sutherland carried them through crowds of people with whom it is impossible to avoid close comparison. This is why the disparate, often shadowy figures we have encountered along the way – people such as cousin Eva Levy, the Silberfeld uncles, the Metcalfes of Astonette in Toowoomba, Olive Keys, Laurie E. Smith, Alice Ward, H. Westall Guest, Madame Alexis, Abel Isaacson, Harry Thompson, Miss Ward Gillespie and the Siegenbergs of the Chicago and Winter Garden – assume such importance to this little narrative. Like the eponymous hero in Joseph Conrad's 1900 masterpiece *Lord Jim*, Rubinstein jumped over, past or away from all of them. She left behind their households, premises or *milieux* and, at times, their Australasian cities, towns and communities – successively, and with a degree of courage and an appetite for risk that boggles the mind.

For Jim, the downward jump from the deck of an apparently sinking ship was a fatal misstep, which he replicates at ever greater distances from the civilised world. For Helena Rubinstein, each jump, each departure, led her rapidly upwards, into greater and ever more powerful centres of influence, but with a consistency and continuity that are simply astonishing. For once, O'Higgins hit the nail on the head: 'Flight was her method. And flight fanned her ambitions and fed her energies.'[1] With every departure, Rubinstein pushed against successive obstacles, while, at the same time, drawing energy from them. Close comparison has therefore been our friend throughout this journey.

Figure 28. Heavily doctored photomontage, showing Helena Rubinstein with a selection of the portraits of herself that she owned and displayed at 625 Park Avenue, New York, c. 1958. From top, left to right: Salvador Dalí, Christian Bérard, Graham Sutherland, Roberto Montenegro, Marcel Vertès, Pavel Tschelitchew, Candido Portinari, Raoul Dufy, Margherita Russo and Marie Laurençin.

In 1964, the late Susan Sontag's now famous essay 'Notes on "Camp"' first appeared in the *Partisan Review*.[2] Sontag made no mention of Helena Rubinstein, and it seems highly improbable that Rubinstein was ever made aware of Sontag, or the essay, or even the concept of camp sensibility, which, as Sontag points out, had rarely been discussed in print. Instead, discussion of camp and the concept of camp itself were mostly restricted to a closed and secretive homosexual subculture. However, what jumps out and hits one over the head today is the degree to which, almost always passing through the prism of male observers and conforming to many of Sontag's observations, one could easily choose to see Rubinstein, her business, her self-presentation, her interior decorating, costume and jewels as almost quintessentially camp. 'Camp', Sontag wrote, 'is the answer to the problem: how to be a dandy in the age of mass culture.' The artifice, the exaggeration, the surface glitter, the thirst for glamour, the self-consciousness, the irony, the archness, the stylisation, the playfulness, the 'theatricalization of experience', the outrageously doctored portrait photographs, the white-coated performance in 'laboratories' – all these connect with the camp sensibility. So too, I think, do Sutherland's portraits of her, and in much the same ways. O'Higgins's handling of Rubinstein's ghosted memoir and his own memoir were both definitely camp. 'Camp taste,' wrote Sontag, 'is by its nature possible only in affluent societies, in societies or circles capable of experiencing the psychopathology of affluence.' The origin of the term appears to be literal, and therefore references appropriation: pitching your tent upon someone else's territory the better to pretend to own it for a while, and to transform it into your sandpit or adventure playground.

In one of her most suggestive *aperçus*, however, Sontag drew a sort of parallel between the action upon urban culture of, on the one hand, camp sensibility, and, on the other, what she described as 'Jewish moral seriousness':

> The peculiar relation between Camp taste and homosexuality has to be explained. While it's not true that Camp taste *is* homosexual taste,

there is no doubt a peculiar affinity and overlap. Not all liberals are Jews, but Jews have shown a particular affinity for liberal and reformist causes. So, not all homosexuals have Camp taste. But homosexuals, by and large, constitute the vanguard – and the most articulate audience – of Camp. (The analogy is not frivolously chosen. Jews and homosexuals are the outstanding creative minorities in contemporary urban culture. Creativity, that is, in the truest sense: they are creators of sensibilities. The two pioneering forces of modern sensibility are Jewish moral seriousness and homosexual aestheticism and irony.)

No doubt deliberately provocative, Sontag's analogy would nevertheless seem to have particular relevance to Helena Rubinstein. It brings to mind Picasso's equally provocative remark about the costume she wore at *La Californie* in November 1955: 'You look like a marvellous transvestite – '*un travesti*' – dressed for the *Bal des Quat-z-arts*.'

However, if we follow Sontag's original ideas to their logical conclusion, are we not in danger of, first, trivialising Rubinstein and her many achievements in business, and, second, attributing to her Jewishness a 'moral seriousness', much less a 'liberalism', to neither of which Rubinstein herself ever to my knowledge laid claim? You could argue that for decades Rubinstein did indeed create a 'sensibility', and even that 'Beauty is Power' was a kind of propaganda, but that neither the sensibility nor the propaganda derived from her Jewishness. Her portraits by Sutherland may strike us as camp, but they are obviously, as I hope I have shown, many other things also.

At the same time, I think it is important to acknowledge that this study positively and unapologetically rejoices in camp. History is written by individuals, and I will gladly affirm that my five-year swan-dive into the Edwardian and later worlds of Rubinstein in Australia and New Zealand would not have happened had it not been fuelled by numerous moments of personal delight arising from that form of nostalgia with which we retrieve often surprising, even bizarre flecks of brightly coloured detail out of the jumble of the past: the fact, for example, that in Collins Street, Melbourne, in

1905 you could take from Miss Fredman zither lessons according to Max Albert's normal system. Or those trapeze artists and playful elephants standing on drums with which Elsa Schiaparelli adorned Rubinstein's short Patou pink evening coat for Sydney in 1938. Or Alice Ward and her Egyptological Salon Charmazelle, or Dr Williams' Pink Pills for Pale People. The hundreds of hours I have spent navigating Trove, mostly in the peaceful hours before dawn, have been a joyous form of *Gedankenspiel*, of mind play. In other words, I am proud to own the camp sensibility, but to claim for it also a seriousness of purpose, one that is also other-oriented. Indeed, this book could be described as a sustained and unapologetically affectionate act of *regard* with respect to Helena Rubinstein: a complex, often contradictory woman who obviously celebrated difference and modernity, but from whom *regard* was so often and so stubbornly withheld, even at times by those closest to her.

Figure 29. Helena Rubinstein surrounded by bogus nuns on the set of Warner Brothers' *The Nun's Story*, starring Audrey Hepburn and Peter Finch, at Cinecittà Studios in Rome, 1957.

EPILOGUE

The past is not a foreign country. Coleraine in Victoria has hardly changed since Rubinstein arrived there in 1896, and Uncle Bernhard Silberfeld's weatherboard store and adjoining dwelling still stand at the western end of Whyte Street (on the south side). Three years ago, the local people were muttering gloomily about the recent drought, just as their predecessors did at the time of Federation. I spent some time standing on the platform of the pretty little railway station contemplating Helena Rubinstein's arrival, her passage through the small ticket office and out the other side, into the warm and thankful embrace of Eva Levy. Doubling back, my mind turned to her decision to leave in 1899, a year of *at best* economic uncertainty, and her bold determination to go her own way, alone, and never to return.

Figure 30. Helena Rubinstein with luggage, 1942.

Rubinstein would probably have succeeded in business no matter where she started her business, but the fact that she did so in Australasia was fortuitous. Other than the topmost tier, the social strata of Australia and New Zealand were, as we have seen, far more porous than the defining equivalents 'at home', where businesses like Rubinstein's tended to thrive only in London. From the beginning, however, Rubinstein grasped the value of operating in multiple markets. She travelled farther and far more often than most other Australian and New Zealand women, covering enormous distances by rail and ship, almost always unaccompanied. It is no accident that when she established her first public company in Melbourne in 1909, it was not a single enterprise, but that soon afterwards Grafton Street, Mayfair, became the hub for mutually sustaining branches of the same business in Paris and, a little later, New York. This was merely an expansion, albeit a vast one, of her *modus operandi* in Australasia, and it is striking that she never turned her back on the two little countries that allowed her to build that head of steam.

Figure 31. Helena Rubinstein with jewel case at La Guardia, New York, in 1946, boarding a plane bound for Paris.

EPILOGUE

Figure 32. Helena Rubinstein in Hong Kong, 1957.

By the time Graham Sutherland painted her portraits, Rubinstein, her corporation and their entire ethos and rationale were all under threat, the kind of threat that is impossible to imagine before it presents itself, fully formed and banging aggressively at your front door. Think PanAm. Think Kodak and BlackBerry. There were plentiful grounds for concern. The tight control Rubinstein had always exercised over the formulation, production, presentation and distribution of her products – to say nothing of maintaining a workforce of tens of thousands – was becoming ever costlier and more cumbersome. For all of its fifty-year success, her business model was beginning to look increasingly inelastic and not particularly nimble. It was becoming harder for her to *keep* control, more often than not from the famous fluorescent lucite bed in 625 Park Avenue. The prospect of diversification, meanwhile, of introducing cheaper lines in the face of aggressive competition or expanding into new markets, seems to have held little appeal. Instead, Rubinstein pressed on, and remained at the helm of the company until the end of her life, adhering to essentially the same business practices centred upon New York, London and Paris.

Having always been synonymous with that company, and the company for five decades having been so dependent upon the projection of her personal identity, Helena Rubinstein died at home in Park Avenue on 1 April 1965. She was ninety-two and a half. She had suddenly been brought low when she was badly hurt in a vicious burglary the previous year. She never recovered from it. The business did not survive her for long. Unfortunately coinciding with the 1973 oil embargo, the corporation was packed up and sold *en bloc* to Colgate-Palmolive for $142.3 million. Not seven years later, Colgate-Palmolive lobbed the Helena Rubinstein Corporation to Albi Enterprises Incorporated for $20 million, a shocking, humiliating discount. If, in its heyday, Rubinstein's company had ever had something as novel as a well-maintained risk register, it would surely have filled with dread any non-executive company director today. By the time Sutherland painted her portraits in 1956–57, Rubinstein had lost nothing *except* momentum. For the first thirty years, however, beginning in 1903, she had nothing to lose *but* momentum. With considerable generosity, Australia and New Zealand gave Rubinstein the gift of that crucial head start.

In the last few days before I finished writing this book, I spoke on the telephone with a dear old family friend, Moira Westfold. She was in wearisome covid lockdown in Melbourne, as I was in Canberra. Moira asked me what I had been up to lately, and I told her a little about this book. Without the slightest further hint or prompt from me, Moira straightaway described her vivid recollection of an occasion during her childhood in the early 1940s when she and her mother came from Geelong up to Melbourne and made straight for the Helena Rubinstein salon on the third floor of the Myer Emporium in Bourke Street. There, Moira's mother bought herself a stash of Valaze – 'you know, the one in the pretty little jar with two Greek heads in profile on the lid'. Moira used the correct pronunciation of Valaze and described in exact detail Rubinstein's original flagship product, as it was by then marketed. I was preparing to hand a finished draft of this book to my editor, pleased to be about to unfold for him an Edwardian pageant of our Australasian past, but thanks to Moira Westfold, 'the present quietly put its hand through the printed page of history and said, "It is here. It is now." History is not events, but people. And it is not just people remembering, it is people acting and living their past in the present.'[3] History is also Rubinstein's decision at the beginning of 1903 to register with the Commissioner of Trademarks in Melbourne the Polish label copy for her single product Valaze. That that product, long since repackaged and remarketed over and over again, should still be remembered with affection in Melbourne in August 2022, attests to the enduring reach and sheer scale of Helena Rubinstein's achievement.

Acknowledgements

My greatest debt of gratitude is to the three benefactors to whom this volume is dedicated, but to these I must also add the Chairman, Dr Helen M. Nugent AC, and successive members of the National Portrait Gallery Board during my tenure as Director (2014–19), without whose support and encouragement this modest work would not have been undertaken in the first place. Lately, however, the baton passed briefly to the National Museum of Australia, so to the Director, Dr Mathew Trinca AM, I also extend my warmest thanks. This is therefore a project born of not one but two national cultural institutions in Canberra.

As well, numerous colleagues and friends have read long portions of the manuscript – or the whole at very different stages – and have returned enormously helpful comments, suggestions and advice, either with a specialist eye for detail or else as 'cold' readers whose opinions I trust. Others have generously answered obscure queries. To all I am grateful: the Paris-based embroidery and textile designer Nadia Albertini; Rebecca Badenoch of the Melbourne firm of Culshaw Miller Badenoch Lawyers; Gavin Bannerman, Director of Queensland Memory, State Library of Queensland in Brisbane; Helen Bird of the Swinburne Law School in Melbourne; Jennifer Bott AO; Hamish Bowles, European editor-at-large for American *Vogue*; Christopher Breward, sometime Visiting Professor of Cultural History at the Edinburgh

ACKNOWLEDGEMENTS

College of Art; Jillian Broadbent AC FRSN; Eileen Chanin; Douglas Chilcott; Stephen Coppel, Curator of modern prints and drawings at the British Museum; Louise Doyle at the National Archives of Australia in Canberra; Dr Mary Eagle; my former colleague Sarah Engledow; William Farmer AO and the Reverend Elaine Farmer; Professor Belinda Fehlberg of the School of Law at the University of Melbourne; Ken Fitzgerald and Graeme Wallis of the Coleraine Local Historical Centre and Museum in Coleraine, Victoria; the Hon. Justice Stephen Gageler AC of the High Court of Australia; my former colleague Joanna Gilmour; Professor Diana Cavuoto Glenn, formerly of Flinders University in Adelaide; Sir Andrew Grimwade CBE; Michael Gronow QC; Fiona Gruber; Marguerite Hancock; Louise Hand PSM; Associate Professor David Hansen of the Centre for Art History and Art Theory in the School of Art at the Australian National University, Canberra; Dr Deborah Hart, Henry Dalrymple Head Curator, Australian Art, at the National Gallery of Australia; Philip Harvey; Professor Michael Hatt of the University of Warwick; my former colleague Bruce Howlett; Mellissa Huber, Assistant Curator in the Costume Institute at the Metropolitan Museum of Art in New York; Associate Professor Alison Inglis AM of the School of Culture and Communication at the University of Melbourne; Helen Ibbitson Jessup; Daryl Karp AM, formerly Director of the Museum of Australian Democracy in Canberra; Professor Anthony Julius; Daniel Katz of Daniel Katz Limited, London; Terence Lane; Paul Latimer of the Swinburne Law School in Melbourne; John Leroux, Manager of Collections and Exhibitions, and Celine Gorham, Registrar, at the Beaverbrook Art Gallery, Fredericton, New Brunswick; the Reverend Dr John S. Levi AC, Rabbi Emeritus of Temple Beth Israel in Melbourne; Stuart Lochhead, formerly of Daniel Katz Limited, London; Gregory Lubczenko; Patrick McCaughey; Karen Macdonald, Reference Librarian, and Simon Underschultz, Research Library and Archives Special Collections Officer at the National Gallery of Australia; John McPhee; Alastair Marks; Gaspard de Massé of the Service Archives at the House of Balenciaga in Paris; Joan R. Mertens, lately Curator of Greek and Roman Art at the Metropolitan Museum of Art in New York;

ACKNOWLEDGEMENTS

Dr Amy Meyers, formerly Director of the Yale Center for British Art in New Haven, Connecticut; Steven Miller at the Art Gallery of New South Wales in Sydney; the Hon. Justice David O'Callaghan; Barry Pearce, Emeritus Curator of Australian Art at the Art Gallery of New South Wales; my former colleague Stephen Phillips; Emeritus Professor John Poynter AO OBE, formerly Ernest Scott Professor of History at the University of Melbourne, 1966–75, and Deputy Vice-Chancellor, 1975–90; Dr Romita Ray, Associate Professor, Art History, in the Department of Art & Music Histories, Syracuse University, New York; Kelly Read; Georgia Richter; my former colleagues Margaret Shaw and Libby Coates in the National Portrait Gallery Reference Library; Dr Gene Sherman AM; Suzanne Slesin of Pointed Leaf Press, New York; Dr Geoffrey Smith; Dr Benjamin Thomas of Trinity College in the University of Melbourne; Daniel Thomas AM, Emeritus Director of the Art Gallery of South Australia in Adelaide; Hamish Trumble; Nick Trumble; Simon Trumble; Tom Trumble and Gabrielle Munzer; Gerard Vaughan AM, formerly Director of the National Gallery of Australia in Canberra; John Wares of Mr Wares in the Block Arcade, Melbourne; Daryl Watson; Moira Westfold; Jin Whittington, formerly Information Manager (Librarian) at the Art Gallery of South Australia in Adelaide; Katarzyna K. Williams of the Centre for European Studies at the Australian National University; Dr Mark Williams; my former colleague Ruth Wilson; Daniel Samotus Zbytek of the Embassy of Poland in Canberra, and Igor Uria Zubizarreta, Director of Collections at the Cristóbal Balenciaga Museoa (Fundación Cristóbal Balenciaga) in Getaria, Spain.

At a critical moment, Grant Hamston came to my rescue in the Trescowthick Information Centre at the State Library of Victoria in Melbourne.

In March 2019, a three-week residency in the writers' cottage at Bundanon, the late Arthur and Yvonne Boyd's magnificent property on the Shoalhaven River at Illaroo, New South Wales, allowed me to accomplish the chunky middle part of the job of writing. To the chairman, board, CEO and staff of the Bundanon Trust I extend my thanks for that superb gift of dedicated space, time, peace and quiet.

ACKNOWLEDGEMENTS

Through the second half of 2021, Cynthia Troup read and re-read the nearly finished manuscript and gave me enormously helpful editorial assistance, the effect of which was to coax me in the direction of seeing the wood for the trees. Here in Canberra, Sarah Martin, Genna Ward, Bill and Elaine Farmer, Matthew G. Robinson and Anthony Barhouche, and Will Hilton-Thorp and Ginny Hoy have through the past three strange years provided me with personal and practical support that is impossible to overstate.

I have been fortunate indeed to have been able to place my manuscript in the hands of the La Trobe University Press imprint of Black Inc. in Melbourne. To Morry Schwartz AM, Chris Feik, Denise O'Dea and the rest of the Black Inc. team, thank you.

To the extent that, as I said in the beginning, this volume seeks to correct numerous errors, and partly to fill in some conspicuous blanks, I have voluntarily raised the bar of accuracy to a somewhat bracing height. The conventional author's disclaimer is therefore more than usually necessary. Any errors or lapses of judgement herein are my own.

Afterword

Jaynie Anderson

Angus Trumble (1964–2022) was one of the most memorable writers on art that Australia has known. Angus was born into a distinguished family of Melbourne lawyers. His parents, Peter and Helen Trumble, were descendants of Scottish and Irish settlers in East Gippsland. He was the youngest of four sons, their genius baby brother. He went to school at Melbourne Grammar, where on graduating he won the Barry Humphries Prize for Liberal Arts in 1981, sharing certain abilities with the donor.

In 1982 he enrolled in a Bachelor of Arts degree, in fine arts and history, at the University of Melbourne, with classics and English as minor subjects. At Trinity College, where he resided, Professor John Daley remembers that Angus went in for the Wigram Allen Essay Prize, an award of some financial and intellectual significance. When Angus announced the title of his essay, 'A Marxist interpretation of Jemima Puddle-Duck', his peers were deflated by the title alone, which predicted inevitable success. Dr Adam Jenney remembers that later, when Angus was the secretary of the Trinity College Dialectic Society, he invited Barry Humphries to speak. As a gift, Angus gave Humphries a Trinity scarf, which Humphries loved and was seen wearing in his next television interview.

Angus graduated with first-class honours in 1985, receiving the Dwight Final Examination Prize in both fine arts and history, a unique achievement. He did equally well in his minor subjects, classical civilisation and English, which he dropped after achieving first-class honours in them. His final-year thesis was on the 'Iconography of the crucifixion in the aftermath of iconoclasm: the evidence of Byzantine cloisonné enamel'. This surprising choice revealed an enthusiasm for deeply religious art and for the complex problems of interpretation which were at the root of Christian experience. The acknowledgements in his thesis went far beyond thanking his supervisor, Margaret Riddle, and revealed a gift for cultivating friendships across the Faculty of Arts and with scholars overseas. Even as an undergraduate, Angus was a superb writer on art, always entertaining. After graduating he won a fellowship to be an intern at the Peggy Guggenheim Museum in Venice from 1986 to 1987.

When he returned from Venice, he was appointed *aide-de-camp* to the governor of Victoria, Davis McCaughey, from December 1987 until December 1991. McCaughey was an Irish-born theologian of great charm, learning and integrity. Angus blossomed socially and intellectually in his new role and wrote a first book, jointly authored with Davis and Naomi Perkins, *Victoria's Colonial Governors: 1839–1900* (1993). He was charming, ably abetting Jean McCaughey at the dinner table with conversation and on the croquet field, as she vanquished guests at Government House. There Angus met many remarkable people and realised he could successfully write about almost anything. Even here, as the Honourable Linda Dessau recounted at a memorial service for Angus at Trinity College, Melbourne, Angus created legends so strong that all future aides were given his advice (now to be found on his blog, *The Tumbrel Diaries*, under the heading 'A Day at Government House'). Previously Angus had been dressed by his mother, but from his Government House days he always stood out in a crowd, with his charming, inimitable sense of dress that he wore with aplomb on his tall, thin frame.

When Angus commenced postgraduate studies, he chose for his MA (1992) at the University of Melbourne the quirky and difficult subject of the exquisite eight panels, *tavolette,* representing the miracles of San Bernardino (1473) in the Galleria Nazionale dell'Umbria, one of which may be by Perugino himself; the others are attributed to his friends or workshop. The choice reveals that he was fascinated by beauty allied with difficulty, and reflected the curiosity of a quizzical High Church Anglican about proving miracles. Having won a trio of Australian scholarships (the Australian and Italian Postgraduate Research Award, the Lizette Bentwitch Scholarship and a fellowship from Trinity College) he went to the Hertziana Library in Rome, the most serious institution for Italian art history in the world, where he became the unofficial pupil of the director, Richard Krautheimer, a legendary German art historian, and spent one of the happiest years of his life, looking at Quattrocento Italian art in Rome, Perugia and Venice. Equipped with an MA in Renaissance art, in 1994 he won a Fulbright Scholarship to the Institute of Fine Arts, New York, always regarded as the birthplace of American museum directors.

I first met Angus Trumble in 1992, when he invited me to publish a lecture I gave on 'Rubens' eroticism provoked by David Jaffé's exhibition, *Rubens and the Italian Renaissance*' in *The Bulletin*, a periodical for the friends of the Museum of Art and the Department of Fine Arts. Angus was its editor, and he did not hesitate to illustrate the cover with a provocative detail of a white swan's yellow beak and fluffy neck penetrating Leda's mouth. Much later, in the four years that Angus was director of the National Portrait Gallery in Canberra, the gallery's biennial *Portrait* magazine became the liveliest art history journal in Australia. As usual, Angus elicited outrageous contributions and wrote many articles himself, including 'Study in Scarlet' (2018), which gave us a glimpse of this book.

Angus's museum career commenced with his appointment as associate curator (later curator) of European art at the Art Gallery of South Australia, Adelaide, from 1996 to 2001, where he curated some important and influential exhibitions. Two especially received international critical acclaim, *Bohemian London* in 1997 and *Love and Death: Art in the Age of Queen Victoria* in 2002, which resulted in an invitation to apply for a position at the Yale Center for

British Art. Years later Angus recalled that the curator of Asian ceramics, Dick Richards, had one of the best 'eyes' he had ever encountered and that his curatorial skills deeply influenced Angus.

At Yale, Angus curated fourteen major exhibitions, the first being on the draughtsman who accompanied Captain James Cook on his voyage in the Pacific, *William Hodges: The Art of Exploration* (2005). According to David Attenborough, Hodges was the most unjustly neglected artist of the eighteenth century, and his exotic scenes of the Pacific were revelatory. The most famous of Angus's exhibitions was *Edwardian Opulence: British Art at the Dawn of the Twentieth Century* (2013), celebrating the visual arts, creation, consumption, display and dazzling fashion during the reign of Edward VII, the eldest son of Queen Victoria, with remarkable loans from the British Royal Collection and other London museums. The brilliantly illustrated catalogue remains unsurpassed as an exploration of the period and it was enhanced by Angus's flamboyance.

While at Yale, Angus talked about his own writing process – how he needed to immerse himself completely and rub up against a deadline in a terrifyingly close way. This way, he said, he could tap into the energy and clarity of thought that were needed to find the shape of the words he needed. He explored his love of New York, describing with characteristic joy how much he loved driving into Manhattan, seeing the city open before him as he approached – and then hurtling through its streets, tapping into the city's energy. He was an energetic and generous colleague in Yale's art history department.

In 2007 Angus was diagnosed as HIV-positive. At that point, realising he was immune-compromised, he wrote what he described as 'an extraordinarily grandiose document', with detailed instructions for his funeral. At the end, he predicted various ways in which he might die, to be printed in the order of service: 'He had the honour to follow in the footsteps of those fine men and women who were infected by the human immunodeficiency virus but, somewhat ironically, died instead as a result of a lightning strike/ car crash/ terrorist incident/ absurd domestic accident/ non-sexually-transmitted coronavirus (delete whichever).' In the end, his predictions failed to come true, as he died of a heart attack.

Apart from his curatorial duties, he wrote two witty, exuberant books of social history, which were reprinted in numerous editions (Melbourne, London, New York), and in China: *A Brief History of the Smile* (2003) and *The Finger: A Handbook* (2010). He was immensely popular as a reviewer for *Apollo*, *The Burlington Magazine*, *The Times Literary Supplement* and many other journals. He had the knack of fearlessly exploring subjects in a way that was different to others.

In 2014, Angus returned to Australia as director of the National Portrait Gallery, Canberra, which he led from 2014 to 2018 with his habitual panache and remarkable wardrobe. During his directorship, he secured major acquisitions, oversaw the gallery's restructuring and presented many diverse exhibitions. He was elected a fellow of the Australian Academy of the Humanities in 2015.

In 2022, Angus was inducted as a fellow of Trinity College at the University of Melbourne, an honour of which he was extremely proud. His portrait by the exacting draughtsman Evert Ploeg has been acquired by the college. It contains many delightful symbols of *trumbology*, as he coined the cult of his family. Angus had earlier been portrayed by Yale-based artist Jonathan Weinberg in the pose of François Boucher's nude odalisque, a painting which members of his family all wish to inherit. The experience of sitting for a nude portrait surely encouraged the provocative 2015 exhibition *Bare: Degrees of Undress*, which explored portraiture, nudity and intimacy and was, as might be imagined, an unforgettable success.

Dr Felicity Harley-McGowan, an art historian at Yale, remembers a story Angus recounted about the day he walked out of the Center for British Art and found an elderly man fallen in the street. The man's vagrant-like appearance had attracted the attention of a police officer, but when Angus approached, he recognised a distinguished (then retired) professor of art history. It is easy to slip into a kind of reverie, now that Angus has died, about how he may have reflected on his own mortality in that moment, and on the fleeting nature of life.

Angus was a person of deep faith. Our work consumes us, the art drives us, and we hope that in writing about art we might contribute something to the greater good of humanity. Angus had an enormous impact – through his energy, his drive, his razor-sharp and beautiful observations, his seemingly boundless creativity. He was thankfully spared the faltering steps of his older Yale colleague, but he was taken too soon.

In the dramatic instructions he left for his funeral, Angus remembered meeting Olivier Messiaen at Government House. Among the moving hymns and prayers Angus chose, he determined that he would love to have, for the postlude, Messiaen's *Transports de joie*: 'something ethereal, very modern, completely mad and theatrical: let's go out with a bang and a wallop! But is there anyone in Canberra who can actually play it? Being a somewhat eccentric choice for one's own funeral, it might make sense to explain to the congregation exactly why I wanted it, but of course, if sheer practicalities more or less rule it out – no problem.' Messiaen did prove too difficult.

At the time of his death, Angus was aged fifty-eight, a senior research fellow at the National Museum of Australia. We will never see his like again.

Endnotes

Author's Note

1   HR, p. 23.

Introduction

1   In 1925, T.S. Eliot added to his *The Waste Land* (1922) a dedication to Ezra Pound, in acknowledgment of Pound's vital editorial assistance, as well as a phrase from Dante Alighieri, '*il miglior fabbro*', meaning literally 'the better craftsman' (*Purgatorio*, canto XXVI, verso 117). The compliment was originally intended for the late twelfth-century Occitan troubadour Arnaut Daniel.

2   *Postera crescam laude* (from the Odes of Horace, III.xxx) means something like 'I shall rise in the esteem of future generations.' This Latin phrase has been the motto of the University of Melbourne since 1854. See Trumble (a), p. 5.

3   Robin Givhan, 'Angela Merkel's Lasting Impression', *The Washington Post*, 15 July 2021.

4   For this insight I am indebted to Cynthia Troup.

5   As recently as September–October 1986, the Museu de Arte de São Paulo in Brazil could assert (with the full support of her company, which was taken over by Albi Enterprises Incorporated in 1980): '*Se para Jean Cocteau Helena Rubinstein era "Imperatriz da Beleza," para Toulouse Lautrec, Vuillard e Bonnard foi musa, para Auguste Renoir foi modelo, para Picasso, Matisse, Dufy, Dalí, Derain, Rouault, Braque…foi amiga. Helena Rubinstein foi una mulher de ciência, uma empresária e uma grande protetora dos artistas com quem conviveu e apoiou.*' (If to Jean Cocteau Helena Rubinstein was 'Empress of

Beauty', to Toulouse Lautrec (etc.) she was muse, to Renoir a model, to Picasso (etc.) she was a friend. She was a woman of science, an impresario and a great patron of artists with whom she lived and whom she supported.) São Paulo, p. 1. The claim about Henri de Toulouse-Lautrec is especially egregious. He died on 9 September 1901, just when Helena Rubinstein was working as a waitress at the Maison Dorée in Swanston Street and/or the Chicago and Winter Garden in the Block Arcade, Collins Street, Melbourne. Helena Rubinstein never sat for Pierre-Auguste Renoir, Vuillard or Bonnard. L'Oréal acquired the Helena Rubinstein brand in stages between 1984 and 1988. Although they still exist elsewhere and online, ironically Helena Rubinstein products are no longer available over Australian counters. At the date of publication it seems this may be about to change.

6 Gruber, *passim*.

7 Royal jelly: HR, pp. 86–7. Marriage to Titus: For reasons that are not entirely clear to me, Woodhead, p. 77, doubted Madame's own clear statement that, following his formal proposal at the Café Royal, she married Titus in London: HR, p. 39. Woodhead suggests instead that they were married in Sydney. However, the official record is unequivocal. Helena Rubinstein married Edward William Titus at the General Registry Office, Strand, London, on Tuesday 28 July 1908. Marriages solemnised at the Register Office in the District of Strand in the County of London, 1908, no. 102.

8 Netto, *passim*.

9 Parke-Bernet and Parke-Bernet (a), (b), (c), (d), (e), (f) and (g).

10 National Gallery of Australia, Canberra, 80.2285.

11 Hayes, *passim*.

12 https://trove.nla.gov.au/newspaper. See also Te Puna Mātauranga o Aotearoa National Library of New Zealand's https://paperspast.natlib.govt.nz/newspapers and the British Library's www.britishnewspaperarchive.co.uk.

13 Thursday 20 October 1904, p. 6.

14 'Overland Passengers', Thursday 6 October 1904, p. 5.

15 Section 51 (v) of the *Constitution of Australia Act* assigned to the Commonwealth power over telephone and 'other like services', which from 1901 fell under the purview of the postmaster-general's office in Melbourne. See Chris Healy, 'Telephone', in EM, p. 711.

16 Peter Collingwood, 'Radio', in EM, p. 587.

17 Although invented by the French in the middle of the eighteenth century, and originally used to describe much of southeast Asia and Oceania, the term

Australasia was by the time of Federation used on both sides of the Tasman Sea to describe seven British colonies *en bloc*: New Zealand and the six others that on 1 January 1901 merged to form the Commonwealth of Australia.

18   As regards the structure and content of such a mass of evidence, the social historian of Edwardian Australia may also now benefit from important recent work in the much broader fields of microhistory, lists, taxonomy and cataloguing. See, for example, Belknap, *passim*.

19   G.P. Walsh, 'Sands, John', in ADB, Vol. 6: 1851–1890, R–Z, p. 86.

20   S&McD (a), 1904, p. 21.

21   Queen Bee, 'Women's Home Industries', *The Australasian*, Saturday 1 September 1906, p. 523.

22   'Artist, Sitter and Portrait: Mr Graham Sutherland and Miss Helena Rubinstein', *Sphere*, Saturday 7 December 1957, p. 32.

23   New York: The Viking Press, 1971 (hereinafter *Madame*).

24   Ibid., pp. 289–90.

25   Ibid., p. 214.

26   See Rutland, pp. 132–3; Woodhead, pp. 36–54; Slesin p. 212. To Woodhead we owe a great deal for supplying much missing information about Helena Rubinstein's early years in Kraków. Far less reliable are Fitoussi and Brandon. See also Klein's important exhibition catalogue for the Jewish Museum in New York. Slesin contains much valuable, previously unpublished pictorial material.

27   Towards the end of the long period of research for this book, I chanced upon James Bennett's excellent and exhaustive blog https://cosmeticsandskin.com. This covers the whole of Helena Rubinstein's career: Bennett (a), Bennett (b), Bennett (c) and Bennett (d). With regard to her Australian years, Mr Bennett has obviously raked over the same ground every bit as thoroughly as I have, and sometimes far more so. He has also collated a wealth of visual material in connection with Valaze. Most importantly, he has accumulated a full list of Helena Rubinstein's products as and when they were introduced. His is a colossal piece of work which deserves to be applauded, and to which I am indebted.

28   Philip Ziegler, *Mountbatten: The Official Biography*, London: Collins, 1985.

Part I—Veni, Vidi (I came, I saw)

1   26 February, p. 5. *The New Zealand Times* was wrong about Alexander the Great. The Latin phrase *veni, vidi, vici*, one of the most famous from antiquity, does indeed mean 'I came, I saw, I conquered.' However, according to

Suetonius (*Iul.* 37.2), this was an inscription displayed in Rome by Julius Caesar during his ceremonial triumph over Pontus in 46 BCE.

1. The Sutherland Portrait

1 HR, p. 95. I have found no trace of any published remark comparing Sutherland's portraits with a 'Renaissance masterpiece', only with Diego Velázquez, which is pretty good. However, that unsigned notice in *The Listener*, 24 October 1957, is decidedly vinegary, and also describes Graham Sutherland as an English Giorgio de Chirico, an observation that was clearly meant to be withering.

2 Clark, p. 42. But see also Secrest, pp. 106–7.

3 Thuillier, pp. 60–78.

4 Hayes (a), *passim*.

5 Martin, pp. 175–8.

6 Woodhead, pp. 368, 467.

7 Julius, p. 13. Julius (a), *passim*.

8 It is of relevance, here, to note John Hayes's characterisation of Sutherland's portrait as being like 'a tanned, Indian idol with blue-black hair, heavily bejewelled …', Hayes, no. 17.

9 *Madame*, p. 227.

10 Ibid., pp. 227–8.

11 Ibid.

12 Ibid., p. 229.

13 Ibid., pp. 232–3.

14 Ibid., p. 186.

15 Cameron, p. 51, cit. Thuillier, pp. 167–8. For the euphemism 'middle European', see Kaplan, pp. 12–13.

16 Woodhead, p. 154, citing Vickers, p. 206; Mellor, p. 52, and Albrecht, p. 19.

17 Roberts, p. 459.

18 Berthoud, p. 60.

19 Clifford (a), p. 92.

20 NFSA, No. 1108390. https://soundcloud.com/nfsaaustralia/helena-rubinstein-interviewed, accessed many times.

21 Woodhead, p. 368.

22 Ibid., pp. 3–4, 13, 80.

23 Woodhead, pp. 13, 80.

24 Tassi, nos. 67, 68 and 69, p. 225. See also Man, nos. 62, 63, 64.

25 *Madame*, pp. 232, 230. Berthoud (p. 229), however, states that the Sutherlands first met Helena Rubinstein in Paris on 26 April 1956, and that Sutherland returned to Paris for more sittings in September.

26 Ibid., pp. 231–3.

27 Berthoud, p. 60 n. 8, 229. Sutherland's insurers eventually paid £2600. Ibid.

28 Hayes (a), nos. 59–65, pp. 63–5. Berthoud, p. 60.

29 14 April 1957, p. 18, cit. Berthoud, p. 230. See also Alley, p. 141.

30 Berthoud, p. 230.

31 Ibid.

32 *Madame*, p. 214. Hayes, p. 65.

33 Sutherland and Bacon were close friends in the 1940s and early 1950s, when the friendship became strained: Hammer, p. 1.

34 The picture measures 180.3 × 111.8 cm. Gift of the Beaverbrook Foundation. Acc. no. 1959–433. Beaverbrook paid £3,500 for the group. Berthoud, p. 231.

35 New York, Metropolitan Museum of Art: C.I.69.16a, b. Woodhead, pp. 153, 255.

36 Bowles, p. 25.

37 Parke-Bernet. It is tempting to associate one or either of the rings with lot 22 (p. 3) and lot 92 (p. 25), but the pearls are more safely identified with lot 84, pp. 22–3, the many diamonds being mounted in the platinum clasp which is not visible in the portrait.

38 Woodhead, p. 153–5.

39 *Madame*, p. 233. See also John Rothenstein to the Rt. Hon. Lord Beaverbrook, Tate Gallery, 1 October 1957.

40 *Madame*, pp. 233–5.

41 Berthoud, p. 230.

42 Included among these were the 35-carat square-cut emerald and diamond ring, lot 102 in Parke-Bernet.

43 Hayes (a), p. 13.

2. Embarkation and Landfall

1. National Archives of Australia, Canberra (NAA), A1, 1907/4551. The Commonwealth *Naturalisation Act 1903* specifically provided for naturalisation as a British subject, not as an Australian citizen. The concept of Australian citizenship did not come into being until the *Nationality and Citizenship Act* was given royal assent in 1948.
2. Poynter and Thomas, p. 18, favour the latter possibility.
3. Barnard, p. 28.
4. Grimwade, *passim*. See also Poynter, *passim*.
5. p. 49.
6. 'Toilet Hints', *Leader* (Melbourne), Saturday 14 July 1900, p. 39. For all of this I am indebted to Bennett (a).
7. According to the ship's manifest Ceska Rubinstein was seventeen (she was actually twenty-two), and Lola Beckmann, the daughter of Gusta Rubinstein's sister, Rosalie Silberfeld Beckmann, was nineteen. Ceska and Lola sailed from Bremen, whereas Helena Rubinstein joined the ship at Genoa, as she had in 1896. As for the missing years, Patrick O'Higgins puzzled over them without much success: 'This leaves a gap of several years unaccounted for in Australia by Madame Rubinstein in her biography. What was she up to?' *Madame*, p. 149.
8. Woodhead, p. 439.
9. *Madame*, p. 237, and Woodhead, p. 24.
10. Public Record Office of Victoria, Melbourne. VPRS 947, fiche 309.
11. Ibid., fiche 113.
12. National Archives of Australia, Canberra (NAA), A1, 1907/4551.
13. Marriages solemnised at the Register Office in the District of Strand in the County of London, 1908, no. 102.
14. 4 October 1957.
15. HR, p. 11.
16. Pope-Hennessy.
17. Pope-Hennessy (a), p. 56.
18. *The Age*, 9 July 1900, p. 1.
19. *The Age*, 2 June 1902, p. 3.
20. 'On and Off the Stage' *Table Talk*, 2 January 1902, p. 22.

21   Poynter, p. 476.
22   HR (a), p. 12.
23   HR, p. 13.
24   Woodhead, p. 31.
25   HR, p. 13.
26   Woodhead, p. 32.
27   HR, p. 17.
28   Ibid, p. 18.
29   Ibid., pp. 18–19, 24.
30   Woodhead, p. 33.
31   Fitoussi, p. 40; Woodhead, p. 35.
32   Glockemeier, *passim*.
33   Bradshaw, p. cxlv.
34   'The Prinz Regent Luitpold', *The Argus*, 17 September 1896, p. 4. HR, p. 21, almost trebled the duration of the voyage.
35   Jewish rites: *The Argus*, 1 June 1889, p. 1. Insolvency: 'New Insolvents', *The Argus*, 20 February 1892, p. 7. Reginald Michael Levy was born in Austin Street, Hawthorn (Melbourne), on 8 April 1890. He died in St Kilda East in 1971, aged eighty-one. Frederick Reuben Levy was born in Whyte Street, Coleraine, on 4 June 1891. He died in Murrumbeena in 1943, aged fifty-two. Theodore Harold Levy was born in 1893 or 1894. He died in Toorak in 1978, aged eighty-four.
36   *The Age*, 5 August 1896, p. 3. Eva Levy remained with her father for the rest of his life. Bernhard Silberfeld died in Robe Street, St Kilda, on 25 June 1923: *The Argus*, 27 June 1923, p. 1, 'in his 87th year'. He had sold the business in June 1911 – still 'Messrs Silberfeld Brothers' – as well as the premises and land in Coleraine: *Hamilton Spectator*, 24 June 1911, p. 4. In May 1913, Bernhard subscribed £10 to the 'Distressed Polish and Other Jews' Relief Fund': *Jewish Herald*, 7 May 1913, p. 2.
37   Woodhead, p. 33.
38   Bradshaw, p. lxvii.
39   HR, p. 21.
40   Ibid.
41   *Mail* (Adelaide), 3 December 1938, p. 36.

42 HR, p. 19.

43 Ibid., p. 24.

44 Ibid.

45 HR, p. 12. *Madame*, pp. 41 and 47; see also Woodhead, pp. 34 and 440.

46 Bernhard (formerly Baruch Moyzesz, born 1839/40), the eldest, set out in 1870 aboard the *Hampshire*, when he was about thirty. Louis (formerly Aryeh Leib Louis, born 1854/55) followed ten years later aboard the famous *True Briton*, when he was about 25 – he was fourteen years younger than Bernhard – and John (formerly Jacob Herz, born 1856/57) came six years after that, aged about 30, aboard the New Zealand Shipping Company's *Arawa*.

47 The ship's manifest lists him as Mr S. Beavsky, aged twenty. 'German Mail Steamer Karlsruhe', *The Argus*, 3 April 1899, p. 4.

48 Suzanne D. Rutland, 'Jewish Immigration, 1881–1933', in AP, p. 528.

49 Ibid., p. 529.

50 Suzanne D. Rutland, 'Jewry in Australia', in OCAH, p. 360, and Rutland (a), pp. 22–35.

51 Anthea Hyslop, 'Myer, Simcha (Sidney) Baevski', ADB, Vol. 10: 1891–1939, Lat–Ner, 1986, pp. 657–8.

52 Rutland (a), pp. 25–28.

3. Working with Children

1 HR, p. 22.

2 Scorching desert wind: Woodhead, p. 40. Maxene: Fabe pp. 21–2. Pioneering outback town: Woodhead, p. 38. Nicky Haslam, '"Helena Rubinstein: The Woman Who Invented Beauty", by Michèle Fitoussie – review', *The Spectator*, 13 April 2013.

3 Always from this address, at the end of 1882 Richards and Silberfeld advertised for 'waterproof coat makers; learners; also, 50 Buttonhole Hands': *The Age*, 20 December 1882, p. 1. A follow-up notice ten days later narrowed this field to 'girls wanted, to learn waterproof coat making': *The Age*, 30 December 1882, p. 3, and again on 8 January 1883, p. 1. Eighteen months later, Richards and Silberfeld were seeking 'Buttonhole Hands, first class', a 'slop cutter', a good machinist and 'tailoresses': *The Age*, 11 March 1884, p. 1; 21 March 1884, p. 8, and 5 May 1884, p. 1. A slop cutter was effectively a tailor of cheap, ready-made clothes.

4 'At L. Richards's, 126 Franklin Street, near Swanston Street – Apprentices wanted for waterproof coat making.' *The Age*, 9 January, 1885, p. 3.

5   *The Age*, 26 April 1887, p. 3.
6   16 December 1890, p. 4, and 18 December 1890, p. 4.
7   Poynter, p. 475.
8   National Archives of Australia, Canberra (NAA) A712, 1892/T 8137 (Bernhard Silberfeld, 1839/40–1923); NAA A712, 1892/U 8184 and NAA A712, 1901/O 9992 (Louis Silberfeld, 1854/55–1908), and NAA A712, 1895/A 5675 (John Silberfeld, b. 1856/57).
9   p. 15.
10 *The Herald*, 8 May 1947, p. 6, and *The Argus*, 9 May 1947, p. 2.
11 HR, p. 19.
12 By 1871, all the Australian colonies had enacted divorce legislation closely modelled on the parent *Matrimonial Causes Act* (1857). In Victoria, a *Divorce and Matrimonial Causes Act* was given royal assent in July 1861. The Act empowered Supreme Court judges to grant decree nisi divorces. This was followed by a *Divorce Act* that provided for more specific grounds – drunkenness, violence, desertion, etc. – and a consolidated *Marriage Act* (both 1890). Finlay, pp. 103–27.
13 Poynter, p. 475. *Madame*, p. 146. A girl who assisted Miss Crouch was Professor John Poynter's step-grandmother.
14 In 1837, John Bryan had been the first European to follow in the footsteps of the explorer Major Thomas Mitchell. As always, Helena Rubinstein was apt to imply a sizeable disparity in scale and distance. See Spreadborough & Anderson, p. 123. This location is very close to the Coleraine Racecourse, with which we have seen that Uncle Bernhard Silberfeld was closely associated as a steward since 1891.
15 HR, p. 23.
16 Kiddle, p. 434.
17 HR, pp. 23–4.
18 'The Wool Land', *The Sydney Morning Herald*, 19 November 1909, p. 5.
19 Woodhead, p. 38.
20 Brown, p. 202.
21 Fletcher, p. 231.
22 Clarke, *passim*. See also Turner, p. 12.
23 Clarke, *passim*. See also Gibbs, *passim*, and Turner (a classic), *passim*.
24 Writing to the *The Argus* on 4 January 1899 ('A Woman's Salary', p. 5),

'Penelope' opened the floodgates. 'Liberty' followed in *The Argus*, 12 January 1899, p. 6. See also 'Thirty Pounds a Year', *The Australasian*, 7 January 1899, p. 37; 'The Governess and the Cook', *Geelong Advertiser*, 11 January 1899, p. 3; 'Servants v. Governesses', *The Herald* (Adelaide), 11 February 1899, p. 6, and a harsh critique of 'Penelope' by 'Mosquito' in *The Bendigo Independent*, 7 January 1899, p. 3. According to 'Mosquito', '"Penelope" is not a hard-up governess at all, but a hard-up clergyman having a quiet, but sarcastic dig at the wealthier members of his flock for not better remunerating him for doing their work for them'.

25 'Governesses', *Table Talk*, 31 July 1885, p. 8. See also 'Tutors and Governesses', *Truth*, 18 November 1900, p. 7.

26 'The Misadventures of a Governess', *The Sydney Mail and New South Wales Advertiser*, 11 March 1899, p. 563

27 Fairbairn.

28 HR, pp. 24–25; *Madame*, p. 147; Woodhead, pp. 42–45, makes a valiant effort to beat a path from Meltham into the extended vice-regal household of Lord and Lady Lamington, however she is right about the Fairbairns' social connections in Queensland (p. 43).

29 This last point may be an allusion to the Fairbairns of Meltham and/or Burnside, 'out Western way' being technically applicable to Geelong but, as usual, implying far greater scale and distance. Iris, 'Valaze', *The Critic* (Adelaide), 9 May 1903, p. 27. Any doubts about how Helena Rubinstein managed to avail herself of the hospitality of Iris's regular column, 'The Gay Metropolis', may be dispelled by the fact that it was headed: 'Invitations to concerts and social events should be addressed to Iris, *The Critic*, No. 5 Detmold Chambers, Collins Street, Melbourne' or 'The Gables, Toorak'.

30 According to 'Woman's World', 'Mrs Metcalfe arrived today from Toowoomba, and is to be the guest of her sister, [Mary Frances] Mrs [Francis Cheney] Bolton ... (Indooroopilly) ... Mr and Mrs Steve Fairbairn, of Beaconsfield Station [at Ilfracombe, near Longreach], with their little son and his nurse, have arrived in town, having come by train from Bundaberg ... Mr and Mrs Fairbairn propose to pass the greater part of the summer at Merton, their seaside residence near Geelong': 'Social Gossip', *The Brisbane Courier*, 12 October 1895, p. 6. See also 'Golf Notes', *The Brisbane Courier*, 2 September 1901, p. 7.

31 Hancock (a), pp. 166–8; McCaughey, p. 145.

32 Alison Fairbairn married Captain J.A. Stewart Balmain of the 15th (King's Own) Hussars, aide-de-camp to the Governor-General, Lord Northcote, in

1906. Queen Bee, 'A Brilliant Wedding: Balmain–Fairbairn', *The Australasian*, 19 May 1906, p. 1188. Esther Fairbairn was a bridesmaid at that wedding. Later, she married Lieutenant-Colonel Leonard Wheatley DSO of the Argyll and Sutherland Highlanders, sometime military secretary to the Governor-General, Lord Forster.

33   Hansen, n.p.

34   'Toowoomba Police Court', p. 7.

35   Ibid.

36   There was also an older boy, Theophilus James (Theo), the only child of Mr Metcalfe's first marriage in 1889 to Isabel, *née* Taylor. The wealthy Taylors stood at the peak of Toowoomba society, but so too did the wealthy Brodribbs. Isabel Metcalfe died in 1890, eleven days after the birth of Theo, her only child.

37   p. 3.

38   1892, 4 Q.L.J. 145 per Lilley CJ, for which see also Macleod, pp. 253, 255–6.

39   David Carment, 'Groom, Sir Littleton Ernest', ADB, Vol. 9: 1891–1939, Gil–Las, 1983, pp. 130–33.

40   State Library of Queensland, Brisbane; John Oxley Library, Queensland Memory, Acc. 27296 (Box 15647), hereinafter Laurie Smith.

41   Ibid., pp. 94–5, 160–1.

42   Ibid., pp. 1, 22, 49.

43   *The Darling Downs Gazette*, 16 March 1907, p. 8.

44   Laurie Smith, pp. 85 (senna); 105 (castor oil); 63, 89 (mustard).

45   Frank Brodribb died suddenly after a fishing expedition on 28 June 1904, less than a fortnight before the diary commences on Monday 11 July. Mr and Mrs Brodribb were by 5 June 1904 installed at Kyora, their house near the beach at Southport, and had been intending to stay there for the winter months: *The Queenslander*, 11 June 1904, p. 9. Born in Hobart Town, Francis (Frank) Claudius Brodribb (1820–1904) married Ellen Louisa (1828–1905), the eldest daughter of Henry Baker of Upper Gower Street, London. The wedding took place at St Andrew's Church, Brighton (Melbourne) on 2 May 1860.

46   Long afterwards, José married first (7 July 1913) an Anglo-Irish peer, John Evans-Freke, tenth Baron Carbery (1892–1970). Lord and Lady Carbery had a daughter, the Hon. Fabienne José Evans-Freke (1916–2007), an unfortunate name for any child to bear. The Carberys divorced in 1919. Lady Carbery remarried (15 February 1922) to Basil John Montford Bebb (1892–1952). A son,

Simon Montford Bebb (1922–2008) arrived at the end of that year. Mrs Bebb died on 14 June 1977.

47 Laurie Smith, p. 181.
48 Ibid., p. 46.
49 Ibid., p. 48.
50 J. Ann Hone, 'Michaelis, Moritz', in Douglas Pike (ed.), ADB, Vol. 5: 1851–1890, K–Q, 1974, pp. 245–6. I am most grateful to Alastair Marks, a Michaelis descendant, for guiding me through this complicated territory.

4. Taking the Measure of Melbourne

1 Trumble (b), pp. 24–31. Lindy Woodhead's estimate of 2.2 million in 1901 (p. 45) is fanciful.
2 De Serville, pp. 82–105, and De Serville (a), pp. 15–41.
3 McNicoll, *passim*.
4 Blainey (b), p. 143.
5 In 1918, the Parliament at Westminster enacted legislation that (1) gave the right to vote to women over the age of thirty who met a property qualification, and (2) allowed women to be elected to the House of Commons.
6 Peiss, p. 95, citing HR (a), p. 331.
7 Hancock, pp. 81–2.
8 *Constitution of Australia Act 1900* (63 and 64 Vict. c. 12), Section 125.
9 4 CLR 949 (1906), p. 951. I am indebted to the Hon. Justice Stephen Gageler AC of the High Court of Australia for drawing my attention to this case.
10 Woodhead, p. 47.
11 'Overworking Waitresses', *The Age*, 4 January 1901, p. 7; *Prahran Chronicle*, 5 January 1901, p. 4.
12 'A Waitress's Wages', *The Age*, 17 May 1901, p. 3.
13 8 December 1900, p. 1192.
14 See in this instance the case of Bartholomew O'Callaghan, 'Police Court', *Geelong Advertiser*, 30 May 1908, p. 3.
15 Rita Ehrlich, 'Restaurants and Cafés', EM, p. 600. Blainey (a), pp. 399–406.
16 *Madame*, pp. 149–50. See also 'Cosmetic Queen: Visit is a Sentimental Journey', *The Australian Women's Weekly*, 3 April 1957, p. 15. Helena Rubinstein had spent some days in Sydney, and continued on to New Zealand. Her

previous visit to Australia was here said to have taken place in 1939. In fact, she arrived at the end of November 1938. See 'Beauty Expert's Hints', *Table Talk*, 1 December 1938, p. 38.

17 *Madame*, pp. 149–50.

18 'Boarding House Robbery', *The Age*, 1 December 1904, p. 12.

19 'The Maison Dorée', *The Sportsman*, 27 August 1901, p. 8; 'Fact and Rumour', *Melbourne Punch*, 22 August 1901, p. 18; 'The Maison Dorée Café and Restaurant', *Australian Town and Country Journal*, 2 November 1901, p. 56.

20 *The Age*, 8 March 1894, p. 2., viz. a detailed advertisement for the sale of Mr Siegenberg's property and furnishings at premises in South St. Kilda. He was presumably a casualty of the Depression of the 1890s. He made his will on 26 April 1897, died only a few days later on 8 May, and left everything to his wife: real estate £40, residue £2400.

21 'Weston's African Medical Wonder', *Ovens and Murray Advertiser*, 12 December 1896, p. 4.

22 'World of Women', *The Argus*, 26 September 1940, p. 8.

23 Interview with Emeritus Professor John Mulvaney AO CMG, presented by Robyn Williams and produced by Polly Rickard. ABC Radio National, 29 April 1999.

24 Mulvaney, p. 11.

25 'Ladies' Letter', *Melbourne Punch*, 21 September 1905, p. 420. This was obviously several years after Helena Rubinstein had left the Siegenbergs' service.

26 *The Argus*, 12 January 1907, p. 11; *The Age*, 12 January 1907, p. 5; *The Australasian*, 12 January 1907, p. 60.

27 *The Brisbane Courier*, 4 May 1909, p. 7; *Examiner* (Launceston), Monday 31 May 1909, p. 7; *The Mercury* (Hobart), Monday 7 June 1909, p. 7; *The Darling Downs Gazette*, Thursday 8 July 1909, p. 7; *The Bendigo Independent*, Saturday 31 July 1909, p. 10; *The Maryborough Chronicle, Wide Bay and Burnett Advertiser*, Saturday 14 August 1909, p. 7; *The Geraldton Express*, Monday 13 September 1909, p. 4; *The Ballarat Star*, Friday 1 October 1909, p. 4; *The Advocate* (Melbourne), Saturday 30 October 1909, p. 5; *The Traralgon Record*, Friday 5 November 1909, p. 6; *Euroa Advertiser*, Friday 5 November 1909, p. 3, and *The Daily News* (Perth), Thursday 13 October 1910, p. 5. The blitz was still going as late as summer 1914: *The Riverine Grazier* (Hay, New South Wales), Friday 6 February 1914, p. 4.

28 London: the author, c. 1908.

29 I have not yet been able to trace any surviving copy of this booklet.

30 Poynter, p. 476.

31 *Madame*, p. 150.

32 Blainey (c), pp. 203–22.

33 Max Albert (1833–1882) was a famous German (originally Bavarian) zither virtuoso, composer and teacher. 'Foreign Notes', *The Musical Times*, vol. 23, no. 476 (1 October 1882), pp. 557–9.

34 *The Argus*, Saturday, 11 June 1904, p. 9; *The Age*, Wednesday, 10 January 1906, p. 4.

35 *The Age*, Thursday 17 October 1907, p. 5.

36 HR.

37 Born in Frensham, Surrey, in 1852 or 1853, Mr Dedman next appears in 1881 as an insolvent restaurant-keeper in Adelaide. He then turns up in Launceston, Tasmania, in 1885 as a 'tobacconist', this time in the Bankruptcy Court whence he was discharged in December. At this point, aged thirty-two or thirty-three, rescue came to Mr Dedman in the form of marriage to a widow, Annie Theresa, Mrs Frank Marriott. In marriage, as in business, Mr Dedman was improvident. Mrs Dedman proceeded to bear him nine children. Unfortunately, having eventually moved to Ingham Street, Sydney Road, Coburg, in Melbourne, the first Mrs Dedman died there of a sudden heart attack on 22 April 1898.

38 Insolvent restaurant-keeper: *The Express and Telegraph* (Adelaide), Wednesday 24 August 1881, p. 1. Tobacconist in Launceston: 'Commercial', *Launceston Examiner*, Friday 27 November 1885, p. 2, and 'Commercial', Monday 14 December 1885, p. 2. Marriage to Mrs Frank Marriott: *Launceston Examiner*, Tuesday 15 June 1886, p. 1. Nine children: Six were still alive in 1920: Victor, Edith, Louis, Lilian, Marjorie and Claude. The eldest son and namesake was killed in a railway accident, aged seventeen, in 1905. 'Box Hill Railway Fatality', *The Argus*, Friday 3 February 1905, p. 6. Death of the first Mrs Dedman: 'Sudden Death', *The Age*, Monday 25 April 1898, p. 7, and 'Sad Death of Mrs Dedman', *The Coburg Leader*, Saturday 30 April 1898, p. 2. Remarriage to Anne Jean Baxter: *The Weekly Times*, Saturday 5 May 1900, p. 34. Death of Mr Dedman: Deaths in the District of Melbourne East in the State of Victoria, 1920, no. 11210. Senile dementia: Deaths in the District of Koroit in the State of Victoria, 1933, no. 12829. By this time her name is given as 'Ann Jane'.

39 *Melbourne Punch*: Thursday 2 November 1905, p. 621.

40 *Cyclopedia of Victoria*: Smith, p. 153.

41 Smith, p. 153.

42 Thursday 29 June 1899, p. 627. See also 'Engagements', *Melbourne Punch*, Thursday 10 November 1898, p. 455. On Thursday 21 December 1905 in St Mary's, Stawell, Miss Alice Monk, 'daughter of Mr and Mrs Frederick Monk, of Richmond' married Mr Arthur Nuttall, which seems to have brought to an end her business association with Alice Ward. See 'Weddings', *Leader*, Saturday 30 December 1905, p. 38. Their only child, a daughter (Lorna), was born on Thursday 4 October 1906. *The Age*, Monday 15 October 1906, p. 1. Mrs Nuttall died on Wednesday 15 November 1944. *The Age*, Friday 17 November 1944, p. 7.

43 'Fashion's Frivols', *The Critic* (Adelaide), Saturday 6 August 1898, p. 22.

44 *Melbourne Punch*, Thursday 20 January 1898, p. 58. Madame Alexis's earliest appearance seems to have been in 'Engagements', *Melbourne Punch*, Thursday 25 March 1897, p. 234. Her last appearance as 'Madame Alexis' is in *Melbourne Punch*, Thursday 17 May 1900, p. 478, but the Oriental Massage Company continued at the same address until August 1907. See *Table Talk*, Thursday 15 August 1907, p. 22, whereupon she and it both disappeared.

45 'A "Beauty" Tip for Cup Time', *Melbourne Punch*, Thursday 26 October 1899, p. 428.

46 London: Simpkin, Marshall, 1897.

47 'New Novel by Marie Corelli', *Evening Journal* (Adelaide), Monday 5 April 1897, p. 375. Nevertheless, the book enjoyed widespread success, soon inspiring colonial poets. See, for example, the terrible eight-stanza 'Reincarnation of Ziska-Charmazel' by J.G. Barker of Tasmania: 'Original Poetry', *The Queenslander* (Brisbane), Saturday 26 March 1898, p. 593. In 'Sporting Notes from Home', meanwhile, 'Robin Hood' reported in May 1899 that the thoroughbred racehorse Charmazel (K. Cannon) had run unsuccessfully in the Royal Two-Year-Old Plate at the Kempton Spring Meeting at Sunbury-on-Thames, Surrey: *The Australasian*, Saturday 17 June 1899, p. 1306. For Orientalism in colonial Australia, see chapter 20, 'Isis Unveils in Australia: Lemuria and Feminism', Docker, pp. 207–21.

48 'Fact and Rumour', *Melbourne Punch*, Thursday 30 October 1902, p. 622.

49 HR, p. 26.

50 'A Beauty Institute', *Table Talk*, Thursday 7 December 1905, p. 19. On 20 May 1892, *The British Architect* ('Notes on Current Events') had wondered, as indeed I have: 'What is "art" green? A certain lady, writing in the interests of artistic homes, tells us she had a prejudice against "art" green until a certain gentleman persuaded her into the love of it. Alas, what nonsense is talked in

the name of art! Pea green, olive green, emerald green, blue green, yellow green, and all the other greens – which green is "art green"?' p. 369.

51 *The Sydney Morning Herald*, Wednesday 26 April 1905, p. 10.

52 The other actresses included Emmy Wehlen, Gwendoline Brogden, May Blayney, Madge Fabian, Kate Cutler, Iris Hoey, Jean Aylwin, Phyllis Dare, Lilian Braithwaite, Irene Vanbrugh, Dorothy Ward, Mabel Russell and the Hungarian star of operetta Sári Petráss. Hunter Brothers: 'Beautiful Bracelets for Beautiful Wrists', *Wagga Wagga Advertiser*, Thursday 6 April 1905, p. 3. Stewart Dawson: *The Sunday Times* (Sydney), Sunday 31 October 1909, p. 12. Modern Art Jewellery: *Evening News* (Sydney), Monday 17 December 1900, p. 7. Robur Tea: 'Miss Nellie Stewart Calendar', *The Australasian*, Saturday 23 December 1909, p. 12. Dunlop Rubber: 'Beautiful Art Calendar for 1910 (Miss Nellie Stewart), *Melbourne Punch*, Thursday 9 December 1909, p. 33. Miss Alice Crawford: *Table Talk*, Thursday 18 March 1909, p. 27.

53 'A Woman's Letter', *The Bulletin*, vol. 26, no. 1326, 13 July 1905, p. 16.

54 *Melbourne Punch*, Thursday 3 August 1905, p. 165.

55 Ibid., Thursday 14 September 1905, p. 385.

56 'Complexions of Australian Girls', *Table Talk*, Friday 29 March, p. 15.

57 *Melbourne Punch*, Thursday 22 November 1906, p. 767.

58 Klein, p. 79.

59 Melbourne: *Melbourne Punch*, Thursday 23 June 1904, p. 23. Sydney: *The Sydney Morning Herald*, 21 May 1904, p. 14. Brisbane: *The Queenslander*, Saturday 21 and 28 May 1904, both p. 7. Perth: *The Daily News*, Saturday 27 August 1904, p. 6.

60 'How to Become Beautiful', *The Express and Telegraph* (Adelaide), Saturday 30 July 1904, p. 6.

5. Valaze™

1 National Archives of Australia, Canberra, Series A11731, 7834.

2 The original text omitted the Polish diacriticals. *Liszaje* literally means 'lichens', but blemishes more generally. I am grateful to Dr Katarzyna K. Williams of the Centre for European Studies at the Australian National University, and to Daniel Samotus Zbytek of the Embassy of Poland in Canberra for providing this clarification.

3 'Freckles. – To disperse them take one ounce of lemon juice, a quarter of a dracham of powdered borax, and half a dracham of sugar; mix and let stand

for a few days in a glass bottle till the liquor is fit for use, then rub on the hands and face occasionally.' 'Recipes', *The Manning River Times and Advocate for the Northern Coast Districts of New South Wales*, Saturday 7 June 1902, p. 2.

4   'What Freckles Show', *Ovens and Murray Advertiser*, Saturday 27 December 1902, p. 2. The same poem, apparently a Christmas cracker, was widely syndicated: *Benalla Standard*, 23 December 1902, p. 2; *The Traralgon Record*, 23 December 1902, p. 2; *Bairnsdale Advertiser and Tambo and Omeo Chronicle*, 25 December 1902, p. 2, and *Ovens and Murray Advertiser*, 27 December 1902, p. 2.

5   *The Darling Downs Gazette*, Saturday 28 June 1902, p. 5.

6   'A Cure for Freckles', *The World's News* (Sydney), Saturday 21 June 1902, p. 13.

7   'Didn't Want Freckles', Ibid., p. 24.

8   For all of this I am profoundly indebted to Dr Mark Williams, barrister and solicitor. Written communication with the author.

9   Vol. 19, no. 1 (May 1923), pp. 86–7, cit. Clifford (a), p. 88.

10 London: *Truth*, 1910.

11 '"Those devils in Washington!" Madame railed.' *Madame*, pp. 152–3.

12 I am indebted to Gregory Lubczenko for guiding me through this unfamiliar terrain.

13 *Madame*, p. 151.

14 HR, pp. 26, 28.

15 *The Argus*, Friday 27 February 1903, p. 8. This is the earliest advertisement placed by 'Helena Rubinstein & Co.' in a daily newspaper.

16 'What is Valaze?' *Table Talk*, Thursday 26 February 1903, p. 22.

17 *The Argus*, Saturday 14 May 1904, p. 17. A number of cheap jewellers and engravers, several of whom were Jewish, also traded in O'Connor's: Alfred Ashmore, *Mornington and Dromana Standard*, Saturday 1 May 1909, p. 22; C.J. Smith, *Leader*, Saturday 1 April 1905, p. 40; James Parry, *Jewish Herald*, Friday 20 March 1908, p. 8; Melen Myers and Frank Evans, *The Age*, Thursday 31 December 1903, p. 8. For Phillips the pawnbroker ('Civil servants, clerks, warehousemen, and others promptly accommodated'): *The Age*, Monday 3 July 1899, p. 10, and Monday 27 October 1902, p. 9. Mr Brocket the solicitor and a dentist, Valentine Jordan: *Leader*, Saturday 3 June 1899, p. 2. There were also Mr J.W. Porter, 'patent target maker' together with, conveniently, the offices of the Victorian Rifle Association, which latter fitted neatly with J.K. Smith's Sports Emporium next door. For Porter: *Leader*, Saturday 12 August

1899, p. 14, and the VRA: *The Age*, Saturday 24 February 1900, p. 11. S&McD (a) add to the mix Solomon Davis, gold broker (first floor); Lorenzo Myers, cigar manufacturer, and Albert Albertine, engraver, along with four 'manufacturing jewellers', all crammed onto the second floor. Cluster marketing in retail is nothing new.

18   *Table Talk*, Thursday 1 October 1903, p. 20.

19   Mrs Wilmer: *Melbourne Punch*, Thursday 11 April 1901, p. 23. I.G. Beaver: Isidor George Beaver (1859–1934) eventual architect of the Wattle Path *Palais de Danse*, which opened in 1922, a forerunner of the St Moritz Ice-Skating Palais (1939–82). Other architects in the Fourth Victoria Building included Robert Henry Solly (1883–1968); the Melbourne branch of the pressed-metal designers Wunderlich Limited, and G.W. Vanheems, who designed Vaucluse College, Richmond (1897–1904). Parisian School of Dress-Making: *The Argus*, Tuesday 8 December 1903, p. 1, and *The Age*, Thursday 20 October 1904, p. 1. The Fourth Victoria building society: *The Age*, Monday 30 November 1903, p. 9; Modern and Permanent Building and Investment Society: *The Argus*, 16 September 1904, p. 3; Hepburn Alluvial Mining Company Limited: *The Ballarat Star*, Wednesday 3 February 1904, p. 6, and the Automobile Club of Victoria (third floor): *Table Talk*, 24 March 1904, p. 23.

20   'Miss Helena Rubinstein', *Table Talk*, Thursday 4 August 1904, p. 19

21   *The Ballarat Star*, Saturday 28 November 1903, p. 4.

22   *Melbourne Punch*, Thursday 2 November 1905, p. 28.

23   *Leader*, Saturday 28 December 1907, p. 47.

24   But see Clark and Clark (a), *passim*, both of which (apart from Alice Ward and H. Westall Guest) point to important London antecedents.

6. To Europe and Back

1   'Local and General', *The Daily Telegraph* (Launceston), Saturday 1 April 1905, p. 4.

2   'Miss Helena Rubinstein', *Table Talk*, Thursday 19 January 1905, p. 23.

3   Ibid.

4   Barnard, pp. 42–3.

5   *The Northern Miner*, 1 December 1908, n.p.

6   'A Beauty Institute', *Table Talk*, Thursday 7 December 1905, p. 19.

7   'Beauty Culture', *Australian Town and Country Journal* (Sydney), Wednesday 11 December 1907, p. 67.

8   Bennett (a).

9   All four are in the collection of the Library of the Wellcome Institute for the History of Medicine in London, and are now digitised: Paschke, Unna, Lassar and Berthelot.

10 For estimates of distance, duration and fares, see Bradshaw, which reflects a vast continental rail network that had hardly changed in the previous ten years.

11 Ibid., p. lxv.

12 'Social', *The Brisbane Courier*, Saturday 8 October 1904, p. 14, and 'Social', *The Brisbane Courier*, Monday 10 October 1904, p. 2.

13 Duke of Cornwall and York: 'Rivals for the Duke – Sydney v. Melbourne', *The Bendigo Independent*, Thursday 14 February 1901, p. 2. Weather: 'Intercolonial Cricket. Melbourne v. Sydney', *The Sydney Stock and Station Journal*, Friday 16 March 1900, p. 4. Monsoonal rain: 'Weather Prophets', *Advocate* (Melbourne), Saturday 28 February 1903, p. 25.

14 John W. East, *Queen Street, 1900: A Study of the Victorian Architecture of Brisbane's Principal Thoroughfare*, Brisbane, 2020, p. 1.

15 'Golf', *The Inquirer and Commercial News* (Perth), Friday 5 May 1899, p. 14.

16 'Social Gossip: Personalities', *The Queenslander*, Saturday 15 October 1904, p. 9.

17 p. 43.

18 'Advertising Rates', *Balonne Beacon* (St George on the Darling Downs), Saturday 2 January 1909, p. 8.

19 See also HR, pp. 42–3, a suggestively similar trope.

20 'Comrade Mary', 'In a Woman's Mind', *The Worker* (Brisbane), Saturday 22 October 1904, p. 5.

21 *The Queenslander*, Saturday 30 June 1906, p. 13.

22 'Australians Abroad', *The Brisbane Courier*, Thursday 22 October 1908, p. 7.

23 'Le Beau Monde', *The Darling Downs Gazette*, Monday 22 February 1909, p. 8

24 'Entertainment at Menzies", *Melbourne Punch*, Thursday 6 December 1906, p. 840.

25 *Victoria Government Gazette*, no. 115, Wednesday 22 September 1909, p. 4263.

26 Ibid., p. 4315. At this date, under existing corporation laws in Australia, which were in lockstep with earlier ones enacted at Westminster, a proprietary limited company could have as few as one shareholder.

27 *The Critic* (Adelaide), Saturday 2 January 1904, p. 27 and Wednesday 4 January 1905, p. 16.

28 The Western Australian blitz began with *The Western Mail* (Perth), Saturday 15 August 1903, p. 40. Mrs Buscombe: *Kalgoorlie Western The Argus*, Tuesday 20 October 1903, p. 41. Madame Helen: *The Western Mail* (Perth), Saturday 9 January 1904, p. 41.

7. New Zealand

1 p. 5.
2 'Valaze', *The New Zealand Mail*, 31 January 1906, p. 26. But see also *The New Zealand Times*, 27 January 1906, p. 12; *The Auckland Star*, 23 January 1906, p. 6; *The New Zealand Herald*, 24 January 1906, p. 3, and *The Otago Daily Times*, 24 January 1906, p. 7. There are many others.
3 'Medical: Beauty for New Zealand Women', *The New Zealand Times*, 29 January 1906, p. 2.
4 'Beautiful Women Use Valaze', *The New Zealand Herald*, 13 February 1906, p. 7.
5 *The Lyttelton Times*, 2 February 1907, p. 2.
6 *The New Zealand Times*, 26 February 1907, p. 1, and *The Evening Post*, 28 February 1907, p. 1.
7 'Rubinstein Valaze Tour', *The Auckland Star*, 10 February 1908. 'Miss Ward Gillespie', *Wanganui Chronicle*, 4 February 1908.
8 Auckland: *The Auckland Star*, 11 February 1908, p. 3. Wanganui: *The Wanganui Herald*, 31 January 1908, p. 5. Palmerston North: *Manawatu Standard*, 31 January 1908, p. 5. Christchurch: *The Lyttelton Times*, 26 February 1908, p. 8. Personally despatched: *Manawatu Standard*, 31 January 1908, p. 3.
9 *The Sydney Morning Herald*, Saturday 30 January 1909, p. 10; *The Argus*, Thursday 28 January 1909, p. 7; *Table Talk*, Thursday 28 January 1909, p. 28; *Melbourne Punch*, Thursday 28 January 1909, p. 125; *The Australasian*, Saturday 30 January 1909, p. 293.
10 Klein, p. 57, incorrectly ascribes the drawing to the Swedish artist August Hagborg, but the version that was printed in *Table Talk* carries the clearly legible signature 'Otto Hagborg.'
11 'Miss Helena Rubinstein', *Table Talk*, 4 August 1904, p. 19
12 'An Interview with Mdlle Rubinstein', *Table Talk*, 23 May 1907, p. 10.
13 *The Queenslander*, 8 December 1900, p. 1192.

8. Business as Art

1   Another version of latter, *Secrets (Confidences)* or *Inspiration*, 1934–35, has been in the collection of the Barnes Foundation in Philadelphia since 1936. Parke-Bernet (a), lot 24, pp. 38–9. Included in the Parke-Bernet estate sale in 1966 were *Intérieure d'Els Quatre Gats à Barcelone*, 1899–1900 (private collection); *Tête d'un garcon*, 1906 [Paulo] (Carnegie Museum of Art, Pittsburgh, Pennsylvania); *Homme nu aux mains croisées* (gouache), spring 1907; *Etudes pour nu à la draperie – I and II* (Studies for *Les Desmoiselles d'Avignon*), 1907 (both Museum of Modern Art, New York); the cubist *Nature morte – verre et pomme*, 1911; *Figure – collage*, c. 1912–13, and *Guéridon avec compotier* (gouache), 1920 – an extremely impressive group. Ibid: *Els Quatre Gats*, lot 27, pp. 38–9 (see also Ocaña, p. 273); Paulo, lot 33, pp. 56–7; *Mains croisées*, lot 34, pp. 58–9 (Daix and Rosselet, no. 50, p. 200); *Nu à la draperie – I*, lot 39, pp. 68–9 (Daix and Rosselet, no. 82, p. 206); *Nu à la draperie – II*, lot 40, pp. 68–9 (Daix and Rosselet, no. 84, p. 206); *Verre et pomme*, lot 45, pp. 78–9; collage, lot 50, pp. 88–9 (subsequently in the Hope and Abraham Melamed collection, Milwaukee, Wisconsin; *Impressionist and Modern Art – Works on Paper*, Christie's, New York, 6 November 2014, lot 5); *Guéridon*, lot 53, pp. 94–5.

2   *The Sun* (Sydney), 3 November 1938, p. 32.

3   Christian House, 'A Magic Trick Explained', *The Art Newspaper*, vol. 28, no. 305, October 2018, p. 16.

4   HR, p. 96.

5   Roberts, p. 459.

6   *Madame*, p. 222.

7   *The Sun* (Sydney), 31 October 1938, p. 9.

8   'Madame Suzy, Magician of Millinery', *The Australian Women's Weekly*, 5 October 1935, p. 10.

9   Helen Seager and A.F.D. Rodie, 'The Prince and the Not-So-Paupered: Big Business and Romance Blend Easily for Madame Rubinstein. A Candid Interview', *Smith's Weekly* (Sydney), 12 November 1938, p. 11.

10 'Famous Beauty Specialist Arrives in Australia', *The Australasian*, 19 November 1938, p. 25.

11 'The World of Women: A Princess Unpacks Lovely Gowns', *The Argus*, 8 November 1938, p. 5.

12 *Smith's Weekly*, 12 November 1938, p. 11.

13 'Beauty and Business', *The Sydney Morning Herald*, 27 October 1938, p. 26.

14 'Famous Beauty Authority', *The Labor Daily*, 31 October 1938, p. 8.
15 1 November 1938, p. 3.
16 *Smith's Weekly*, 12 November 1938, p. 11.
17 'On Honeymoon Tour', *The Argus*, 4 November 1938, p. 6.
18 'Cocktails at the Menzies', *The Argus*, 5 November 1938, p. 31.
19 'Expert's Views On Beauty and Diet', *Advertiser*, 29 November 1938, p. 7.
20 Clifford, *passim*, and Clifford (a), pp. 83–108.
21 Klein, pp. 61–2.
22 Klein, p. 68. Daniel Thomas remembers clearly attending one of the Parke-Bernet sales in New York in 1966, when the illuminated lucite sleigh bed caused quite a stir. It appeared as lot 307 in Parke-Bernet (c), pp. 44–5.
23 *The New York Sun*, 16 April 1943.
24 Hayes, no. 5.
25 Heathcote, p. 37; Gleeson, pp. 197–9.
26 HR, p. 30.
27 Heathcote, p. 38.
28 Art Gallery of New South Wales, *William Dobell: Paintings from 1926 to 1964* (15 July–30 August 1964), Sydney: AGNSW, 1964, n. p.
29 Freeman, pp. 66–8.
30 Ibid., p. 74; Parke-Bernet, lot 102; for the earrings, see Slesin, p. 33, perhaps Parke-Bernet, lot 134; *cfr*. TarraWarra: Heathcote, p. 74.
31 Woodhead, pp. 28, 71.
32 Roberts, p. 459.
33 Karen Rosenberg, 'An Art Trove Built on Mascara and Cold Cream', *The New York Times*, 30 October 2014..

Epilogue

1 *Madame*, p. 154.
2 Susan Sontag, 'Notes on "Camp,"' *Partisan Review*, vol. 31, no. 4 (Fall 1964), pp. 515–30.
3 J. Bronowski, *The Ascent of Man*, London: BBC, 1973, p. 269.

Chronology

25 December 1872	On 25 December HR is born in Szeroka Street, Kazimierz, Kraków, in what is the northernmost province of Galicia in the Austro-Hungarian Empire (modern Poland).
c. 1892/93	HR leaves her parents' home and stays at first in Kraków with one of her Silberfeld aunts, Rosalie Beckmann. Soon afterwards, she moves to Vienna and lives with another Silberfeld aunt, Helena Splitter.
1896	In August, HR proceeds by train from Vienna to Genoa. She sails thence to Melbourne aboard the *Prinz-Regent Luitpold*. In September, she arrives at Port Melbourne and proceeds by train to Coleraine in the Western District of Victoria, by way of Ararat and Hamilton.
c. 1899/90	HR leaves Coleraine and lives and works briefly in Sandford, near Casterton, before leaving the region for good. She possibly serves as governess to the Fairbairn children either at Meltham, Gheringhap, near Geelong, or shuttling between Oma, Toorak, and another Fairbairn estate, Burnside (which was adjacent to Meltham).
1900/1902	HR serves as governess to the Metcalfe children at Astonette, Toowoomba, Queensland, then moves to Melbourne and possibly serves briefly as governess to the grandchildren of Moritz Michaelis at Linden, St Kilda.

She then works as a waitress, first at the Maison Dorée restaurant and oyster saloon in Swanston Street and then at the Chicago and Winter Garden Tea and Luncheon Rooms in the Block Arcade.

1902   HR prepares to establish her company in two upstairs rooms in O'Connor's Buildings, 138 Elizabeth Street, Melbourne.

1903   In February, HR registers her Valaze trademark and commences trading. On 1 October she moves to the Fourth Victoria Building, 243 Collins Street, and in early December she is consulting at Miss Jones's rooms in Camp Hill Chambers, Ballarat.

1904   In September, HR is consulting in Sydney at Washington H. Soul Pattinson's Chemist, Phoenix Chambers, Pitt Street. On 5 October she arrives in Brisbane via Wallangarra and Toowoomba and remains there for about a fortnight, consulting from a room above Messrs McGuffie & Co., Chemist, Queen Street. On 20 October she passes through Toowoomba en route to Sydney and is briefly reunited with the Metcalfe family.

1905   In February, HR sails to Europe on her fact-finding mission. In April, in her absence, HR advertises for the first time her Sydney business, this time in her own premises in Phoenix Chambers, 158A Pitt Street, presumably established immediately prior to her departure for Europe. In September she returns to Melbourne with her sister Ceska and her cousin Lola Beckmann, and moves to a suite of rooms on the first floor of W.H. Glen & Co.'s Music and Piano Warehouse (Glen's), 274 Collins Street, Melbourne.

1906   In February and March, HR travels to New Zealand and visits pharmacies in Auckland, Wanganui, Wellington, Christchurch and Dunedin.

1907   In late February, HR visits Wellington, opens a salon at 9 Brandon Street, and hires at least two staff, including Miss Ward Gillespie, 'sole Australasian representative'.

	In March and April she visits Christchurch and Dunedin. On 22 May she is granted a certificate of naturalisation as a British subject and shortly after sails to Europe.
1908	HR opens her first London salon at 24 Grafton Street, Mayfair. On 28 July she marries Edward Titus at the General Registry Office, London. The earliest commissioned portrait of HR is executed in London or Paris by Otto Hagborg and reproduced in *Table Talk* (Melbourne).
1909	HR acquires the Maison Champbaron and opens a Paris salon at 255 rue Saint-Honoré. She makes a return visits to Sydney, Melbourne and New Zealand, and in September Helena Rubinstein Pty Ltd is incorporated in the state of Victoria. In December, her son Roy Titus is born in London.
1912	In May, another son, Horace Titus, is born in Surrey, an event that probably gave rise to the commission of two lithographic portraits of HR by Paul-César Helleu, which appeared in Paris in the same month's issue of *Le Théâtre*.
1914	HR, Titus and their children move to New York.
1915	HR opens her first New York salon at 15 East 49th Street.
1916	HR opens salons in Philadelphia, New Orleans and San Francisco.
1918	HR moves her New York salon to 46 West 57th Street and opens a salon in Atlantic City, New Jersey.
1920	HR opens Boston salon.
1921	HR moves her Paris salon to 126 rue du Faubourg Saint-Honoré.
1926	HR incorporates her company in the United States.
1927	HR moves Paris salon to 52 rue du Faubourg Saint-Honoré and opens another in Milan.
1928	HR moves New York salon to 8 East 57th Street. In December she sells her controlling interest in the company to Lehman Brothers. She opens salons in Vienna and Toronto.

CHRONOLOGY

1929	HR opens a Madrid salon. In October, Wall Street crashes.
1931	HR reacquires full control of the company from Lehman Brothers.
1932	HR divorces Edward Titus.
1934	HR opens salon in Seattle, Washington.
1936	HR moves her New York salon to 715 Fifth Avenue.
1937	HR redesigns and refits her salon at 52 rue du Faubourg Saint-Honoré.
1938	In June, HR marries Prince Artchil Gourielli-Tchkonia in Baltimore, Maryland. In October and November she visits Australia and New Zealand.
1939	HR closes her Vienna salon.
1940	In February, HR moves her Sydney salon to 82 Castlereagh Street. She visits Mexico City and is photographed with Diego Rivera and Frida Kahlo.
1942	Salvador Dalí paints a portrait of HR in New York.
1955	HR sits for Pablo Picasso in Cannes. On 21 November, HR's husband, Artchil Gourielli-Tchkonia, dies.
1956	In May and September, HR sits for Graham Sutherland in London and Paris.
1957	HR visits Japan and while there is portrayed in at least three drawings by Andy Warhol. In March/April she visits Australia and New Zealand for the last time. In March she sits for her portrait by William Dobell, which he enters in that year's Archibald Prize; it is awarded the *Australian Women's Weekly* Portrait Prize. HR establishes the Helena Rubinstein Travelling Art Scholarship under the auspices of the Art Gallery of New South Wales in Sydney.

	In late summer she inspects both versions of her portrait by Graham Sutherland. In October–December Sutherland's portraits of HR are exhibited at the Tate Gallery in London; Lord Beaverbrook acquires one for the Beaverbrook Art Gallery in Fredericton, New Brunswick. HR retains the other.
1958	On 18 April, HR's son Horace Titus dies in Greenwich, Connecticut. Later that year, Frank Hodgkinson (1919–2001) is awarded the first Art Gallery of New South Wales Helena Rubinstein Travelling Art Scholarship.
1959	The Helena Rubinstein Foundation presents the Helena Rubinstein Pavilion for Contemporary Art in Tel Aviv to the State of Israel; in connection with this, HR lunches with Foreign Minister Golda Meir and dines with Prime Minister David Ben-Gurion.
1964	National Gallery of Victoria acquires William Dobell's portrait of HR through the Felton Bequest.
1965	In March, *My Life for Beauty* is published in London. On 1 April, HR dies in New York.
1965–1966	Parke-Bernet sales of HR's art collections, furniture, jewels and other collections in New York.
1973	The Helena Rubinstein Corporation is purchased by Colgate-Palmolive for $142.3 million.
1980	Colgate-Palmolive sells the Helena Rubinstein Corporation to Albi Enterprises Inc. for $20 million.
1984–88	L'Oréal acquires the Helena Rubinstein brand in stages 'for several hundred million francs'.
2011	The Helena Rubinstein Foundation winds up its operations in New York and disposes of its remaining assets, including the seated portrait by Graham Sutherland.

List of Figures

Figure 1. Helena Rubinstein on holiday in France, with Chrysler Plymouth and Peugeot automobiles, c. 1932, by an unknown photographer. Courtesy of Fashion Institute of Technology, SUNY, Gladys Marcus Library Special Collections and College Archives, US.NNFIT.SC.284.1.1.08.029.

Figure 2. Helena Rubinstein with *Horse*, c. 1911–15, by Elie Nadelman (1882–1946), in the 'treasure room' at 645 Park Avenue, New York, with carpet designed by Jean Lurçat (1892–1966), 1936, by George Maillard Kesslère (1894–1979). Courtesy of Fashion Institute of Technology, SUNY, Gladys Marcus Library Special Collections and College Archives, US.NNFIT.SC.284.1.1.11.022.

Figure 3. Helena Rubinstein and Patrick O'Higgins in Paris, 1960, by an unknown photographer. Courtesy of Fashion Institute of Technology, SUNY, Gladys Marcus Library Special Collections and College Archives, US.NNFIT. SC.284.1.1.18.019.

Figure 4. Surrealistic photomontage, 1930s, by Cecil Beaton (1904–1980). Reproduced from the lost original by Charmante Studio, 210 Fifth Avenue, New York, n.d. Courtesy of Fashion Institute of Technology, SUNY, Gladys Marcus Library Special Collections and College Archives, US.NNFIT. SC.284.1.1.12.025. © Estate of Cecil Beaton / Condé Nast.

Figure 5. Three portrait studies of Helena Rubinstein, 1956, by Graham Sutherland. Graphite, charcoal, black ink on paper. © The Trustees of The British Museum, London, GS1980, 1011.140. © Estate of Graham Sutherland.

Figure 6. *Portrait of Helena Rubinstein*, 1956, by Graham Sutherland. Graphite, charcoal, black ink on paper. © The Trustees of The British Museum, London, GS1980,1011.210. © Estate of Graham Sutherland.

Figure 7. *Portrait of Helena Rubinstein III*, 1960, by Graham Sutherland. Lithograph on paper. © The Trustees of The British Museum, London, GS1980.1011.211. © Estate of Graham Sutherland.

Figure 8. Helena Rubinstein posing at the Tate Gallery with both versions of her portrait by Graham Sutherland, 1957. Courtesy of Fashion Institute of Technology, SUNY, Gladys Marcus Library Special Collections and College Archives, US.NNFIT.SC.284.1.1.23.012.

Figure 9. Helena Rubinstein posing *en fête* with (left to right) Viscount and Viscountess Hambleden, Douglas Cooper, Nela Rubinstein, Kathleen Sutherland, Artur Rubinstein and Graham Sutherland, Grafton Street, Mayfair, 25 November 1957, by or for Central Press Photos Ltd. Courtesy of Fashion Institute of Technology, SUNY, Gladys Marcus Library Special Collections and College Archives, US.NNFIT.SC.284.1.1.23.014.

Figure 10. Helena Rubinstein and Graham Sutherland, Grafton Street, Mayfair, 25 November 1957, by or for Central Press Photos Ltd. Courtesy of Fashion Institute of Technology, SUNY, Gladys Marcus Library Special Collections and College Archives, US.NNFIT.SC.284.1.1.23.013.

Figure 11. Helena Rubinstein's application to the Commonwealth Department of External Affairs in Melbourne for Naturalisation as a British subject, May 1907. National Archives of Australia, Canberra, Series A1, 1907/4551.

Figure 12. Helena Rubinstein (standing) with three of her seven sisters and their mother, seated to right, in Kazimierz, Kraków, c. 1890–92, by an unknown photographer for Atelier K. Courtesy of Fashion Institute of Technology, SUNY, Gladys Marcus Library Special Collections and College Archives, US.NNFIT.SC.284.1.4.3.11.001.

Figure 13. Bremen-based Norddeutscher–Lloyd fast twin-screw steamer *Prinz-Regent Luitpold* in Sydney Cove, c. 1900, by Henry King (1855–1923). From glass-plate negative. Museum of Applied Arts and Sciences (Powerhouse Museum), Sydney. The Tyrell Collection, 85/1285-29.

Figure 14. Helena Rubinstein in Vienna, c. 1895–96, reproduced from a lost original by an unknown photographer by Peter A. Juley & Son, photographers, New York, n.d. Courtesy of Fashion Institute of Technology, SUNY, Gladys Marcus Library Special Collections and College Archives, US.NNFIT.SC.284.1.1.09.012.

Figure 15. Federal Coffee Palace, Collins Street, Melbourne, c. 1890–92, by Charles Rudd (1849–1901). Albumen silver photograph. State Library of Victoria, Melbourne, H2001.60/43.

LIST OF FIGURES

Figure 16. The signature of Frederick Sheppard Grimwade (1840–1910), who stood sponsor for Helena Rubinstein's application to the Commonwealth Department of External Affairs in Melbourne for naturalisation as a British subject, May 1907. National Archives of Australia, Canberra, Series A1, 1907/4551.

Figure 17. Helena Rubinstein while fact-finding in Vienna, 1905, by an unknown photographer, by or for Mertens, Mai & Cie, photographers, Vienna. Courtesy of Fashion Institute of Technology, SUNY, Gladys Marcus Library Special Collections and College Archives, US.NNFIT.SC.284.1.1.09.001.

Figure 18. Helena Rubinstein in her Saint-Cloud laboratory, c. 1958, by an unknown photographer. Courtesy of Fashion Institute of Technology, SUNY, Gladys Marcus Library Special Collections and College Archives, US.NNFIT.SC.284.1.1.01.019.

Figure 19. Helena Rubinstein's application for registration as trade mark of the distinctive label copy of Valaze. February 1903. National Archives of Australia, Canberra, Series A11731, 7834.

Figures 20 and 21. Helena Rubinstein dressed by the House of Worth, Paris, c. 1909, by an unknown photographer. Courtesy of Fashion Institute of Technology, SUNY, Gladys Marcus Library Special Collections and College Archives, US.NNFIT.SC.284.1.1.09.004.

Figure 22. Helena Rubinstein and Pablo Picasso at Picasso's Villa La Californie, Cannes, 1955, by an unknown photographer, possibly Patrick O'Higgins. Courtesy of Fashion Institute of Technology, SUNY, Gladys Marcus Library Special Collections and College Archives, US.NNFIT.SC.284.1.1.22.008.

Figure 23. *Portrait of Helena Rubinstein XIX (27-11-1955)* by Pablo Picasso, 1955. © Succession Picasso / Copyright Agency, 2023.

Figure 24. Street view of Helena Rubinstein's Grafton Street salon, 1926, designed by Erno Goldfinger, by an unknown photographer. British Architectural Library, Royal Institute of British Architects, London, RIBA 28460.

Figure 25. *Heroic Noon* and *Evening*, murals for 625 Park Avenue, 1942, by Salvador Dalí, by an unknown photographer. Courtesy of Fashion Institute of Technology, SUNY, Gladys Marcus Library Special Collections and College Archives, US.NNFIT.SC.284.1.1.05.001.

Figure 26. *Madame Rubinstein in Kyoto, Japan* by Andy Warhol, c. 1957. Black ink, white highlights on paper, 42.5 × 55.9 cm. Williams College Museum of Art, Williamstown, Massachusetts; Gift of Richard F. Holmes, class of 1946, M.2005.17.37. © Andy Warhol Foundation for the Visual Arts, Inc. ARS / Copyright Agency, 2023.

Figure 27. *Portrait of Helena Rubinstein* by Paul César Helleu, 1912. Lithograph, originally reproduced in the May 1912 issue of *Le Théâtre*. Image courtesy of Fine Art Images / Heritage Images / Alamy.

Figure 28. Heavily doctored photomontage, c. 1958, showing Helena Rubinstein with a selection of the portraits of herself that she owned and displayed at 625 Park Avenue, New York, c. 1960, by an unknown photographer. From top, left to right: Salvador Dalí, Christian Bérard, Roberto Montenegro, Marcel Vertès, Pavel Tschelitchew, Candido Portinari, Raoul Dufy, Margherita Russo and Marie Laurençin. Courtesy of Fashion Institute of Technology, SUNY, Gladys Marcus Library Special Collections and College Archives, US.NNFIT.SC.284.1.1.06.002.

Figure 29. Helena Rubinstein surrounded by bogus nuns on the set of Warner Brothers' *The Nun's Story* (1959), starring Audrey Hepburn and Peter Finch, at Cinecittà Studios in Rome, 1957, by an unknown photographer. Courtesy of Fashion Institute of Technology, SUNY, Gladys Marcus Library Special Collections and College Archives, US.NNFIT.SC.284.1.1.21.013.

Figure 30. Helena Rubinstein with luggage, 1942, by an unknown photographer. Courtesy of Fashion Institute of Technology, SUNY, Gladys Marcus Library Special Collections and College Archives, US.NNFIT.SC.284.1.1.13.023.

Figure 31. Helena Rubinstein with jewel case at LaGuardia Airport, New York, boarding a TWA Lockheed Constellation bound for Paris, 1946, by an unknown photographer, probably for George Valentine Enell and Associates, photographers, New York. Courtesy of Fashion Institute of Technology, SUNY, Gladys Marcus Library Special Collections and College Archives, US.NNFIT.SC.284.1.1.14.030.

Figure 32. Helena Rubinstein in Hong Kong, 1957, by an unknown photographer. Courtesy of Fashion Institute of Technology, SUNY, Gladys Marcus Library Special Collections and College Archives, US.NNFIT.SC.284.1.1.16.007.

Colour Plates

Plate 1. *Helena Rubinstein in a Red Brocade Balenciaga Gown*, 1956–57, by Graham Sutherland OM (1903–1980). Oil on canvas, 156.8 × 92.7 cm. National Portrait Gallery, Canberra. Purchased with funds provided by Marilyn Darling AC, Tim Fairfax AC and Sid Myer AM (the Sid and Fiona Myer Family Foundation), 2015.118. © Estate of Graham Sutherland.

Plate 2. *Portrait of Helena Rubinstein*, 1956–57, by Graham Sutherland. Oil on canvas, 180.3 × 111.8 cm. Beaverbrook Art Gallery, Fredericton, New Brunswick. Gift of the Beaverbrook Foundation, 1959–216. © Estate of Graham Sutherland.

Plate 3. Evening ensemble, c. 1956, by Cristóbal Balenciaga (1895–1972) of the House of Balenciaga, in altered state. Silk brocade. The Costume Institute of the Metropolitan Museum of Art, New York. Gift of Mala Rubinstein, 1969, C.I.69.16a.b. Courtesy Art Resource, New York.

Plate 4. Evening ensemble, c. 1956, by Cristóbal Balenciaga (in altered state) (detail). Silk brocade, probably created for Gustav Zumsteg at the House of Abraham in Zurich. The Costume Institute of the Metropolitan Museum of Art, New York. Gift of Mala Rubinstein, 1969. C.I.69.16a.b. Courtesy of Art Resource, New York.

Plate 5. Detail from *Helena Rubinstein in a Red Brocade Balenciaga Gown*, 1956–57, by Graham Sutherland OM (1903–1980). Oil on canvas, 156.8 × 92.7 cm. National Portrait Gallery, Canberra. Purchased with funds provided by Marilyn Darling AC, Tim Fairfax AC and Sid Myer AM (the Sid and Fiona Myer Family Foundation), 2015.118. © Estate of Graham Sutherland.

Plate 6. Advertisement for Helena Rubinstein from *Gazette du Bon Ton*, no. 6, p. ix, c. 1914, with illustration by by Emilio Ayres (1890–1916). Image courtesy of RijksMuseum.

Plate 7. Advertisement for Helena Rubinstein from a French magazine, 1920s. Image courtesy Retro AdArchives / Alamy.

Plate 8. *Portrait of Princess Artchil Gourielli (Helena Rubinstein)*, 1943, by Salvador Dalí (1904–1989). Oil on canvas. Private collection. © Fundació Gala-Salvador Dalí. VEGAP / Copyright Agency, 2023; image courtesy of Sotheby's / Bridgeman Images.

Plate 9. *Portrait of Helena Rubinstein*, 1957, by William Dobell (1899–1970). Oil on composition board, 95.4 × 95.6 cm. National Gallery of Victoria, Melbourne, Felton Bequest 1964, 1391-5. © William Dobell / Copyright Agency, 2022.

Bibliography

Adams, Brian. *Portrait of an Artist: A Biography of William Dobell*, Melbourne: Hutchinson, 1983.

ADB: Douglas Pike et al. (eds), *Australian Dictionary of Biography*, 18 vols, Melbourne: Melbourne University Press, 1966–2012.

Albrecht, Donald. *Cecil Beaton: The New York Years*, New York: Skira Rizzoli, 2011.

Alley, Ronald. *Graham Sutherland*, London: Tate Gallery, 1982.

Arcangeli, Francesco. *Graham Sutherland*, New York: Harry N. Abrams, 1975.

Barnard, Edwin. *Emporium: Selling the Dream in Colonial Australia*, Canberra: National Library of Australia, 2015.

Barton, Robert D. *Reminiscences of an Australian Pioneer*, Sydney: Tyrrell's, 1917.

Bassett, Marnie. *The Hentys: An Australian Colonial Tapestry*, London: Oxford University Press, 1954.

Beaverbrook Art Gallery. *Paintings*, Fredericton: University Press of New Brunswick, 1959.

Belknap, Robert E. *The List: The Uses and Pleasures of Cataloguing*, New Haven and London: Yale University Press, 2004.

Bennett, James. 'Helena Rubinstein', *Cosmetics and Skin,* http://cosmeticsandskin.com/companies/helena-rubinestin.php

Bergman-Carton, Janis. 'Negotiating the Categories: Sarah Bernhardt and the Possibilities of Jewishness', *Art Journal*, vol. 55, no. 2 (Summer 1996), pp. 55–64.

Bernays, Doris Fleischmann (ed.). *An Outline of Careers for Women*, New York: Doubleday, Doran, 1928.

Berthelot, Marcellin. *Les origines de l'alchimie*, Paris: G. Steinheil, 1885.

Berthoud, Roger. *Graham Sutherland: A Biography*, London: Faber and Faber, 1982.

Bevan, Scott. *Bill: The Life of William Dobell*, Sydney: Simon & Schuster, 2014.

Blainey (a): Geoffrey Blainey,. *Black Kettle and Full Moon: Daily Life in a Vanished Australia*, Melbourne: Penguin/Viking, 2003.

Blainey (b): Geoffrey Blainey, *A History of Victoria*, Melbourne: Cambridge University Press, 2005.

Blainey (c): Ann Blainey, *I Am Melba: A Biography*, Melbourne: Black Inc., 2009.

Bowles: Hamish Bowles, *Balenciaga and Spain*, New York: Skira Rizzoli, 2011.

Bradshaw: *Bradshaw's Continental Railway Guide and General Handbook*, London: Henry Blacklock & Co, 1913.

Brandon: Ruth Brandon, *Ugly Beauty: Helena Rubinstein, L'Oréal, and the Blemished History of Looking Good*, New York: HarperCollins, 2011.

Brown: P.L. Brown, '"Meltham" Near Geelong', *Victorian Historical Magazine*, vol. 31, no. 4, May 1961, pp. 200–2.

Bullock: Alan Bullock (ed.), *Makers of the Twentieth Century*, London: Weidenfeld & Nicolson, in conjunction with Artus Publishing, 1981.

Burne-Jones: Georgiana Burne-Jones, *Memorials of Edward Burne-Jones*, London: Macmillan, 1904.

Cameron: Roderick Cameron, *The Golden Riviera*, London: Weidenfeld & Nicolson, 1975.

Chapman & Stillman: Heather Chapman and Judith Stillman, *Lost Melbourne*, London: Pavilion Books, 2015.

Clark: Kenneth Clark, *The Other Half: A Self Portrait*, London: John Murray, 1977

Clark (a): Jessica P. Clark, 'Beauty on Bond Street': Gender, Enterprise, and the Establishment of an English Beauty Industry, 1850–1910, Washington, D.C.: Georgetown University PhD dissertation, 2012.

Clark (b): Jessica P. Clark, 'Pomeroy v. Pomeroy: Beauty, Modernity, and the Female Entrepreneur in *fin-de-siècle* London', *Women's History Review*, vol. 22, no. 6, 2013, pp. 877–903.

Clarke: Patricia Clarke, *The Governesses: Letters from the Colonies, 1862–1882*, Melbourne: Hutchinson of Australia, 1985.

Clifford: Marie J. Clifford, Brand Name Modernism: Helena Rubinstein's Art Collection, Femininity, and the Marketing of Modern Style, 1925–1940, Los Angeles: UCLA PhD dissertation, 1999.

BIBLIOGRAPHY

Clifford (a): Marie J. Clifford, 'Helena Rubinstein's Beauty Salons, Fashion, and Modernist Display', *Winterthur Portfolio*, vol. 38, no. 2/3, summer–autumn 2003, pp. 83–108.

Comay: Joan Comay, *Who's Who in Jewish History after the period of the Old Testament*, London: Weidenfeld & Nicolson, 1974.

Cooper: Douglas Cooper, *The Work of Graham Sutherland*, London: Lund Humphries, 1961.

Daix and Rosselet: Pierre Daix and Joan Rosselet, *Picasso: The Cubist Years, 1907–1916: A Catalogue Raisonné of the Paintings and Related Works,* London: Thames and Hudson, 1979.

De Serville: Paul de Serville, *Port Phillip Gentlemen and Good Society in Melbourne Before the Gold Rushes*, Melbourne and Oxford: Oxford University Press, 1980.

De Serville (a): Paul de Serville, *Pounds and Pedigrees: The Upper Class in Victoria, 1850-80*, Oxford: Oxford University Press, 1991.

Docker: John Docker, *The Nervous Nineties: Australian Cultural Life in the 1890s*, Oxford: Oxford University Press, 1991.

Domnitz: Myer Domnitz, *The World of Jewish Faith*, London: Longman, 1980.

Donaldson: Elizabeth Donaldson, *William Dobell: An Artist's Life*, Wollombi, New South Wales: Exisle Publishing, 2010.

Eagle: Mary Eagle, *A Tribute to William Dobell*, Canberra: Australian National University, The Drill Hall Gallery, 1999.

Brown-May, Andrew and Shurlee Swain (eds), *The Encyclopedia of Melbourne*, Melbourne: Cambridge University Press, 2005.

Fabe: Maxene Fabe, *Beauty Millionaire: The Life of Helena Rubinstein*, New York: Thomas Y. Cromwell Company, 1972.

Fairbairn: Steve Fairbairn, *Fairbairn of Jesus: An Autobiography* London: John Lane, The Bodley Head, 1931.

Finlay: Henry Finlay, *To Have but Not to Hold: A History of Attitudes to Marriage and Divorce in Australia, 1858–1975*, Sydney: The Federation Press, 2005.

Fitoussi: Michèle Fitoussi, *Helena Rubinstein: La Femme qui inventa la beauté*, Paris: Bernard Grasset, 2010 (*Helena Rubinstein: The Woman Who Invented Beauty*, London: Gallic Books, 2013).

Fitoussi (a): Michèle Fitoussi (ed.), *L'Aventure de la beauté*, Paris: Flammarion in association with the Musée d'art et d'histoire du Judaïsme, 2019.

Fletcher: Anthony Fletcher, *Growing Up in England: The Experience of Childhood,*

1600–1914, New Haven and London: Yale University Press, 2008.

Freeman: Virginia Freeman, *Dobell on Dobell*, Sydney: Ure Smith, 1970.

Garden: Don Garden, *Victoria: A History*, Melbourne: Thomas Nelson Australia, 1984.

Gibbs: Mary Ann Gibbs, *The Years of the Nannies*, London: Hutchinson, 1960.

Gleeson: James Gleeson, *William Dobell*, London: Thames & Hudson, 1964.

Gleeson (a): James Gleeson, *William Dobell: A Biographical and Critical Study*, Sydney and London: Angus & Robertson, 1981.

Glockemeier: Georg Glockemeier, *Zur Wiener Judenfrage*, Vienna and Leipzig: Verlag Johannes Günther, 1936.

Goldin: Marco Goldin, *Sutherland ritratti*, Milan: Electa, 1996.

Graff: Terry Graff, *Masterworks from the Beaverbrook Art Gallery*, Fredericton, New Brunswick: Goose Lane Editions, 2013.

Grimwade: Russell Grimwade, *Flinders Lane: Recollections of Alfred Felton*, Melbourne, Melbourne University Press, 1947.

Gruber: Fiona Gruber, 'Graham Sutherland's Portrait of Helena Rubinstein', *Australian Book Review*, 25 October 2016.

Hammer Martin Hammer, *Bacon and Sutherland*, New Haven and London: Yale University Press, for the Paul Mellon Centre for Studies in British Art, 2005.

Hancock: W.K. Hancock, *Australia*, London: Ernest Benn, 1930.

Hancock (a): Marguerite Hancock, *Colonial Consorts: The Wives of Victoria's Governors, 1839–1900*, Melbourne: Melbourne University Press (The Miegunyah Press), 2001.

Hansen: David Hansen, *Dempsey's People: A Folio of British Street Portraits, 1824–1844*, Canberra: National Portrait Gallery, 2017.

Haslam: Nicky Haslam, '"Helena Rubinstein: The Woman Who Invented Beauty", by Michèle Fitoussie – review', *The Spectator*, 13 April 2013.

Hayes: John T. Hayes, *Portraits of Helena Rubinstein*, London: National Portrait Gallery and the Helena Rubinstein Foundation, 1977.

Hayes (a): John T. Hayes, *Portraits by Graham Sutherland*, London: National Portrait Gallery, 1977.

Hayes (b): John T. Hayes, *The Art of Graham Sutherland*, Oxford: Phaidon, 1980.

Heathcote: Christopher Heathcote, *Discovering Dobell*, Adelaide: Wakefield Press in association with TarraWarra Museum of Art, 2017.

HR: Helena Rubinstein, *My Life for Beauty*, London: The Bodley Head, 1965.

HR (a): Helena Rubinstein, *Beauty in the Making*, London: the author, c. 1908.

HR (b): Helena Rubinstein, 'Manufacturing – Cosmetics', Bernays, p. 331.

HR (c): Helena Rubinstein, *The Art of Feminine Beauty*, New York: Horace Liveright, Inc., 1930.

Hylton: Jane Hylton, *William Dobell: Portraits in Context*, Adelaide: Wakefield Press, 2003.

Inglis: Alison Inglis, 'Deathless Beauty: Poynter's *Helen*, Lillie Langtry and High Victorian Ideals of Beauty', in Trumble, pp. 71–82.

Inglis (a): Andrea Inglis, *Beside the Seaside: Victorian Resorts in the Nineteenth Century*, Melbourne, Melbourne University Press, 1999.

Joubert: Hélène Joubert, *Helena Rubinstein: Madame's Collection*, Paris: Skira, 2021.

Julius: Anthony Julius, 'England's Gifts to Jew Hatred', *Spectator*, vol. 285, no. 8988, 11 November 2000, p. 13.

Julius (a): Anthony Julius, *Trials of the Diaspora: A History of Anti-Semitism in England*, Oxford: Oxford University Press, 2010.

Jupp, James (ed.). *The Australian People: An Encyclopedia of the Nation, Its People and Their Origins*, Cambridge: Cambridge University Press, 2001.

Kaplan: Morton A. Kaplan, 'Senator Fulbright and the Arrogance of Power', *International Journal on World Peace*, vol. 12, no. 1, March 1995, pp. 12–13.

Kiddle: Margaret Kiddle, *Men of Yesterday: A Social History of the Western District of Victoria, 1834–1890*, Melbourne: Melbourne University Press, 1961.

Klein: Mason Klein, *Helena Rubinstein: Beauty is Power*, New York: The Jewish Museum, 2014.

Lassar: Oskar Lassar, *Zur Therapie der Hautkrebse*, Berlin: L. Schumacher, 1893.

McCaughey: Davis McCaughey, Naomi Perkins and Angus Trumble, *Victoria's Colonial Governors, 1839–1900*, Melbourne: Melbourne University Press (The Miegunyah Press), 1993.

Macleod: Thomas Macleod, *The Queensland Criminal Reports*, Brisbane: Law Book Company, 1913.

McNicoll: Ronald McNicoll, *Number 36 Collins Street: Melbourne Club, 1838–1988*, Melbourne: Allen & Unwin/Haynes in conjunction with the Melbourne Club, 1988.

McQueen: Humphrey McQueen, *Social Sketches of Australia, 1888–2001*, third edition. St Lucia: University of Queensland Press, 2004.

Madame: Patrick O'Higgins, *Madame: An Intimate Biography of Helena Rubinstein*, New York: The Viking Press, 1971.

Man: Felix H. Man, *Graham Sutherland: Das Graphische Werk, 1922–1970*, Munich: Verlag Galerie Wolfgang Ketterer, 1970.

Martin: Stanley Martin, *The Order of Merit: One Hundred Years of Matchless Honour*, London and New York: I.B. Tauris, 2007.

Mellor: David Mellor (ed.), *Cecil Beaton: A Retrospective*, Boston: Little, Brown, 1986.

Michaelis: Moritz Michaelis, *Chapters from the Story of My Life*, Melbourne: Norman Brothers Printers for the author, 1899.

Mulvaney: John Mulvaney, *Digging Up a Past*, Sydney: University of New South Wales Press, 2011.

Netto: David Netto, 'Is This Park Avenue Penthouse the Best Apartment in New York?' *Town & Country*, 28 April 2017.

OCAH: Graeme Davison, John Hirst and Stuart Macintyre (eds), *The Oxford Companion to Australian History*, Melbourne: Oxford University Press, 1998.

Ocaña: María Teresa Ocaña et al., *Picasso and Els 4 Gats: The Early Years in Turn-of-the-Century Barcelona*, Boston: Little, Brown & Company, 1996.

Parke-Bernet: *Precious-Stone Jewels from the Unique Collection of the Late Helena Rubinstein*, Parke-Bernet, New York, 12 October 1965.

Parke-Bernet (a): *The Helena Rubinstein Collection: Modern Paintings and Sculptures, Part One*, Parke-Bernet, New York, 20 April 1966.

Parke-Bernet (b): *African and Oceanic Art, Part One*, Parke-Bernet, New York, 21 April 1966.

Parke-Bernet (c): *French Furniture and Decorations, Russian Icons, Other Paintings*, Parke-Bernet, New York, 22 April and 23 April 1966.

Parke-Bernet (d): *Modern Paintings and Sculptures, Part Two*, Parke-Bernet, New York, 27 April 1966.

Parke-Bernet (e): *Modern Drawings and Prints*, Parke-Bernet, New York, 28 April 1966.

Parke-Bernet (f): *African and Oceanic Art, Part Two*, Parke-Bernet, New York, 29 April 1966.

Parke-Bernet (g): *African and Oceanic Art, Part Three*, Parke-Bernet, New York, 15 October 1966.

Paschkis: Heinrich Paschkis, *Kosmetik für Ärzte*, Vienna: Alfred Hölder, 1893.

Pearce: Barry Pearce, *William Dobell, 1899–1970: The Painter's Progress*, Sydney: Art Gallery of New South Wales, 1997.

Peiss: Kathy Peiss, *Hope in a Jar: The Making of America's Beauty Culture*, Philadelphia: University of Pennsylvania Press, 1998.

Phillips: P.D. Phillips, *A Treatise on the Insolvency Law in Force in the Colony of Victoria, with an Historical Review of English Bankruptcy Legislation*, Melbourne: J.C. Stephens, Printer, 1899.

Phillips (a): Fred H. Phillips, 'The Beaverbrook Gallery in Fredericton', *Canadian Geographical Journal*, vol. 59, no. 5, November 1959, p. 173.

Pope-Hennessy: James Pope-Hennessy, *Queen Mary, 1867–1953*, London: Allen & Unwin, 1959.

Pope-Hennessy (a): James Pope-Hennessy (Hugo Vickers, ed.), *The Quest for Queen Mary*, London: Zuleika, 2018.

Poynter: John Poynter, *Russell Grimwade*, Melbourne: Melbourne University Press, 1967.

Poynter (a): John Poynter, 'Rubinstein, Helena (1870? [*sic*]–1965), cosmetics manufacturer', *ADB,* vol. 11: 1891–1939, Nes–Smi, 1988, pp. 475–77.

Poynter and Thomas: John Poynter and Benjamin Thomas, *Miegunyah: The Bequests of Russell and Mab Grimwade*, Melbourne: Melbourne University Press (The Miegunyah Press), 2015.

Quinn: Edward Quinn (ed.), *Graham Sutherland: Complete Graphic Work*, London: Thames & Hudson, 1978.

Roberts: Keith Roberts, 'London', *Burlington Magazine*, vol. 119, no. 891, June 1977, p. 459.

Robinson: Cyril Robinston, 'Beaverbrook's Enduring Gift to his Friends', *Weekend Magazine*, vol. 9, no. 37, 12 September 1959, p. 18.

Rubinstein: Hilary L. Rubinstein, *Chosen: The Jews in Australia*, Sydney: Allen & Unwin, 1987.

Rubinstein and Rubinstein: Hilary L. Rubinstein and William D. Rubinstein, *The Jews in Australia: A Thematic History*, Melbourne: William Heinemann Australia, 1991.

Rutland: Suzanne D. Rutland, *Edge of the Diaspora: Two Centuries of Jewish Settlement in Australia*, second revised ed., Sydney: Brandl & Schlesinger, 1997.

Rutland (a): Suzanne D. Rutland, *The Jews in Australia*, Melbourne: Cambridge University Press, 2005.

S&A: Robert Spreadborough and Hugh Anderson, *Victorian Squatters*, Melbourne: Red Rooster Press, 1983.

S&McD: *Sands & McDougall's Melbourne and Suburban Directory for 1898 [1899, 1900, 1901]*, Melbourne: Sands & McDougall, 1898 [1899, 1900, 1901].

S&McD (a): *Sands & McDougall's Melbourne, Suburban and Country Directory for 1902 [1903, 1904, 1905, 1906, 1907]*, Melbourne: Sands & McDougall, 1902 [1903, 1904, 1905, 1906, 1907].

Sagazio: Celestina Sagazio, *Women's Melbourne*, East Melbourne: National Trust of Australia (Victoria), 2010.

São Paulo: Museu de Arte de São Paulo, *I Seleção Helena Rubinstein de Arte Jovem*, São Paulo: Museu de Arte de São Paulo, 1986.

Saunders: Kay Saunders, *Notorious Australian Women*, Sydney: HarperCollins (ABC Books), 2011.

Searle: G.R. Searle, *A New England? Peace and War, 1886–1918*, Oxford: Oxford University Press, 2004.

Secrest: Meryle Secrest, *Kenneth Clark: A Biography*, London: Weidenfeld & Nicolson, 1984

Shann: Edward Shann, *An Economic History of Australia*, Cambridge: Cambridge University Press, 1938.

Slesin: Suzanne Slesin, *Over the Top: Helena Rubinstein, Extraordinary Style, Beauty, Art, Fashion, Design*, New York: Pointed Leaf Press, 2006.

Smith: James Smith (ed.), *The Cyclopedia of Victoria, an Historical and Commercial Review, Descriptive and Biographical Facts, Figures and Illustrations, an Epitome of Progress*, Melbourne: The Cyclopedia Company, vol. 3, 1905.

Soavi: Giorgio Soavi, *Protagonisti: Giacometti, Sutherland, de Chirico*, Milan: Longanesi, 1969.

Sontag: Susan Sontag, 'Notes on 'Camp'', *Partisan Review*, vol. 31, no. 4 (Fall 1964), pp. 515–30.

Souter: Gavin Souter, *Lion and Kangaroo: The Initiation of Australia, 1901–1919*, Sydney: Collins, 1976.

Sutton: Denys Sutton, 'The Precarious Tension of Opposites', *Apollo*, vol. 116, no. 246, August 1982, p. 73.

Svensen: Stuart Svensen, *The Shearers' War: The Story of the 1891 Shearers' Strike*, revised edition. Brisbane: University of Queensland Press, 2008.

Symons: Michael Symons, *One Continuous Picnic: A Gastronomic History of Australia*, second edition. Melbourne: Melbourne University Press, 2007.

Tassi: Roberto Tassi, *Graham Sutherland: Complete Graphic Work*, London: Thames & Hudson, 1978.

Testori: Giovanni Testori, *Sutherland: L'Atelier dei ritratti*, Milan: Gruppo Editoriale Fabbri, Bompiani, 1992.

Thuillier: Rosalind Thuillier, *Graham Sutherland: Life, Work, Ideas*, Cambridge: The Lutterworth Press, 2015.

Trevelyan: G.M. Trevelyan, *English Social History: A Survey of Six Centuries, Chaucer to Queen Victoria*, London: Longman, Green & Co., 1944.

Trueman: Stuart Trueman, 'An Enduring Gift to New Brunswick: The Lord Beaverbrook Art Gallery', *Canadian Art*, vol. 15, no. 4 (November 1958), p. 282.

Trumble: Angus Trumble (ed.), *Love and Death: Art in the Age of Queen Victoria*, Adelaide: Art Gallery Board of South Australia, 2001.

Trumble (a): Angus Trumble, 'Clunky Modern English', *Australian Book Review*, no. 313, July–August 2009, p. 5.

Trumble (b): Angus Trumble, 'A Study in Scarlet', *Portrait*, no. 60, Spring 2018, pp. 16–23.

Turner: E.S. Turner, *What the Butler Saw: Two Hundred and Fifty Years of the Servant Problem*, London: Michael Joseph, 1962.

Unna: Paul Gerson Unna, *Allgemeine Therapie der Hautkrankleiten*, Berlin: Urban & Schwarzenberg, 1899.

Vickers: Hugo Vickers, *Cecil Beaton: The Authorised Biography*, London: Weidenfeld & Nicolson, 1986.

Wardell: Michael Wardell, 'The Beaverbrook Art Gallery', *Atlantic Advocate*, vol. 50, no. 1, September 1959, p. 52.

Waugh: Evelyn Waugh, *Rossetti: His Life and Works*, London: Duckworth, 1928.

West: Katharine West, *Chapter of Governesses: A Study of the Governess in English Fiction, 1800–1949*, London: Cohen & West, 1949.

Woodhead: Lindy Woodhead, *War Paint: Madame Helena Rubinstein and Miss Elizabeth Arden: Their Lives, Their Times, Their Rivalry*, Hoboken, N.J.: John Wiley & Sons, Inc., 2003.

Wykes-Joyce: Max Wykes-Joyce, *Cosmetics and Adornment: Ancient and Contemporary Usage*, London: Peter Owen, 1961.

Index

Page references in **bold** are to illustrations.

Abraham, House of (Zurich) 37
ACI (Australian Consolidated Industries) 45
Adelaide (South Australia) 198
Adenauer, Konrad 24
advertising
    in colonial newspapers and directories 12–14
    costs of 166–67
    for employees 50, 175
    regulation of 136–38
Agnès 36, 196
Albert, Max xii, 106, 107, 183, 214, 244n33
Albi Enterprises Incorporated 218, 231n5, 257
Alexander II (Tsar) 8, 51, 64
Alexis (Madame) 112–13, 120–21, 210, 245n43
Allen (Mrs) 45–46
Mrs Allen's World's Hair Restorer 45–46
Anderson, Selina 93
Annie (housemaid at Astonette) 85
anti-semitism 6, 10, 16, 25–30, 55–56, 59, 78
    See also pogroms
Archibald Prize 256
Arden, Elizabeth 7
Art Gallery of New South Wales (Sydney) 202, 203, 257

Ascot (in Toowoomba) 82, 86
Astonette (in Toowoomba) 79, 81, 82–88, 210, 254
Atlantic City 255
Auckland (New Zealand) 171–75, 181, 184
Australia Felix 70
Australian Book Society 202
Australian Consolidated Industries (ACI) 45
Automobile Club of Victoria 142
Ayres, Emilio 152, **plate 6**

Bacon, Francis 35, 235n33
Baevski, Elcon (later Elcon Myer) 64, 65
Baevski, Simcha (later Sidney Myer) 64, 65
Balenciaga, Cristóbal 3, 19, 36–37, **plates 3 & 4 & 5**
    See also Sutherland, Graham: *Helena Rubinstein in a Red Brocade Balenciaga Gown*
Ballarat (Victoria) 65–66, 78, 82, 145, 173, 254
Bara, Theda 27
Baxter, Anne Jean 106–7
Beaton, Cecil
    and Andy Warhol 206–7
    anti-semitism of 28–30, 201
    nastiness of 17

Beaton, Cecil (*cont.*)
 opinion of Sutherland portrait 34–35, 210
 portrait of HR by 10, 28–30, **29 (fig. 4)**
 suggests Sutherland portrait 27, 35
beauty
 as a duty 120
 and the soul 177, 200
Beauty in the Making (promotional booklet) 104, 181
Beauty Institute 151–53, 162–63, 168, 172
'Beauty is power' x, 1, 120–21, 134–35, 177, 213
Beaver, Isidor George 142, 248n19
Beaverbrook (Lord) 24, 35, 39, 200, 257
Beaverbrook Art Gallery (Fredericton, New Brunswick) 35, 39, 257
Beckmann, Lola (cousin of HR)
 emigration to Australia by 47, 59, 145, 160–61, 236n7, 254
 as employee of HR 151, 158, 171, 183–84
Beckmann, Moritz (uncle of HR) 58
Beckmann, Rosalie (*née* Silberfeld; maternal aunt of HR) 54, 58, 236n7, 253
Beit, William (Mr and Mrs) 82, 86
Bendigo (Victoria) 65
Ben-Gurion, David 7, 257
Bennett, James 46, 160, 233n27
Bérard, Christian 10, **211 (fig. 28)**
Bernhardt, Sarah 94, 118, 152
Berrill (Madame) 15
Berthelot, Marcellin (Dr) 150, 154, 160
biography and biographies (writing of) 2–4, 11–19, 209, 213–14, 218–19
Block Arcade (Melbourne) 47, 106, 111, 142, 145, 164
 See also Chicago and Winter Garden Tea and Luncheon Rooms
Boer War 83, 88, 169
Bonnington's chemist (Christchurch) 174
Bosisto, Joseph 45
Boston 255
Bouché, René 10
Box, John Burnett 156
Brancusi, Constantin 37
Brandon, Ruth 233n26

9 Brandon Street, Wellington 145, 175, 181, 198, 255
Brassey, Sybil de Vere (Lady) 119
Breton, André 7
Brezzo, Charles 101
Brisbane 12, 82, 87, 163–68, 171–73, 184, 254
British Empire 56, 81, 92, 93, 95–96, 165
Brodribb, Beatrice (later Pyne) 79–80
Brodribb, Frank 87, 241n45
Brodribb, Wynnie Prudence (later Mrs Evelyn James Metcalfe) 79–88
Brodzky, Maurice 110
Brothwood (chemist, Sydney) 117
Bryan's or Bryant's Creek, later Koroite Creek (outside Coleraine) xiv, 73, 239n14
The Bulletin 116
Buñuel, Luis 7
Burnside (Fairbairn estate) 253
Buscombe (Mrs) 170

Cameron, Roderick 28, 30, 200
camp sensibility 212–15
Capilla Hair Tonic 115–16
Capote, Truman 206
Carpathian Mountains 51, 132, 140, 144, 174, 187
Castelbarco, Emmanuele 10
Casterton (Victoria) 70, 74, 78, 253
Castles, Amy 50
Celine. *See* Creme Celine
ceresin wax 46
Chanel, Gabrielle ('Coco') 36, 200
Charmazel (racehorse) 245n47
Charmazelle, Salon. *See* Salon Charmazelle
chemist shops 170, 173–75
 See also Bonnington's (Christchurch); Brothwood (Sydney); Clayton, J.W. (Adelaide); Davies Pharmacy (Wanganui); Fletcher (Mrs) (Christchurch); Jones (Miss) (Ballarat); Leary's Pharmacy (Palmerston North); McGuffie & Co. (Brisbane); Salek (Mr) (Christchurch); Soul Pattinson, Washington H. (Sydney); Wilkinson's (Dunedin); Woollams' (Auckland)

Chicago and Winter Garden Tea and Luncheon Rooms (Melbourne) 47, 97–98, 101–3, 145, 254
  See also Siegenberg, Frances
Christchurch (New Zealand) 171, 174–76, 181–82, 184, 254, 255
Churchill, Winston 24
City Chambers (Auckland) 175
City Chambers (City of Melbourne Building) 101, 109
Clark, Kenneth 24
Clayton, J.W. (chemist, Adelaide) 170
Cleverdon and Fay (solicitors) 47–48, 170, 183–84
Cocteau, Jean 28, 231n5
Cohen, Leslie 117–18
Cohen, Michael 15
cold cream 46–47
  See also Valaze
Coleraine (Victoria) xii, xiv, 47, 58, 63–65, 69–78, 89, 215, 253
Coleraine Racecourse 73
Colgate-Palmolive 218, 257
Collins (Mrs) (of City Chambers, Auckland) 175
243 Collins Street, Melbourne (Fourth Victoria Building) 14–15, 116, 142, 145, 147, 161, 171, 198, 248n19, 254
274 Collins Street, Melbourne 106–9, 139, 145, 150, 162, 168, 170, 171, 175, 198, 254
Conder, Charles 140
Conrad, Joseph 60, 210
Cooper, Ceska. *See* Rubinstein, Ceska or Cäcilie
Cooper, Douglas 40, **40 (fig. 9)**
Cooper, Gladys 116
copyright law 130–32
Corelli, Marie 113, 245n47
Cory (Mrs) (housekeeper at Astonette) 85
cosmetics 27, 34, 132–35, 140, 151–52, 200
  artistry of 135–36
  disapproval of 2, 112, 119, 133, 137, 142–43, 165
Costume Institute (Metropolitan Museum of Art, New York) 36–37, 222
Crawford, Alice 116

Creme Celine 109, 110
Curie, Marie 7, 125–26
currency (imperial) xv
Cyclopedia of Victoria 108, 109, 110, 132–34

Dalí, Salvador 7, 10, 199–201, **199 (fig. 25), 211 (fig. 28), 256, plate 8**
Danglow, Jacob (Rabbi) 101
Danglow, Rose (later Mrs Abel Isaacson) 101
Darling Downs (Queensland) 75, 81–84
Davies Pharmacy (Wanganui) 174–75
de Bray, Sybil 116
de Chirico, Giorgio 7, 234n1
de l'Enclos, Ninon 132–33
de Serville, Paul Huège 92
Dedman, Anne Jean (*née* Baxter) 106–7
Dedman, Annie Theresa (*née* Downes) 244n37
Dedman, William Hine James 106–7, 244n37
department stores 6, 65, 175, 199, 218
depression (1890s) 8, 45, 64–65, 92, 243n20
Dobell, William 10, 202–6, 257, **plate 9**
Dr Williams' Pink Pills for Pale People xii, 141, 214
Drapery and General Importing Company of New Zealand Ltd (D.I.C.) 175
drought, Federation 70, 92, 215
Dufy, Raoul 10, **211 (fig. 28)**, 231n5
Dunedin (New Zealand) 171, 174–75, 181–84, 254, 255
Dunlop Rubber Company 116

Eight Hours Act (1916) 97
  See also labour movement; wages
electric therapies 107, 155–58, 162, 167–68
Elizabeth Arden 7
138 Elizabeth Street, Melbourne (O'Connor's Chambers) 11, 74, 100, 102, 106, 127, 139–42, 164, 170, 198, 247n17, 254
Elliott, Maxine 116
Éluard, Paul 7
Epstein, Jacob 10
Ernst, Max 7, 20
eucalyptus oil 45

INDEX

Fabe, Maxene xv, 69
Fairbairn, Alison 240n32
Fairbairn, Angela 75
Fairbairn, Esther 241n32
Fairbairn, Ian 75
Fairbairn, Steve 75, 78, 80–81, 240n30, 253
Falk Studios 111
Fashion Institute of Technology (New York) 30, 66, 125, 189, 259–62
Federal Coffee Palace (Melbourne) 95–**96** (**fig. 15**)
Federation of Australia (1901) 2, 13, 56, 80, 92–96, 103, 130, 136, 164, 233n17
Fellowes, Daisy (the Hon. Mrs Reginald Fellowes) 24
Felton, Alfred 45, 203
Felton Bequest 203, 257
Felton Grimwade & Co. 43–46, 89, 97, 105, 131–32, 149, 188, 203
Female Middle Class Emigration Society (London) 75–76, 77
Finch, Peter **214** (**fig. 29**)
Fitoussi, Michèle xv, 233n26
Fitzgerald, F. Scott 7
Fletcher (Mrs) (chemist, Christchurch) 175
Forter, Boris 27
Fourth Victoria Building. *See* [243] Collins Street, Melbourne
freckles 109–13, 127–30, 145, 246n3
    See also Valaze
Fredman (Miss) (zither teacher) xii, 106–7, 214
Freud, Sigmund 55
zu Fürstenberg, Maximilian Egon 24

Gaston-Lucien 188
Gaunt, G.F. (Miss) 15
Gay, Edward F. 142
Geelong (Victoria) 66, 75, 78, 80–82, 218
Genoa 56–60, 89, 108, 159, 161, 253
George (gardener at Astonette) 85
Gilmore, Mary 202
Gilot, Françoise 192
Givhan, Robin 3–4
Glen & Co. Music and Piano Warehouse (Melbourne) 43, 106–10, 113–14, 145, 151, 183, 254

Glockemeier, Georg 55
gold rush 64, 92
Golden Key Pharmacy 118
Goldfinger, Ernő **198** (**fig. 24**)
Goldstein, Jacob 93
Goldstein, Vida 93
Goodman (Lord) 24
Gourielli-Tchkonia, Artchil (second husband of HR) 8, 16, 49, 195–96, 197, 256
    death of 27, 191
governesses 75–77, 80–88, 97, 186
24 Grafton Street, Mayfair **40** (**fig. 9**), **41** (**fig. 10**), 84, 152, 176, 177, 180, 183–84, 216, 255
Great Depression (1930s) 8–9, 256
Greenwich Village (New York) 7
Grimwade, Frederick Sheppard 43–45, 89, 105, **105** (**fig. 16**), 143, 169, 203
Grimwade, Phelia (Mrs Norton Grimwade) 169
Grist, Ethel 103
Grist, Frank 103
Grist, Harry 102–3
Grist, Isabella (*née* Hutchings) 103
Groom, Littleton Ernest (Sir) 84
Guest, H. Westall 117–21, 210
Guest, Olive 119

Hagborg, Otto 176, 250n10, 255
hair and hairdressing 108–12, 114, 115–16, 119, 121
hair removal 107, 158
Hambleden (Viscount and Viscountess) 40, **40** (**fig. 9**)
Hamilton (Victoria) 66, 70, 74, 78, 253
Hancock, Marguerite 94
Hansen, David 81
Harlaxton House (near Toowoomba) 79
Harleston (in Caulfield) 43, 89
Harris, Kamala 4
Haslam, Nicky 69
Helen (Madame) 170
Helena Rubinstein & Co.
    in Adelaide 116–17, 170
    advertising by 20, 139–40, 166–67, 170, **plates 6 & 7**. *See also* Helena Rubinstein & Co.: promotional activities of

278

INDEX

in Brisbane 163–69, 171
as employer 5, 16, 94, 183–84
expansion into Sydney 145, 163–64, 171
founding of xiii, 4, 11, 14–15, 91–92, 97–107, 139–40, 142–43, 254
in Hobart 170
HR's sale and repurchase of shares in (1928, 1931) 9
incorporation in the USA 255
international expansion of 5, 123, 184–85, 195, 216, 254–56
in Kalgoorlie 170
in Launceston 170
in London 5, 8, 27, 123, 152–53, 160, 176–79. *See also* [24] Grafton Street, Mayfair
L'Oréal purchase of 6, 232n5, 257
in New Zealand 5–6, 21, 145, 171–73, 254–55
ownership of 5, 6, 9, 217–18, 231–32 n5, 256, 257
in Perth 120, 170
premises/addresses of: in Brisbane 163–64, 168, 171
premises/addresses of: in London 152, 176, 180, 183, 198–99, **198 (fig. 24)**, 255. *See also* [24] Grafton Street, Mayfair
premises/addresses of: in Melbourne 14–15, 106–10, 139, 142, 145, 164, 171, 181–83, 198, 254. *See also* [138] Elizabeth Street, Melbourne; [243] Collins Street, Melbourne; [274] Collins Street, Melbourne; Glen & Co.
premises/addresses of: in New York 255–56
premises/addresses of: in Paris 152, 184, 198–99, 255. *See also* [255] rue Saint-Honoré; Saint Cloud
premises/addresses of: in Sydney 163–64, 171, 198, 254, 256. *See also* [158A] Pitt Street
premises/addresses of: in Wellington 175, 255. *See also* [9] Brandon Street, Wellington
profitability of 98, 143–45, 184–86, 197

promotional activities of 1, 114–16, 119–21. *See also* Helena Rubinstein & Co.: advertising by
sale of to Colgate-Palmolive 218, 257
See also Rubinstein, Helena
Helena Rubinstein Corporation 218, 257
See also Helena Rubinstein & Co.
Helena Rubinstein Foundation 202, 205, 257, 258
Helena Rubinstein Incorporated. *See* Helena Rubinstein & Co.
Helena Rubinstein Pavilion for Contemporary Art (Tel Aviv) 7, 257
Helena Rubinstein Pty Ltd xiii, 170, 185, 255
See also Helena Rubinstein & Co.
Helena Rubinstein Travelling Art Scholarship 257
Helleu, Paul-César 10, 207, **207 (fig. 27)**, 255
Hemingway, Ernest 7
Hepburn, Audrey **214 (fig. 29)**
Her Majesty's Theatre (Melbourne) 94
Herzl, Theodor 55
Hillary, Edmund 7
Hobart (Tasmania) 170
Hodgkinson, Frank 257
Holocaust 8, 51, 55–56
homosexuality 212–13
Hopetoun, Hersey Alice (Countess of)
Hough (Mr) (domestic servant to Queen Mary) 49
House of Abraham (Zurich) 37
Hoyningen-Huene, George 37
Hughes, Kent (Dr) 156
Hunter Brothers (jewellers) 116

interior décor 113–15, 150, 151, 157, 198–99, 245–46n50, 256
Isaacson, Abel 99–101, 103, 104–5
Isaacson, Rose (*née* Danglow) 101
Isaacson, S. 101
Israel 1, 7, 257

Jackson (Miss) (tutor at Astonette) 85
J.C. Williamson's Theatre Royal (Melbourne) 94
Jewish Museum (New York) 208

Jews and Jewry 212–13
  in Australia 64–65, 89
  in Britain 64–65
  in Kraków 8
  in Melbourne 88
  in Russia 8
  in Victoria 64–65
J.K. Smith's Sports Emporium 139, 247n17
John, Augustus 24
Jones (Miss) (chemist in Ballarat) 145, 173, 254
Joyce, James 7–8
Julius, Anthony 26

Kahlo, Frida 19, 256
Kaorite Creek xiv, 73
Karlsruhe (ship) 47, 48, 64, 151, 162
Kazimierz (Poland). *See* Kraków
Kean, Charles and Ellen 94
Kellaway, Thomas 15
Kesslère, George Maillard **11 (fig. 2)**
Keys, Olive 82–85, 88, 210
Kirkland, I. Lindsay (Miss) 15
Knoedler's Gallery 200, 201
Kolin, Henry (nephew of HR) 9
Kolin, Mala (later Mala Rubinstein; niece of HR) 9, 37
Kolin, Oscar (nephew of HR) 9
Kolin, Regina (*née* Rubinstein, sister of HR) xv, 8–9, 51
Koroit (Victoria) xiv, 107
Koroite Creek, formerly Bryan's or Bryant's Creek (outside Coleraine) xiv, 73, 239n14
Kraków (Poland)
  HR's birth in 43, 48, 253
  HR's emigration from 58–60, 89–90
  HR's relatives in 58–59, 64, 75, 160, 162, 253
  Jewish quarter of 8, 50–54
  photograph taken in xv, **53 (fig. 12)**

Labouchère, Henry 136
labour market 49–50, 95, 97, 186
  See also governesses; wages; waitresses; women's rights and status
Lacaton, Josephine 101
'Lady Kitty' 111

Lamington (Lord and Lady) 78–79, 240n28
lanolin 45–47, 74
Lanvin, Jeanne 36
Lasaar (Professor) 154, 159–60
Lassar, Oska (Professor). *See* Lasaar (Professor)
Launceston (Tasmania) 170, 244n37
Laurençin, Marie 10, **211 (fig. 28)**
Lawrence, D.H. 7
Lawrence, Ida 120
Leary's Pharmacy (Palmerston North) 175
Lehman Brothers 9, 256
Levy (Mrs) (of Cahors, Macleay Street, Sydney) 117–18
Levy, Eva (*née* Silberfeld; maternal cousin of HR) 57–59, 63–64, 71–73, 88, 215, 237n36
Levy, Frederick Reuben 237n35
Levy, Louis Leopold (husband of Eva Levy) 58–59, 71, 88
Levy, Reginald Michael 237n35
Levy, Theodore Harold 237n35
Liebreich, Oscar (Professor) 46
Linden (in St Kilda, Melbourne) 88–89, 254
Lipnitzki, Boris 125–27, 135, 145, 197
List, Emmie (Dr) 150, 159
litigation and lawsuits 82–84, 131, 136, 137, 156
London 5, 8, 123, 152–53, 160, 176–79
  See also [24] Grafton Street, Mayfair
Loos, Anita 17
L'Oréal 6, 231–32 n5, 257
Lum, Rowena ('Binny') 31, 54, 138–39
lung food 140–41
Lurçat, Jean **11 (fig. 2)**
Lykuski (or Lykusky), Josef (Dr) 43, 131, 144, 148–49, 160–61
  achievements of 174
  introduction to 52
  name of 139
  veracity of 46–47, 117, 187
  See also Valaze
Lyster's Opera Company 94

MacDonald, Helen 104
Madame Alexis 112–13, 120–21, 210, 245n44

INDEX

Madame: An Intimate Biography of Helena Rubinstein (by Patrick O'Higgins, 1971) 15–18, 26–27, 99–100, 105–6, 138–39, 210–12, 236n7
   See also My Life for Beauty; O'Higgins, Patrick
Madame Olga 117, 121
Madame Suzy 36, 196
Madden, Gertrude Frances (Lady)
Madrid 256
Maesmore Morris (Mrs Gertrude) 180
Maison de Beauté Valaze (London) 180
Maison Dorée oyster saloon (Swanston Street, Melbourne) 47, 96–101, 254
make-up. *See* cosmetics
'Mamie' 112–13
Man, Felix 34, 36
Marcoussis, Louis 10
Marley (Miss) (dancing teacher) 85
Marriott, Annie Theresa 244n37
Mars (Mademoiselle) (Anne Françoise Hyppolyte Boutet Salvetat) 133
Martel, Nellie 93
Matisse, Henri 20, 231n5
Maugham, Somerset 24, 35, 40
McGuffie & Co. (chemists, Brisbane) 163–65, 168, 171, 173, 254
Medgyes, Ladislas 201
Meir, Golda 1, 3, 7, 257
Melba, Nellie 63, 94, 106–7
Melbourne Cup 112–13
Melbourne Glass Bottle Works 45
Melbourne Punch 108–11, 113–14, 120
Meltham (near Gheringap, Victoria) 75, 78, 80–81, 253
Menzies Hotel (Melbourne) 99, 101, 105, 107, 169, 197, 202
Merino (Victoria) 64, 71
Merkel, Angela 3–4
Metcalfe, Debonnaire Prudence 83, 85–88
Metcalfe, Evelyn James (Mr and Mrs) 79–88
Metcalfe, Isabel 87
Metcalfe, José 83, 85–87, 241n46
Metcalfe, Theophilus ('Theo') 87, 241n36
Metcalfe, Wynnie Prudence (Mrs Evelyn James Metcalfe, née Brodribb) 79–88
Michaelis, Edward 89

Michaelis, Hallenstein & Co. 89
Michaelis, Moritz 88–90, 254
Milan 255
Minnie (laundry maid at Astonette) 85
Miró, Joan 20
misogyny 6, 28
Missingham, Hal 203
Mitchell, Thomas (Major) 70, 239n14
Modern Art Jewellery Co. (Sydney) 116
Modigliani, Amedeo 20
Modjeska (Helena Modrzejewska) 52
Molyneux 36, 196
'Mona' 112–13
Monk, Alice Emma 109, 114, 245n42
   See also Salon Charmazelle
Montenegro, Roberto 10, **211 (fig. 28)**
Moore-Bentley, Mary 93
Mount Koroit and Dundas Station (Victoria) xiv
Mrs Allen's World's Hair Restorer 45–46
Mulvaney, John 102
Murdoch, Euphemia 97
Murdoch, John Smith 84
My Life for Beauty (HR's memoir ghost-written by Patrick O'Higgins, published 1965) xiv, 15–16, 18, 49, 78, 156, 191, 212, 257
   See also O'Higgins, Patrick
Myer, Elcon (*né* Elcon Baevski) 64, 65
Myer, Sidney (*né* Simcha Baevski) 64, 65
Myer Emporium 218

Nadelman, Elie 10, **11 (fig. 2)**
National Archives of Australia (Canberra) 43, **44 (fig. 11)**, 104, 130
National Film and Sound Archive of Australia (Canberra) 31, 138
National Gallery of Australia (Canberra) 10
National Gallery of Victoria (Melbourne) 202, 257
National Library of Australia (Canberra) 11
National Portrait Gallery (Canberra) 18
National Portrait Gallery (London) 205
Nazism 8, 9, 51, 56
New Orleans 255
New Zealand 95, 181, 184–85, 254–55
niche marketing 121

INDEX

Nin, Anaïs 8
Noel (Dr) 117
Norddeutscher–Lloyd line 57, **57 (fig. 13)**, 60, 147
Norman, Henry Wylie 79
Northcote, Henry Stafford (first Baron Northcote) 48, 240n32
The Nun's Story **214 (fig. 29)**
Nuttall, Alice Emma 245n42

O'Connell (Miss) 119
O'Connor's Chambers. *See* [138] Elizabeth Street, Melbourne
O'Higgins, Patrick 15–18, **17 (fig. 3)**, 25, 39, 46, 64, 72, 99–100, 205
  See also Madame: An Intimate Biography of Helena Rubinstein; My Life for Beauty
Olga (Madame) 117, 121
Oma (in Toorak, Melbourne) 253
opaline glass 19
Oriental Massage Company 112, 245n44
  See also Alexis (Madame)

Palmerston North (New Zealand) 175
Palotta, Grace 104, 116
Pankhurst, Christabel 93
'Pansy' 168–69
625 Park Avenue, New York 10, **11 (fig. 2)**, 191, **199 (fig. 25)**, 200, 202, 210, **211 (fig. 28)**, 217
Parke-Bernet Galleries (New York) 10, 38, 251n1, 252n22, 257
Paschkis, Heinrich (Dr) 154, 159–60
Pashki (Dr) 154, 159–60
Pasteur, Louis 150
Patou, Jean 196, 214
Pavlova, Anna Matveyevna 63
Péret, Benjamin 7
Perth (Western Australia) 120, 170
pharmaceuticals 45–46, 160, 173
pharmacies. *See* chemist shops
Philadelphia 255
Picasso, Pablo 7, 10–11, 19, 37, 191–95, **193 (fig. 22)**, **194 (fig. 23)**, 213, 256
158A Pitt Street, Sydney 145, 161, 173, 175, 181, 254

pogroms 8, 50–51, 56, 64
Poiret, Paul 36
Pokitonoff, Mathilde (Dr) 154, 160
Pokitonoff, Mathilde von Wulfert (Dr) 154, 160
Pompadour (Madame de) 132–33
Pompidou, Claude (Mme) 7
Pompidou, Georges (Prime Minister of France) 7
Portinari, Candido **211 (fig. 28)**
Potocka, Emanuela Pignatelli (Countess) 159
Poynter, John 51, 72
Prinz-Regent Luitpold (steamship) **44 (fig. 11)**, 47, 48, **57 (fig. 13)**, 60–63, 78, 80, 104, 162
Proust, Marcel 200, 201
Pyne, Beatrice (*née* Brodribb) 79–80
Pyne, Charles (Captain) 79–80

The Queen's Face Food 116–17

Ray, Man 7, 10, 19
Rhein (ship) 151
Richards, W. (Mr) 115
Richards and Silberfeld 70, 238n3
Richardson, John 193
Rivera, Diego 19, 256
Robert, Keith 192
Roberts, Tom 103
Robur Tea Company 100, 103–4, 116, 139
Röhm & Haas 201
Roosevelt, Franklin Delano 138
Roque, Jacqueline 192
Rosenberg, Karen 208
Rothschild, Élie de (Baron) 24
Rotorua (New Zealand) 174
Royal Society of Portrait Painters 24
Rubinstein, Anton Grigorevich (pianist and composer) 12
Rubinstein, Artur (pianist) 40, **40 (fig. 9)**
Rubinstein, Ceska or Cäcilie (sister of HR; later Cooper) 51
  depiction of xv
  emigration to Australia of 47, 145, 160–61, 236n7, 254
  as employee of HR 27, 171
  expertise of 151, 158, 183–84

INDEX

Rubinstein, Erna (sister of HR) xv, 51
Rubinstein, Gitel ('Augusta' or 'Gusta'; mother of HR) xv, 51–53, **53 (fig. 12)**, 57–58, 63
Rubinstein, Helena
  age of 43–44, 48–49
  as art collector 9, 10–11, 19–20, 30, 202, 209
  biographies of 2–3, 5–6, 15–16, 195, 233 nn26 & 27. *See also* Bennett, James; Brandon, Ruth; Fabe, Maxene; Fitoussi, Michèle; *Madame: An Intimate Biography of Helena Rubinstein; My Life for Beauty*; O'Higgins, Patrick; Slesin, Suzanne; Woodhead, Lindy
  birth name of (Chaja; חיה) 48, 54
  birth of 43–44, 48, 253
  business acumen of. *See* Helena Rubinstein: financial acumen of
  children of 8. *See also* Titus, Horace; Titus, Roy
  and clothing 3–4, 36–37, 169, 188–89, 195–96, 203–4
  death of (1965) 5, 218, 257
  divorce from Edward Titus (1932) 8, 256
  as domestic servant 47, 49–50, 58–59, 72
  education of 54, 72–73, 77–78, 197
  emigration to Australia of 43–44, 47–48, 56–63, 65–66
  as employer 16, 197, 217
  estate sale of 10–11, 19–20, 30, 38, 252n22, 257. *See also* Parke-Bernet Galleries (New York)
  ethics of 16, 47–49. *See also* Rubinstein, Helena: mythologising of
  exhibitions about xiv, 15, 23, 38, 205, **211 (fig. 28)**, 257
  financial acumen of 9, 16, 20, 28, 48, 108, 145, 216–18
  first love of (Stanisław) 54, 59
  frugality of 20
  as governess 50, 69–90, 98, 254
  homes of: in Coleraine 89
  homes of: in Kraków 48, 50–53, 253
  homes of: in Melbourne 43, 89, 99–100, 103
  homes of: in New York 10, **11 (fig. 2)**, 191, **199 (fig. 25)**, 200–202, **211 (fig. 28)**
  homes of: in Paris 7
  and jewellery 10, 25, 28, 30, 37–39, 189, 197, 201, 204–5, **216 (fig. 31)**
  life trajectory of 8–11, 18–19, 210–11, 215–18
  marriages of 7, 8, 49, 168–69, 181, 188, 195, 232n7, 255, 256. *See also* Gourielli-Tchkonia, Artchil; Titus, Edward
  and the media 11–14, 20, 36
  as mother 16
  mythologising of xiv, 2, 6–7, 12–14, 18, 78–79, 159, 181
  naturalisation of, as British in Australia (1907) 43–44, **44 (fig. 11)**, 47–48, 105, **105 (fig. 16)**, 184
  in New York **11 (fig. 2)**
  in New Zealand 5–6, 21
  opinion of Sutherland portrait 23, 39–40
  parents of xv, 54, 160. *See also* Rubinstein, Gitel; Rubinstein, Naftaly Hertzel
  as philanthropist 169
  portraits of 4, 8, 9, 10–11, 188–89, 200–211, **211 (fig. 28)**, 255, **plates 1–5**. *See also* Beaton, Cecil; Dalí, Salvador; Dobell, William; Hagborg, Otto; Helleu, Paul-César; Lipnitzki, Boris; Picasso, Pablo; Sutherland, Graham; Warhol, Andy
  religious beliefs of 89
  royal title of 8
  and science **126 (fig. 18)**, **plate 7**. *See also* scientific claims
  sisters of xv, 38, 51, **53 (fig. 12)**. *See also* Kolin, Regina; Rubinstein, Ceska; Rubinstein, Erna; Rubinstein, Manka; Rubinstein, Pauline; Rubinstein, Rosa; Rubinstein, Stella
  social life and status of 51–52, 75, 111, 169, 200
  travels of 63, 72, 147–70, 190, 195, 205–6, 215–17, **215 (fig. 30)**

INDEX

Rubinstein, Helena (*cont.*)
  underestimation of 8
  as waitress 47, 50, 90, 96–100
  wealth of 9, 20, 192, 200, 205
  as wife 16
  work ethic of 155
  See also Helena Rubinstein & Co.
Rubinstein, Mala (*née* Kolin; niece of HR) 9, 37
Rubinstein, Manka (sister of HR) xv, 51
Rubinstein, Naftaly Hertzel ('Horace'; father of HR) 51, 54
Rubinstein, Nela (wife of pianist Artur Rubinstein) **40 (fig. 9)**
Rubinstein, Pauline (sister of HR) 51, 184
Rubinstein, Rosa (sister of HR) 51
Rubinstein, Stella (sister of HR, later Oscestowicz) 51, 184
255 rue Saint-Honoré, Paris 48, 84, 152, 184, 188, 255
Russo, Margherita **211 (fig. 28)**
Rutland, Suzanne 65

Sackville (Lord) 24
Saint-Cloud 125–26, **126 (fig. 18)**, 145
Saint-Laurent, Yves 36
Salek (Mr) (chemist, Christchurch) 174
Salon Charmazelle 108–18, 120, 145, 153, 214
  in Sydney 163
  See also Monk, Alice Emma; Ward, Alice Augusta
San Francisco 255
Sandford (Victoria) 74
Sands & McDougall 13–15
Schiaparelli, Elsa 196, 214
Schlumberger, Pierre 24
scientific claims 126–27, **126 (fig. 18)**, 135, 141, 143–44, 150–53, 159–60, 188, **plate 7**
Seattle 256
Sensenberg (Mrs) 100–101
Sert, Misia 200
Shaumer, Maurice Max 88–89
Siegenberg, Frances ('Fanny', *née* Cohn; Mrs John Siegenberg) 101–2, 109–10
Siegenberg, John 101–2, 243n20
Siegenberg, Rose Victoria 101
Silberfeld, Bernhard (*né* Baruch Moyzesz; maternal uncle of HR) xiv, 53, 57–58, 63–65, 70–73, 215, 237n36, 238n46, 239n14
Silberfeld, Eva (maternal cousin of HR). *See* Levy, Eva
Silberfeld, John (*né* Jacob Herz; maternal uncle of HR) 53, 58, 63–65, 72, 89, 238n46
Silberfeld, Louis (*né* Aryeh Leib Louis; maternal uncle of HR) 53, 63–65, 70–72, 238n46
Silberfeld, Rebecca (maternal grandmother of HR) 51
Silberfeld, Sale ('Solomon'; maternal grandfather of HR) 51–52
skin food 79, 134, 136–38, 140–43, 153, 165, 167–68, 172
  See also Valaze
skin peels 150, 154, 157, 159, 163
Slesin, Suzanne xv, 233n26
Smith, James 108, 132
Smith, Laurie E. xiii, 84–88
Smith's Sports Emporium 139, 247n17
Snowball, O.A. (Miss) 15
Sontag, Susan 212–13
Soul Pattinson, Washington H. (chemist, Sydney) 154, 163, 171, 173
South African War 83, 88, 169
South Australian Hotel 198
Splitter, Helena (*née* Silberfeld; maternal aunt of HR) 54, 56, 58, 60, 162, 253
Splitter, Liebisch (uncle of HR) 54, 56, 58, 162
St Kilda 75, 88–90, 97, 101, 254
Standard Dining Rooms (Prahran) 97
Stanisław (HR's first love) 54, 59
Stein, Gertrude 7, 191–92
Stern, Elizabeth 89, 100–101, 103
Stewart, Nellie 94, 115–16, 118, 143
Stewart Dawson & Co. (Sydney, jewellers) 116
Streeton, Arthur 103
surrealism 7, 8, 24, 28–29, 35, 199–201, 209
Sutherland, Graham 9, 15, 18, 23–41, **40 (fig. 9), 41 (fig. 10)**, 189, 191, 194, 200, 209
  career of 24–25

Helena Rubinstein in a Red Brocade Balenciaga Gown (1957) 2, 3, 23–41, 108, 204–5, 209–10, **211 (fig. 28)**, 212–13, 256, 258, **plates 1 & 2 & 5**
    meets HR 25–28, 235 n25
    opinion of HR 202–4
Sutherland, Kathleen (wife of Graham Sutherland) 31, 34, **40 (fig. 9)**
Suzy (Madame) 36, 196
Sweet Nell of Old Drury 115
Sydney **57 (fig. 13)**, 92–93, 116–20, 145
    HR & Co. expansion into 161, 163–64, 171, 181, 184
Sydney Morning Herald 74, 176–80, 197

Table Talk (Melbourne) 110–11, 115, 139–40, 142–44, 151
Tahara (Victoria) 70
Talma and Co. 111, 112
Talma Buildings (Melbourne) 112–13
Tanguy, Yves 7
TarraWarra Art Gallery 204
Tate Gallery (London) 15, 23, **38 (fig. 8)**, 39, 257
Theatre Royal (Melbourne) 103
Thompson, Isabella (*née* Hutchings, then Grist, then Thompson) 103
Thompson, James Henry (Harry) 100–101, 103, 116, 139
Thorne & Littlewood 15
Thornton, Walter 156
Titus, Edward (first husband of HR) 7–8, 49, 168–69, 191, 200, 255, 256
Titus, Horace (second child of HR) 8, 26–27, 255, 257
Titus, Roy (first child of HR) 8, 255
Toklas, Alice B. 191
Toowoomba (Queensland) xiii, 47, 75, 78–88, 254
Toronto 256
Toulouse-Lautrec, Henri de 231–32n5
Towle (Dr) 155
trademarks, registration of xiii, 47, 98, 104, 127–**28 (fig. 19)**, 130–32, 219, 254
Trumble, Angus (1964–2022) 2, 18, 225–30
'*Truth*' Cautionary List for 1910 136–37

Tschelitchew, Pavel 10, **211 (fig. 28)**
Tzara, Tristan 7

Una (Dr) 154, 159
United Service Café 101
    See also Chicago and Winter Garden Tea and Luncheon Rooms
University of Melbourne 93, 105
Uniwersytet Jagielloński (Kraków) 51, 54
Unna, Paul Gerson (Dr) 154, 159

Valaze
    and the Australian climate 119, 127, 178, 186–87
    early sales of 102
    efficacy of 137–38, 177
    and Felton Grimwade 43, 45
    formulation of 45–47, 137–38, 144, 149–50
    and Modjeska (Helena Modrzejewska) 52
    name of 138–39
    price of 114, 141, 143, 145, 165, 185–86
    publicity about 78, 103–4, 116, 127, 132–40, 165
    registration of trademark 104, 127–**28 (fig. 19)**, 130–32, 219, 254
    supplies of 148–49, 184–88
    See also freckles; Lykuski (or Lykusky), Josef (Dr); skin food
Valaze Institute (Melbourne) 43
Valaze Massage Institute (Sydney) 171
Valaze Massage Institute (Wellington) 175
Valentine (gardener at Astonette) 85, 87
van Dongen, Kees 20
Vandyck Studio 114
Vertès, Marcel **211 (fig. 28)**
Victorian Artists' Society (Melbourne) 109, 110
Vienna 8, 149, 176–77, 253, 256, 256
    in the 1890s 54–56
    closes salon in 9, 256
    depiction of HR in 66–67, **66 (fig. 14)**, **124 (fig. 17)**, 188
    fact-finding visit to in 1905 72, 150–51, 154, 159, 168, 177

Vienna (*cont.*)
    HR emigrates via 59, 89, 253
    HR moves to 253
    opens salon in 256
    prestige of 54–56, 99, 176
    relations of HR in xv, 54–56, 58, 75, 90, 162
Vogel, Lucien 152
Voskpasta 159, 172
Vreeland, Diana 17–18

Wade, Bertha 119
wages 50, 60, 72, 76–77, 127, 185–86
Wagga Wagga (New South Wales) 116
waitresses 47, 50, 60, 90, 97–98
Wall Street Crash (1929) 8, 9, 256
Wallangarra (Queensland) 254
Walter, Marie-Thérèse 192
Wanganui (New Zealand) 154, 171, 174–75, 181, 184
War Paint (Broadway musical) 7
Ward, Alice Augusta (Mrs Ralph Ward, *née* Taylor) 108–17, 120–21, 145, 190, 214
    See also Salon Charmazelle
Ward Gillespie (Miss) 175–76
Warhol, Andy 10, 206–8, **206 (fig. 26)**, 256
Warrnambool (Victoria) xiv, 93, 107
Wellington (New Zealand) 21, 118, 145, 171, 174–75, 181–84, 254–55
Westfold, Moira 218–19
W.H. Glen & Co. Music and Piano Warehouse (Melbourne). *See* Glen & Co.

Wilkinson's Chemist (Dunedin) 174, 175
Williams, Mark 132
Dr Williams' Pink Pills for Pale People xii, 141, 214
Williamson, J.C. 94
Wilmer (Mrs) (masseuse) 142
Wilson, Gilbert (Mrs) 169
Wilson, Ruth 6
women's rights and status 5, 93–94, 97, 242n5
    See also governesses; labour market; misogyny; wages; waitresses
Women's Weekly Portrait Prize 205, 257
Woodhead, Lindy 48, 59, 69, 89, 97, 195, 233n26
Woollams' Chemist (Auckland) 173, 175
World War I 8, 36, 55, 82, 120
World War II 8, 9, 24, 36, 197, 201
Worth, House of **189 (figs 20 & 21)**, 190
Worth, Jean-Philippe 188
Wyalla (in Toowoomba) 80

Xerox Corporation 7

Young, William xiv
Youngman & Co. 45

Ziegler, Philip 19
Zumsteg, Gustav 37

www.ingramcontent.com/pod-product-compliance
Lightning Source LLC
Chambersburg PA
CBHW040252170426
43191CB00019B/2385